A Fatal Attraction

CRITICAL MEDIA STUDIES
INSTITUTIONS, POLITICS, AND CULTURE

Series Editor

Andrew Calabrese, University of Colorado

Advisory Board

Patricia Aufderheide, American University
Jean-Claude Burgelman, Institute for Prospective Technological Studies
Simone Chambers, University of Toronto
Nicholas Garnham, University of Westminster
Hanno Hardt, University of Iowa
Gay Hawkins, The University of New South Wales
Maria Heller, Eötvös Loránd University
Robert Horwitz, University of California at San Diego
Douglas Kellner, University of California at Los Angeles
Gary Marx, Massachusetts Institute of Technology
Toby Miller, University of California, Riverside
Vincent Mosco, Queen's University
Janice Peck, University of Colorado
Manjunath Pendakur, Southern Illinois University
Arvind Rajagopal, New York University
Giuseppe Richeri, Università Svizzera Italiana
Kevin Robins, Goldsmiths College
Saskia Sassen, University of Chicago
Dan Schiller, University of Illinois at Urbana-Champaign
Colin Sparks, University of Westminster
Slavko Splichal, University of Ljubljana
Thomas Streeter, University of Vermont
Liesbet van Zoonen, University of Amsterdam
Janet Wasko, University of Oregon

Recent Titles in the Series

The Film Studio: Film Production in the Global Economy
  Ben Goldsmith and Tom O'Regan
Raymond Williams
  Alan O'Connor
Why TV Is Not Our Fault: Television Programming, Viewers, and Who's Really in Control
  Eileen R. Meehan
Media, Terrorism, and Theory: A Reader
  Edited by Anandam P. Kavoori and Todd Fraley
Digital Music Wars: Ownership and Control of the Celestial Jukebox
  Patrick Burkart and Tom McCourt
Culture Conglomerates: Consolidation in the Motion Picture and Television Industries
  William M. Kunz
A Violent World: TV News Images of Middle Eastern Terror and War
  Nitzan Ben-Shaul
Community Media: A Global Introduction
  Ellie Rennie
Urban Communication: Production, Text, Context
  Edited by Timothy A. Gibson and Mark Lowes
Empire and Communications
  Harold A. Innis
A Fatal Attraction: Public Television and Politics in Italy
  Cinzia Padovani

For a complete listing of series titles, visit www.rowmanlittlefield.com.

A Fatal Attraction

Public Television and Politics in Italy

CINZIA PADOVANI

ROWMAN & LITTLEFIELD PUBLISHERS, INC.
Lanham • Boulder • New York • Toronto • Plymouth, UK

ROWMAN & LITTLEFIELD PUBLISHERS, INC.

Published in the United States of America
by Rowman & Littlefield Publishers, Inc.
A wholly owned subsidiary of The Rowman & Littlefield Publishing Group, Inc.
4501 Forbes Boulevard, Suite 200, Lanham, Maryland 20706
www.rowmanlittlefield.com

Estover Road, Plymouth PL6 7PY, United Kingdom

Copyright © 2005 by Rowman & Littlefield Publishers, Inc.
First paperback edition 2007

All rights reserved. No part of this publication may be reproduced, stored in a retrieval system, or transmitted in any form or by any means, electronic, mechanical, photocopying, recording, or otherwise, without the prior permission of the publisher.

British Library Cataloguing in Publication Information Available

The hardback edition of this book was catalogued by the Library of Congress as follows:

Padovani, Cinzia, 1961–
  A fatal attraction : public television and politics in Italy / Cinzia Padovani.
    p. cm.— (Critical media studies. Institutions, politics, and culture)
  Includes bibliographical references and index.
  1. Radiotelevisione italiana. 2. Television programs, Public service—Italy.
3. Television and politics—Italy. 4. Television in politics—Italy. I. Title. II. Series:
Critical media studies.
  PN1992.92.R34P33   2005
  302.23'45'0945—dc22
                                                                              2004005122

ISBN-13: 978-0-7425-1949-7 (cloth : alk. paper)
ISBN-10: 0-7425-1949-X (cloth : alk. paper)
ISBN-13: 978-0-7425-1950-3 (pbk. : alk. paper)
ISBN-10: 0-7425-1950-3 (pbk. : alk. paper)

Printed in the United States of America

∞™ The paper used in this publication meets the minimum requirements of American National Standard for Information Sciences—Permanence of Paper for Printed Library Materials, ANSI/NISO Z39.48-1992.

A Leo

Contents

Foreword	ix
Acknowledgments	xi
Introduction: Public Service Broadcasting: The Party System and Democracy	1
1 Democracy in Italy (1945-2003)	13
2 RAI and the Party System (Part I)	53
3 RAI and the Party System (Part II)	105
4 *Lottizzazione*: A Normal Practice for Public Service Journalists	161
Conclusion: Political Power and the Media	229
Glossary	257
Bibliography	265
Index	275
About the Author	285

Foreword

Giuseppe Richeri, professor of social history of communications, University of Italian Switzerland, Lugano

Broadcasting in Europe has always been very different from what we find in the United States. On one side of the Atlantic, it was born and developed as a cultural and social institution and only after a long period of time did it also become a business. On the other side, it was born as a business and, only later, was recognized for its social and cultural role. The distinctive characteristics of the European broadcasting model are evident in all the European countries, despite powerful national differences. Throughout its history, the Italian broadcasting system has tested the strengths and limits of the European model: from state television and public financing to pedagogic and cultural functions, to interaction with public institutions and political parties, to competition, and now to the present complicity between public and private broadcasting systems.

Within the European radio and television broadcasting arena, the Italian case presents the most complex set of interrelationships among political, sociocultural, and economic variables, the most profound institutional and managerial transformations, and the most rapid process of concentration, all while maintaining the lowest level of technological innovation. This book by Cinzia Padovani reconstructs and interprets with balance and competence the wealth of the elements in play, along with the strenuous evolution of Italian broadcasting. Her work is grounded on a thorough knowledge of the existing literature on the topic, and is based on a detailed investigation of unpublished documents and interviews with firsthand witnesses and participants. Altogether, these resources have produced original findings about a subject that is not well-known and issues that have not before been as thoroughly investigated.

The aspect that makes particularly complex the evolution of Italian broadcasting is its interaction, stronger than in other European nations, with the politics and society of the country. One needs to consider, for example, the role and influence of the Catholic Church and its political party of reference, the Christian Democrats, in the first twenty years of Italian television. One can also look at the function of television in the cultural and linguistic unification of the country, and in the creation of a national identity shared within a national territory characterized by very diverse and relatively unconnected geographical, social, and cultural realities. In recent times, the reorganization of public television in Italy has been forced by necessity to reflect more adequately the political, institutional, and cultural pluralism of Italian society. This has included responding to competition for audience attention after the introduction of privately owned commercial broadcasting services.

I believe that to know Italian broadcasting is a fundamental requisite for anyone who wants to understand contemporary Italian society in more than a superficial manner. This is even more evident when we consider that the transformations of Italian politics in the last decade have led to the appointment as prime minister the most powerful television entrepreneur of the country. According to many critics, Silvio Berlusconi's political achievements are directly related, among other things, to his knowledge and dominance of the television medium in Italy. This includes his understanding of marketing and consumer preferences and behavior, and his managerial skills in creating various forms of collaboration with partners who are attentive to the dynamics of mass media uses, image making, and marketing.

The history of Italian television is, then, relevant not only for comprehending the history of the country but also, in particular, for understanding the present phase of its politics. This book is a valuable resource for anyone wishing to develop such an understanding.

Acknowledgments

I wish to thank Prof. Willard D. Rowland Jr. for helping me delineate the structure of my dissertation and focus on the interplay between politics and media in Italy; this book originates from that initial framework. I also want to express my gratitude to Prof. Andrew Calabrese for believing in the validity of this project since its early stages. His encouragement and feedback were always timely and enlightening. A special acknowledgment goes to Prof. Michael Tracey, who taught me to always look at public service broadcasting as a constituent fabric of any social formation. I want to thank him for supporting my work as a postdoctoral researcher at the University of Colorado at Boulder, which allowed me to complete the manuscript for this work. I am also grateful to my colleague Dr. Wendy Redal for her insights and thought-provoking observations.

I want to express my gratitude to Prof. Giovanni Cesareo for his precious comments on the manuscript, and for helping me understand the intricate relationship between the Italian postwar political system and RAI. A special acknowledgment goes out to Prof. Francesco Siliato for always being available to answer my queries, and for providing me with comments and updates on the most recent developments in Italian broadcasting. I also want to express my gratitude to all the journalists,

USIGRAI union members, and politicians who agreed to be interviewed for this project. Not only did their participation serve to breathe life into an otherwise solitary academic pursuit, but it also served to inform the direction of my research.

I want to express my appreciation to Dr. Anna Maria Russo for translating Prof. Giuseppe Richeri's foreword; to Nancy Mann, at CU-Boulder, for her patient support with refining my writing skills in English; and to my friend Dr. Domenico Mannetta for venturing across Rome, on a stormy Sunday afternoon, to take pictures for the cover. Special thanks also to the personnel of the public library in L'Aquila, Italy, who worked beyond their regular shifts in order to help me find many of the resources necessary to complete this work.

I would have never been able to complete this project had I not been blessed with a very patient seven-year-old boy, Leonardo. Since he was a little child, he has wondered why his mom was always working on her book. He was very pleased when I finally turned in the manuscript, and came with me to the publisher to make sure that I was "really, really done." Special thanks also to my friend Dr. Rodney M. Richards for all his support and encouragement. He worked tireless hours to complete the copyediting. Finally, special thanks to my father, Colombo Padovani, whose insights into Italian politics I have always enjoyed listening to.

Introduction

Public Service Broadcasting: The Party System and Democracy

In the last two decades or so, it has been particularly easy to point to the shortcomings and inefficiencies of public service broadcasters as proof of an inevitably and substantially corrupt nature. This criticism has played in favor of those, from the so-called third way left to the right, who have advocated the market (even if regulated) as a solution to the ills of public services. In a context where "corrupt and outmoded" public services have been contraposed to "efficient and self-regulated" commercial broadcasters, it seemed that conquering the audience, competing with commercial channels, and offering programs increasingly similar to the ones offered by the commercial competitor were not a choice but rather a necessity, a fate, and even the destiny of all public service broadcasters, in Italy as elsewhere.

Around the world, public service media face ideological, political, and technological challenges. At issue is whether they will be able to redefine their role in societies that are increasingly dominated by market values and by a powerful sense that the private realm, rather than collective interests and the public, is the defining sphere of human activity. But on a more fundamental level, at issue is whether public service media can still (if they ever did) enhance democratic practices, and whether or not they can claim any special role in contemporary democracies.

According to the dominant model for the study of public service broadcasting, first elaborated by Nicholas Garnham[1] and the "Westminster School," it is by looking at public service broadcasting institutions as an embodiment of the principles of the public sphere that those institutions can be defended and legitimated, and a clear connection between them and democracy can be established.[2] According to this model, which is based on the Habermasian concept of the public sphere as a space separated from state and market influences, only if one can sustain the notion of public service media as free from those influences can a critical and enlightened public develop and the case be made for the relevance of public service broadcasting in the twenty-first century.

The Italian Case: A Different Framework?

However, the dominant discourse setting the agenda for arguments in defense of public service broadcasting has often "obscured the great diversity of forms that [public service broadcasting] takes at different sites."[3] In the Italian case such a framework may have contributed to interpreting the public service broadcaster RAI, *Radiotelevisione Italiana*, which has often proven to be congenial to the particular political and cultural context where it evolved, as a deviance from the normative ideal of public broadcasting. In fact, I believe that RAI's close association with the political establishment and its long tradition of partisan journalism often enhanced the broadcaster's democratic potential by creating a more pluralistic political culture.

This book describes the history of the Italian public service broadcaster from a much contested vantage point, namely, its relationship with the political party system. That relationship, known as *lottizzazione*, indicates the sharing, or parceling out, of positions of power inside the broadcaster on the part of the Christian Democratic Party (DC) and other parties, primarily the Italian Socialist Party (PSI) and the Italian Communist Party (PCI). This history runs from the time when the Christian Democratic Party had almost full power within RAI (1954-1975), to the time when influence was distributed among parties (1975-1992), to the post-*lottizzazione* phase (1993-), when commercial imperatives became predominant concerns for the broadcaster. The history of RAI parallels that of the Italian democracy, from a time when political parties were powerful institutions and *lottizzazione* was accepted as an expression of pluralism (roughly, before 1993), to the 1990s and early 2000s when parties lost their representative power and legitimacy in society and *lottizzazione* was conceived as an expression of corruption.

While political interference in public service media is certainly not only an Italian phenomenon (in Germany, Belgium, the United Kingdom, and Scandinavian countries the government designates its own representatives at the top of broadcasting institutions), in Italy political parties have not only indicated who would lead the corporation, but also intervened in internal decisions, such as journalists' appointments, career advancement, and, sometimes, even programming. Whereas most Western countries have a judicial tradition of separation between the government and the public broadcaster, in Italy the legislators' will to protect the media from political powers has traditionally been weak. Indeed, media and political concentration has reached unprecedented levels with Silvio Berlusconi, owner of media empire Mediaset (RAI's main competitor), becoming prime minister on two occasions, in 1994 and 2001.

The other distinctively Italian characteristic of RAI's relationship with the party system is that *lottizzazione* has been codified, justified, and legitimated by politicians, journalists, and RAI officials to the point that it has become an integral part of the broadcaster's own identity. In continuous tension between a type of journalism perceived as the bearer of politicians' self-interests and a high-quality journalism proud of its openly declared partisanship, *lottizzazione* has marked the history of the corporation. A plethora of factors made it possible for *lottizzazione* to become normalized, or common sense, in Gramscian terms: Italy's longstanding tradition of political journalism dating back to the eighteenth century, the remnants of the Fascist legislation that had regulated the first radio broadcaster, and the whole nature of the post-World War II democracy, defined as a parties' republic, in which political parties played the fundamental role of mediator between citizens and governmental institutions and thus guarantors of those institutions.

What initially legitimated party interference within RAI was a specific way of considering the role of public service journalism in the Italian democracy. As broadcast journalism grew out of the humanist and partisan tradition of print and party press journalism, the myth of objective reporting was not the dominant paradigm. For individual journalists, far from being something to hide, a party affiliation was, at times, a badge of intellectual seriousness and a source of social legitimacy. For the broadcaster as an institution, top-down political activism, broadly conceived, was the core of its mission. Where American media were conceived as suppliers of popular entertainment or neutral mirrors of society, RAI was meant, paternalistically, to educate and enlighten citizens in order to unify, modernize, and democratize the country. Naturally, then, political groups—during the 1950s and 1960s factions within the DC and later other parties—vied to control the content of RAI's broadcasts. And because the political affiliations of individual journalists were already so visible, it seemed natural that to control broadcast content one needed only to hire people with the "right" ideology. Thus hiring in RAI became an arena of political struggle.

As the DC hegemony grew less monolithic, ideological fiefdoms emerged within RAI. Fairness in journalism was defined not as objectivity—the absence of political bias—but as pluralism—the presence of competing political views. After 1975, RAI gradually came to be organized in such a way that each of its three channels had its own party affiliation, with increasingly formalized political quotas in hiring and promotion—the system known as *lottizzazione*. RAI's first channel, RAI1, remained the DC channel, and RAI2 became the Socialist channel. In 1987, RAI3 was given to the Communists.

But as the centrality of political parties and ideological affiliation decreased during the 1990s, the political system changed. As Italy moved away from a republic of parties toward a more polarized political system, and from a "blocked democracy"[4] with powerful opposition toward a more mature democracy with broad-based coalitions, the ideology surrounding journalism also underwent a profound mutation. Journalism began to gradually detach itself from the previous partisan tradition and to embrace the Anglo-American model of fairness and objectivity in reporting. This trend became particularly evident after the Clean Hands political scandal of 1992 and continues today.

In RAI today the web of interrelationships created through the years among parties, the broadcaster, and its journalists is still in place. But, as a consequence of the changing political and social climates, *lottizzazione* has lost its soul, its poignancy, and the strength of its legitimacy. Market imperatives have replaced the postwar hegemony of moderate Catholicism (1954-1975) and the later one of political parties (1975-1992). And if *lottizzazione* is losing its ideological motivations, RAI's public service mission is also fading away as the broadcaster adopts a scheduling strategy that is mainly geared toward maximizing its audience. Indeed, the diminishing influence of the party system did not correspond to a desire to assume leadership in quality programming, to experiment, to innovate, or to enrich, expand, and reinforce the broadcaster's public service identity. Instead, RAI's alleged freedom from the parties has come to increasingly indicate its subjection to the tyrannies of the market, and eventually, the demise of its public service ethos.

Public Television and the Party System

My thesis—that parties' interference in RAI has, at times, strengthened the role of public service broadcasting, and that partisan journalism has even enhanced RAI's democratic potentials—challenges the dominant view, according to which public service broadcasting should comprise a space separate from both market forces and the state, and journalism should be a "relatively uncoerced" practice. Ultimately, this view rests upon a conception of democracy entailing uniform citizenry, financial and cultural stability, and universal values.[5] But the Italian democracy and its public service broadcaster developed under different circumstances: rather than being stable, our democracy was characterized by frequent government crises, with a powerful opposition and strong antagonism among parties. But then, as political philosopher Norberto Bobbio points out, "transformation is the natural state of a democratic regime: democracy is dynamic whereas despotism is static and always identical to itself."[6]

Undoubtedly, Italian public service broadcasting is an imperfect rendition of the public service broadcasting ideal embodied by such institutions as the British Broadcasting Corporation (BBC). This is so for a variety of reasons: RAI was funded partly by advertising revenues from the beginning, carried for decades the inheritance of the Fascist legislation that had established national radio broadcasting, and has been ruled by a codified and well-established set of relationships with the political party system. RAI carries within it the genetic code (its establishing legislation, the character of the Italian party system, and the professional ideology of its journalists and management) of the democratic system from which it was born and in which it has been raised.

Imperfect, just like the democracy in which it evolved, RAI has nevertheless played important roles in promoting the linguistic and cultural unification of the country, and in creating a national identity and a national culture.[7] Often it has offered high-quality journalism and a variety of perspectives. As leading intellectual and RAI journalist Enzo Forcella points out, "Whatever its opponents say, overall public service broadcasting has been a great success."[8]

An Imperfect Public Broadcaster

Bobbio also argues that Italian democracy, as imperfect as it is, "will always be better than any 'perfect' dictatorship."[9] His conclusion can also apply to public service broadcasting. Indeed, even as imperfect as it is, RAI still offers, or at least has the potential to offer, a much-needed alternative to commercial media. The argument of the lesser evil can also help us not to interpret the history and the current conditions of both democracy and public media as histories of defeats, as institutions doomed to end because they were not in tune with the prevailing neoliberal and postmodern principles and social philosophies. In other words, both democracy and public media are unfinished business rather than once-stable institutions now in decline. As such, public service media need to be approached as evolving phenomena, to be "looked at in each site where [they] exist and in the context of the particular media ecology in which [they] exist,"[10] rather than treated as ideal, but abstract, concepts.

The Genesis of *Lottizzazione*

The idea of the public sphere has fragile roots in Italian social practices and political discourse. Whereas the public sphere is idealized as a place for fostering critical reasoning, Italian public service broadcasting was perceived during the first decades of its life (1954-1960) as a government arm, and since then as a political entity per se.[11] Until the early 1970s, RAI enjoyed a monopoly of local and national broadcasting. Only during the 1970s did local private television and radio broadcasters begin operations, and not until the early 1980s did RAI's monopoly over national broadcasting end. It is hardly surprising, then, that the Christian Democratic Party, the Italian Socialist Party, the Italian Communist Party, and various other minor parties all considered RAI as an arena in which each one of them could establish its own cultural and political influence.

Rather than a public broadcaster in the ideal version of the BBC, RAI was conceived as a terrain of ideological struggles. Rather than liberal ideals, a humanist-Catholic discourse legitimated the conditions of RAI's institutional and cultural dependence on the government and on the main party. Soon after the end of the war, the Vatican, in line with its traditional "scrupulous attention to the organization of ideas,"[12] recognized the value of the new mass media (both radio and television), and the DC ensured its leadership over the broadcaster in order to make of it an "essential moment in the Catholic re-foundation of Italians, as an anticommunist, but also as an anti-liberal force."[13]

From 1947 until 1992 Italy functioned as a "blocked democracy" in which the second-strongest party, the PCI, was never allowed to govern. But by the mid-1970s non-DC Italians were becoming restive under one-party control of the media, and "independent" radio and TV broadcasting were growing. The broadcasting Reform Law no. 103 of 1975 was designed to democratize the system. It removed RAI from direct control by the governmental administration and gave more responsibility to the parliamentary committee in charge of regulating the broadcaster's programming and nominating its directors. This law was both an expression of the characteristic activism of Italian political parties and an attempt to democratize the broadcaster. Indeed, *lottizzazione* was the hybrid result of democratizing forces advocating pluralism and broader social participation in the 1970s, cast in the context of an Italian political culture traditionally not very familiar with libertarian values. Paradoxically from an Anglo-American perspective, but quite logically from an Italian perspective, when innovative social forces advocating more democracy within the public broadcaster attempted to foster pluralism in the 1970s, the Italian party system responded by sharing power among its members. According to the logic of the party system, pluralism was finally reached once each of the three main parties was able to exercise hegemony over its own broadcasting channel. Even among journalists *lottizzazione* was often associated with pluralism, as a sign of improved democratic practices.

Is *Lottizzazione* a Corrupt Practice?

The notion that *lottizzazione* might have encouraged democratic practices is not only controversial in the context of the international community of media scholars, but it has also become problematic in Italy, especially since 1992, as citizens and public opinion have been increasingly suspicious of most that is public and political. A 1997 exchange of comments between leading journalist and media historian Paolo Murialdi[14] and the director of RAI's research department, Celestino Spada,[15] well represents the ongoing disagreement among scholars and media practitioners on whether *lottizzazione* is a threat, a malaise, or a normal condition of the public broadcaster.

On one hand, Murialdi considers *lottizzazione* a major problem, a practice that is "far more pervasive and deeper inside the public broadcaster than in any other institution or public agency,"[16] and laments the lack of an organic history of *lottizzazione*. Indeed, even though national dailies and magazines have continued through the decades to dedicate pages and pages to the analysis of each new appointment in RAI as a sign of parties' interference, there has been a singular lack of critical studies on the subject. But most importantly, Murialdi's criticism of *lottizzazione* is based on what he believes is the role of public service broadcasting, and, in particular, upon the necessity to ensure "freedom, prestige, and professionalism"[17] to public service journalism. He thinks that *lottizzazione* is a deviation from what public service journalism and the public broadcaster should be. For him, *lottizzazione* is a central, historical malaise of the Italian public broadcaster and of its journalism.

On the other hand, Spada minimizes the problem of political influence and argues that enough has already been said and written on it. He proposes that, given the changed political climate of the 1990s, *lottizzazione* is not as relevant anymore as it was before, and that the public broadcaster is now forced to face "other challenges—such as competition in an open market environment—rather than the challenge of the political system."[18] He contends that political interference might be neutralized by securely positioning RAI in the marketplace. For him, economic dependence is the structural problem, whereas party influence is a side effect, a superstructural phenomenon, a mere consequence of economic dependence. Not only is *lottizzazione* not a problem, but it has given more people the opportunity to make their voices heard inside the corporation: "RAI had more thinking heads than it would have had if *lottizzazione* had not existed."[19]

As distant as Murialdi and Spada are in terms of their respective notion of the role of public broadcasting, both their positions contain some part of the truth: it is true, as Murialdi affirms, that the phenomenon has not been comprehensively analyzed; but it is also true, as Spada emphasizes, that *lottizzazione* is a well-known practice covered through the years by weekly magazines and newspapers. On the one hand, it is true that everybody knows about it. The average citizen who pays the mandatory annual fee to RAI, as well as any politician or journalist, has certainly heard about *lottizzazione*. On the other hand, the absence of comprehensive historical and systematic analysis reveals a lack of critical awareness.

Is *lottizzazione* a major, understudied problem, or is it an overemphasized, obsolete pseudo-issue? The scarcity of studies confirms what Murialdi calls the impalpable nature of the phenomenon;[20] even Spada acknowledges that *lottizzazione* in RAI has become "*un dato acquisito, fino al luogo comune,*"[21] so well-known that the phenomenon has hidden itself within the shallowness of common sense, becoming a natural practice in RAI. Certainly, the historical and political reasons that have allowed political party influence to become common sense constitute a vantage point to analyze the role of public service broadcasting in postwar Italian democracy. It also becomes evident that in order to study the normalization of *lottizzazione* and the consequent notion of public service broadcasting as a terrain of ideological struggle, the ideal notion of public-service-media-as-public-sphere is not very helpful. Instead, I will approach the study of *lottizzazione* within the framework of Antonio Gramsci's definition of "organic ideology," organic in the sense that the practice of *lottizzazione* has been "necessary to a determinate structure."[22] Indeed, *lottizzazione* seems to have been such a necessary element in the making of the broadcaster that one could easily argue that its end could signify the collapse of the broadcaster itself. And indeed, the demise of *lottizzazione* in the 1990s is correlated with the demise of RAI's public service identity and its mission.

Research Questions

Murialdi and Spada's opposite positions with regard to *lottizzazione* are stimuli for a series of questions with regard to the nature, the ontological status, of *lottizzazione*: Is it plausible to propose that *lottizzazione* is not, or has not always been, a sign of the corruption of Italian democracy and of public service broadcasting? If *lottizzazione* has been a corrupt practice, what is it that *lottizzazione* has corrupted? Is it still practiced today or is it just a memory of the "ancien régime" of the postwar party system? How could *lottizzazione* have become naturalized? How and why did it blend with journalists' professional culture? Could *lottizzazione* be considered a positive expression of an unavoidable relationship between political power and journalism? Could it be that *lottizzazione* is illustrative of actual power struggles and therefore less misleading than bourgeois idealism about journalistic autonomy? Could it be a characteristic of partisan journalism, the distinguishing element of the Italian journalistic tradition?

In the next four chapters I will attempt to answer these questions. In chapter 1, I explore the historical context of Italian political culture and democracy; in chapters 2 and 3, I detail the history of public service broadcasting in Italy; and in chapter 4, I analyze RAI's journalists' experiences and their professional cultures.

Notes

1. Building upon the work of Jürgen Habermas on the history of the public sphere in modern democracies, the international academic discourse on public service broadcasting has developed in the context traced by Nicholas Garnham in a series of influential writings, in which the author presents the public-sphere-as-public-service-broadcasting association as the theoretical foundation for lending legitimacy to public service media. See Nicholas Garnham, "Public Service versus the Market," *Screen* 5, no. 1 (1983): 6-28; Garnham, "The Media and the Public Sphere," in *Communicating Politics: Mass Communication and the Political Process*, ed. Peter Golding, Graham Murdock, and Philipp Schlesinger (Leicester: Leicester University Press, 1986), 37-54; Garnham, "The Media and the Public Sphere," in *Habermas and the Public Sphere*, ed. Craig Calhoun (Cambridge, Mass.: MIT Press, 1992), 359-376; Garnham, *Emancipation, the Media, and Modernity: Arguments about the Media and Social Theory* (Oxford: Oxford University Press, 2000); and Garnham, "A Reply to Elisabeth Jacka's Democracy as Defeat," in "Rethinking Public Media in a Transnational Era," ed. Gerald Sussman, special issue, *Television and New Media* 4, no. 2 (May 2003): 193-200.

2. Habermas defined the public sphere as the sphere emerging when "the public of 'human beings' engaged in rational-critical debate was constituted into one of 'citizens' wherever there was communication concerning the affairs of the 'common wealth.'" See Jürgen Habermas, *The Structural Transformation of the Public Sphere* (Cambridge, Mass.: MIT Press, 1989), 106-107.

3. Elisabeth Jacka, "Democracy as Defeat: The Impotence of Arguments for Public Service Broadcasting," in "Rethinking Public Media in a Transnational Era," ed. Gerald Sussman, special issue, *Television and New Media* 4, no. 2 (May 2003): 188.

4. "Blocked democracy" refers to a stall in the democratic system that characterized the Italian postwar political scene from 1947 to 1992. Because the *conventio ad excludendum* among the government parties did not allow the Communist Party to be part of any ruling coalitions, the Christian Democrats remained uninterruptedly in power for forty-five years.

5. Michael Tracey proposes that the decline of public service broadcasting is caused by mutating cultural, social, and political contexts in which the founding ideals for public service broadcasting institutions, ideals of human and social progress, and homogeneous and stable nation-states and national communities, belong to a bygone era. See Michael Tracey, *The Decline and Fall of Public Service Broadcasting* (Oxford: Oxford University Press, 1998).

6. Norberto Bobbio, *Il futuro della democrazia* (Turin: Giulio Einaudi, 1984), xv.

7. See Tullio De Mauro, *Storia linguistica dell'Italia unita* (Bari: Laterza, 1962).

8. Enzo Forcella, interview with author, December 8, 1996.

9. Bobbio, *Il futuro della democrazia*, 23.

10. Jacka, "Democracy as Defeat," 188.

11. For a history of RAI's early days, see Paolo Murialdi, *Storia del giornalismo Italiano: Dalle prime gazzette ai telegiornali* (Turin: Gutenberg 2000, 1986); Franco Monteleone, *La radio italiana nel periodo fascista*, 2 volumes (Venice: Marsilio, 1976); Franco Monteleone, *Storia della RAI dagli alleati alla DC 1944-1954* (Rome: Laterza, 1979); Franco Chiarenza, *Il cavallo morente* (Milan: Bonpiani, 1978); and Giovanni Cesareo, *Anatomia del potere televisivo* (Milan: Franco Angeli, 1970).

12. Antonio Gramsci, as reported by Stuart Hall, "Gramsci's Relevance for the Study of Race and Ethnicity," *Journal of Communication Enquiry* 10, no. 2 (January 1986): 21.

13. Cesare Mannucci, *Lo spettatore senza libertà* (Bari: Laterza, 1962), 67.

14. Paolo Murialdi, "Per una ricerca sulla lottizzazione" (Notes toward a research on *lottizzazione*), *Problemi dell'informazione* 22, no. 1 (March 1997). *Problemi dell'informazione* is a leading academic journal in communication and media research in Italy. Paolo Murialdi is a former member of RAI's board of directors (1993-1994).

15. Celestino Spada, untitled author's manuscript, Rome, August 28, 1997, published as "Della lottizzazione e del 'partito Rai'" (About *lottizzazione* and the RAI Party), *Problemi dell'informazione* 22, no. 4 (December 1997): 485-493.

16. Paolo Murialdi, "Per una ricerca sulla lottizzazione," no page number available.

17. Paolo Murialdi, "Idee per vivere felici, non lottizzati e senza canone" (A few ideas to be happy, *lottizzazione* free, and without the annual fee), *Reset*, Milan, no. 43 (December 1997): 14-15.

18. Spada, "Della lottizzazione e del 'partito Rai,'" 485.

19. Celestino Spada, interview with author, RAI headquarters, Rome, January 1997.

20. Murialdi, interview with author, Milan, January 31, 1998.

21. Spada, "Della lottizzazione e del 'partito Rai,'" 485.

22. Antonio Gramsci, *Il materialismo storico e la filosofia di Benedetto Croce*, ed. Istituto Gramsci (Turin: Editori Riuniti, 1975), 59. Gramsci draws a

distinction between arbitrary ideology and organic ideology. In the paragraph "Il concetto di ideologia" (the concept of ideology), he defines arbitrary ideology as only being "able to initiate 'isolated movements,' individual polemics, etc., [whereas organic ideology] is historically necessary and has a 'psychological' value to it; it 'organizes' human masses; it shapes and prepares the terrain in which men operate and become aware of their conditions" (Gramsci, *Il materialismo storico*, 59).

Chapter 1

Democracy in Italy (1945-2003)

Two main aspects of Italian political life have nurtured and legitimated the practice of *lottizzazione* in RAI, *Radiotelevisione Italiana*, since the birth of the public broadcaster in 1954. They are the so-called blocked democracy[1] and the political party system. Both these conditions created an atmosphere conducive, and perhaps even vulnerable, to political and parties' interference inside the public broadcaster.

In this chapter, I underline the main characteristics of the postwar democracy, the role that political parties played in the formation of the republic, the creation of the party system, its evolution, and its crisis.

Contrasting Values and the New Constitution

On August 2, 1943, the royal decree law no. 175 put an end to the Fascist era: it dissolved the House of Deputies, the Fascist House (*Camera dei fasci*), and the House of the Corporations. The viceregal decree law of June 25, 1944, no. 151, established that the institutional forms of the new state would be elected by the Italian people, who would nominate through universal, secret, and direct suffrage a Constitutional Assembly to work on a new constitution. On March 16, 1946, a new viceregal decree law established that, together with the upcoming elections for the constituent assembly, the Italian people would also choose, via referendum, a new institutional form of government. On June 2, 1946, with more than 89 percent of the adult population voting, Italians expressed their preference for the republic against the preexisting Savoj monarchy.[2] An analysis of the vote, however, brings to the surface the heterogeneous, and rather weak, foundations on which the newborn republic was being built: not only was the prorepublican majority fairly small, 54.3 percent prorepublic versus 45.7 percent promonarchy, but the results pointed toward deep-seated contradictions between the progressive north (prorepublic) and the conservative south (promonarchy). These were signs that even the partisan struggles had failed to unify the country, and that two decades of fascism had made the social, economic, and cultural regional differences even more acute than before.

The Catholic and the workers' movements, deeply rooted in the country's variegated popular culture, represented the other contrasting forces mobilizing the masses in the postwar period. These two movements became the foundation for the three main parties: the Christian Democratic Party (DC), on one hand, as the conservative, Catholic party, and on the other hand the Italian Communist Party (PCI) and the Italian Socialist Party of Proletarian Unity (which became the Italian Socialist Party, PSI, in 1947) as the leftist, lay parties. The importance of these three parties soon became evident. Indeed, the votes cast for the members of the Constitutional Assembly left no doubt: altogether, the DC, the PCI, and the PSIUP/PSI received 74 percent of the total votes. From the outset, the new republic and the new constitution reflected conflicting, and often passionate, ideologies—Christian Democratic/Catholic versus Communist/Marxist. In an effort to mediate among such diverse interests, the Constitutional Assembly worked longer than it had been expected. The new constitution was finally approved on December 22, 1947, and became effective on January 1, 1948.

The constitution represented a major rupture with the Fascist and pre-Fascist era. In its spirit and words the influence of leftist forces and social Catholicism, which together represented the political and cultural bloc at the foundation of the anti-Fascist unity, was remarkable. The final version of the constitution was an eclectic document, a testimony to the attempts to create a new democracy based on principles of social justice and solidarity, a sign that Marxism and Catholicism were emerging as the protagonists on the postwar political, social, and cultural scene. For instance, the fundamental principles section specified that the republic must "remove any economic and social obstacle that impedes the free expression of citizenship and of the human person" and that the republic "acknowledges the rights of all citizens to work, and promotes those conditions that make such a right a concrete possibility."[3] Besides freedoms of speech, press, religion, and association, already contained (albeit in the different context of the Savoj representative monarchy) in the *Statuto Albertino*, the constitutional charter adopted after the unification of the Italian kingdom in 1861,[4] the new constitution meant to grant social rights to every citizen, and "envisaged a mixed economy with a significant amount of public participation and state intervention."[5] Particular attention was given to guaranteeing individual freedoms and precluding any excess of power in the hands of the executive. Moreover, the 1948 constitution configured a model of democracy more liberal than the prewar one, and more inclusive: more civil rights for more people, protection for the family and especially for working mothers, protection for children, equality of economic treatment between female and male employees, free access to health care and education, universal suffrage, freedom of speech, and freedom of the press.[6]

The new constitution established a majoritarian electoral system and celebrated the centrality of the parliament, whose members, for the most part, would be elected from party lists. In addition, the founding fathers limited the power of the president of the republic. The central role that the political parties had played in liberating the country from fascism, and the weight they would have in the future development of the democracy, was especially well expressed in title IV, which sanctioned the rights of all citizens to "freely become members of political parties in order to democratically participate to the making of national politics."[7] As the Jacobin ideals of a participatory democracy led by political elites, cherished by the Action Party (the united anti-Fascist party dissolved in 1946), were fading away, the three mass parties were emerging as the new subjects of political life and as an alternative to the elite politics typical of the Liberal, pre-Fascist democracy. Expectations of political, economic, and social transformation were the social and cultural engine that firmly established these parties at the center of the Italian political scene.

However, the centrality of the parties was asserted at the expense of other democratic institutions, such as the Constitutional Court, the regions, the National Council of Economy and Labor, and the *Consiglio Superiore della Magistratura*, institutions that were only superficially described by the founding fathers. The original weakness of such institutions showed the downside of the new parties' democracy, namely, the risk that those parties might become too powerful. A first example of such risk materialized when, after winning the national elections of April 18, 1948, the DC implemented the so-called *ostruzionismo di maggioranza* to prevent the election of minority representatives inside the *Consiglio Superiore della Magistratura*, thereby slowing down the process of electing magistrates in an effort to condition the choice of the five presidential nominees and put forward government proposals.

The Birth of the Parties' Republic

The parties' republic is a definition borrowed from the germinal work of Pietro Scoppola on the history of postwar Italy, and underlines the centrality of political parties in the making of the new democracy.[8] After the war, the DC, the PCI, and the PSIUP/PSI became the mediators between the masses and social and political institutions, also providing recreational and educational activities for their members. After two decades of fascism and a war, political participation was often characterized as a "willful act of adhesion . . . a form of socially oriented behavior often adopted under considerable community pressure."[9]

But these political parties had a difficult and somehow contradictory period ahead of them. Even though there was a strong public desire for innovations and rupture with the past, the years from 1945 to 1948 were a time when the eagerly anticipated institutional changes and the process of de-*fascistizzazione* substantially failed. Such a process, which began with the appointment of a high commissioner on April 13, 1944, was an attempt to remove people who had been previously involved with the dictatorship from positions of power in such sectors as the public administration, the armed forces, newspapers, and radio broadcasting. But de-*fascistizzazione* was short lived. Marking the so-called years of continuity of the state, when the leadership of many Fascist institutions (including radio broadcasting) was reinstated and became an integral part of the new republican system, the amnesty of June 1946 forgave charges for political and military crimes. Moreover, in the wake of the 1948 national elections, the government led by the DC supported the creation of the "special transitional roles" to reinstate those involved with the regime (and maximize electoral gains for the Christian Democrats).

The process of revision and elimination of preexisting Fascist norms was also considerably delayed as years went by before the members of the Constitutional Court were finally appointed. The effects of an outdated legislation on journalists' freedoms were noticeable: in the early 1950s, an increasing number of progressive journalists were still being charged with "opinion crimes" and crimes "against the state" for criticizing the government. Often those crimes were tried on the base of the Fascist code (condemned by the new constitution but not yet formally cancelled) according to which any adult male citizen could potentially be considered a "reservist" and therefore prosecuted as a soldier.[10] In the sector of radio broadcasting, some old norms remained substantially the same in the passage from fascism to the new democracy, thereby securing the new broadcaster, RAI, in the hands of the government until the reform law of 1975.

Literacy Rates and Mass Society

Not only were the political conditions somehow hostile to the formation of democratic mass parties, but a further contradiction was represented by the social and cultural conditions of the country immediately after the war. The kind of society that had taken shape during the two decades of dictatorship was, indeed, spurious: "a non-democratic mass society," as Scoppola has defined it,[11] certainly the most negative starting point for a new democracy. Twenty years of fascism had created a mass society within a totalitarian state whose legitimacy was based on a broad-based consensus supported by the Church, the middle class, and a solid party, the Fascist National Party (PNF). Consensus had been skillfully manipulated by control over the mass media (the national press, in the first instance, and then the state-run radio broadcaster *Ente Italiano Audizioni Radiofoniche*, and the cinema),[12] in a context where levels of illiteracy were much higher than in most other European countries. At the outset of the Fascist era, for instance, approximately 27 percent of Italians were unable to read and write, a percentage that was very close to that of the United Kingdom seventy years earlier.[13]

The traditional disadvantage due to the a high illiteracy rate continued to be a reality through the decades. It was only between 1932 and 1951 that the percentage of Italians who could not read and write dropped from 20.9 percent to 12.9 percent. There was also a considerable gap among various regions, specifically between a richer and more educated north and a poorer and less educated south. That gap remained noticeable through the years[14] and it is reasonable to assume that such difference had an impact on newspaper readership since the beginning of the twentieth century. For instance, from 1900 to 1924, the circulation of the national daily *Corriere della Sera* (from the northern city of Milan) increased more than elevenfold (from 70,000 to 800,000 copies). In contrast, from 1901 to 1922, the circulation of *Il Mattino* (from the southern city of Naples) only increased threefold (from 30,000 to 100,000 copies). As a whole, these numbers continued to be considerably low compared to other European countries for years to come. In 1952, for instance, only 10 percent of the Italian population was reading newspapers, compared to 61.5 percent in the United Kingdom, 35.3 percent in the United States, and 24 percent in France.

The Fascist Inheritance

The notion of democracy itself, on which the new parties and the new republic were based, was a complex and disputed one in postwar Italy, given the different, and at times opposing, Marxist and Catholic political and intellectual traditions at play. Not a democracy established by the political elites, as had been the case in prewar Italy, but also not a democracy based on classical Anglo-American liberal ideas as a practice of participation among equal and informed citizens, the new democracy required the parties to lead, educate, and politicize the masses. Their role was to promote social and cultural integration, to "connect the real country with the institutions of the state, link together people across all regions, mediate between the interests of the masters and those of the workers, and mediate among social classes."[15]

Paradoxically, in order to create a large popular consensus and mobilize broad strata of the population, those parties operated within the same "mechanism put in place by the Fascist Party, thereby following some of the rules of mass politics inaugurated by the dictatorship."[16] Indeed, like the postwar parties, the Fascist National Party (PNF), the first mass party that ever existed in Italy, provided some sense of social connectivity by taking care of pension rights and health care benefits for its members, guaranteeing their loans, and providing recreational activities for their children. Thanks to its organizational structure, the PNF was indeed able to provide a "web of interrelationships throughout the entire nation, and had the institutional role of connecting the center with the periphery, the public administration with the citizens."[17] The DC, PCI, and PSI found themselves having to perform a similar task, inheriting, in some respects, the Fascist concept of a "political party as a substitute for the state."[18] Nested in this original contradiction of democratic aspirations alongside the Fascist inheritance, the new republic developed as a party-based democracy.

The Mass Parties and Their Press

The party press, independent newspapers, radio, and, since 1954, television played an important role in supporting the unity of the main parties and their relevance in the cultural and social life of Italians. Besides its own party newspaper (the daily *Il Popolo*, based in Rome), the DC soon established control over various national newspapers (including *Il Mattino* of Naples and *Il Gazzettino* of Venice), the national news agency, ANSA (*Associazione Nazionale Agenzie di Stampa*), and the new radio and television broadcaster, RAI. Other parties, like the PCI and the PSI, were also strongly committed to use their publications as political but also educational tools. In 1949, the Communist Party began an intense distribution campaign to increase the sales of its paper *L'Unità*. The so-called Friends of *L'Unità* actively participated in the campaign by distributing the newspaper outside factories and schools and, on Sundays, selling it door-to-door. In 1949, *Paese Sera*, another communist national newspaper, was founded; other newspapers close to the Communist Party were *Il Nuovo Corriere*, of Florence, and *Milano Sera*. The PSI resumed the publication of its most important paper, *L'Avanti* soon after the liberation of Rome, while two more socialist newspapers *Il Secolo XIX* and *Il Lavoro* were established in the northwest region of Liguria.

The Postwar Parties

The Christian Democratic Party

The Christian Democratic Party (DC) emerged between the summer and fall of 1942, under the leadership of Alcide De Gasperi and with the blessings of the Vatican. An important characteristic of the new party, which was the heir to the Popular Party founded by Luigi Sturzo in 1919, was its fluidity. Open to vast strata of the population, the DC could count on numerous alliances: the broad support of the middle class in the northeast regions, the support of the vast Catholic peasant masses, the faithful alliance of the small and middle-level landowners in central and southern Italy, the fierce anticommunist support of the moderate right, and, most of all, a friendly pope.

The capillary action of the Catholic bloc, represented by the Vatican and the DC, permeated every aspect of Italians' social and cultural life in the first decade after the end of the war, and the overwhelming victory of the DC at the first national elections of 1948 revealed how effective such action was. In its ability to appeal to vast and somewhat different social strata with competing and contrasting needs, aspirations, and political inclinations, and its ability to secure the control of promonarchy and anticommunist moderate voters, the DC presented itself as a solid center, able to bear the transition from the Fascist era to the post-Fascist one.

The support of the Vatican was crucial to establishing cultural hegemony. During the 1940s, when the Church's political and cultural power peaked, its attention to creating consent through the control of the country's ideological apparati was particularly evident. Besides its influence on public affairs, the Church, led by Pope Pius XII (1939-1958), exercised a spasmodic control over the mass media in an attempt to "domesticate modernity"[19]—initially, its control over the cinema spanned from producing films in the Christian realism style (which, in opposition to the critical stance of neorealist cinema, celebrated the power of charity and confession) to overseeing theaters and distribution. During the mid-1950s control was also secured over the newborn state-run television and radio broadcaster through the appointment of Filiberto Guala, a man very close to the clergy, as the head.

The Communist Party

The PCI's commitment to the partisan war against the dictatorship earned it strong popular support toward the end of the war and in the first postwar years. The Italian Communist Party, which was founded in 1921 with the name of the Communist Party of Italy (Pcd'I), had an electoral base consisting mostly of the working class and some members of the intellectual elite, and could count on a well-established network of members in the industrialized northwestern triangle of Genoa, Turin, and Milan. As has been mentioned above, the PCI (and the rest of the mass parties), borrowed from the Fascist experience a model of the party as an organization that would follow its members from "birth to death," with local networks that promoted not only "propaganda activities, but also recreational and cultural ones, organized by gender and age—in the same way as the PNF."[20] The network of PCI's cells and sections spread quickly around the country as women's cells and workers' cells in factories across Italy were instituted in 1947. By 1954, the number of those cells reached sixty thousand units, double the number in 1945. As a result, the PCI enjoyed a strong internal cohesion.

I mentioned the similarities between the structures of the democratic parties and those of the PNF. However, if it is true that such similarities existed, there were also fundamental differences to be found in the directions of the new parties. Whereas Mussolini's idea of the role of the PNF was for the party to "rule with an iron-like fist and discipline the masses, that are, by nature, static and inert," that of the PCI was to democratize them. The party, with its pedagogical drive to educate and politicize Italians, became a "second society, a place where the circuit of possible interpersonal relations [was] completed."[21] The PCI also played an important role in improving the literacy of its members (12.9 percent of Italians were still illiterate in 1951).[22] Community centers, with libraries and educational programs, were opened even in the smallest villages, and the party's newspaper was distributed in every possible way; Arci (*Associazione ricreativa e culturale italiana*), a communist cultural and recreational network, spread across the country. Thanks to this kind of initiative, thousands of party members had an opportunity to get a better education.

Different was the PCI's political culture with regard to the new media of mass communication. During the first decades of the republic, the Communists did not pay much attention to either radio or television—according to Umberto Eco,[23] out of intellectual elitism—considering interpersonal communication, community programs and the printing press to be more effective, more dense with revolutionary potential, and closer to the needs of the workers. This attitude began to change in the 1960s, and by 1980, the PCI had created its own broadcasting network of independent television stations while claiming a stronger presence within the public broadcaster.

The Socialist Party

The PSI was founded in Genoa in 1892. Before the advent of the Fascist regime, the party made proselytes among the working class, experienced various internal schisms (1921 and 1924), and was then reunited under the leadership of Pietro Nenni in 1930. Not particularly active in the partisan struggles against Fascism, the PSI joined the PCI in the Action Party (1942-1946). At the general elections of June 2, 1946, the Socialist Party confirmed its central position in the political scene, gaining 20 percent of the votes. After 1953, when the dissolution of the centrist majority made it impossible for the DC to govern alone, the PSI became the only viable option as an ally on the left. This position gave the Socialists a strategic role as a hinge of the party system, a role that secured a political surplus value to the party confirming the importance of a powerful non-Marxist left. The events of 1956—including the twentieth Congress of the Soviet Communist Party, Khrushchev's speech denouncing Stalin's practices, and the military intervention of the Soviet Army in Hungary—weakened the relations between the Communists and the Socialists. At the Italian Socialist Party's national assembly in Venice in 1960, the PSI officially detached its domestic and international position from any alliance with communism and formally agreed to join the center-left government. As domestic and international events unfolded during the 1960s (political terrorism and the worsening of the crisis of Soviet communism with the invasion of Czechoslovakia in 1968), the PSI further established its complete autonomy from the PCI. In 1965, reflecting the emerging distinctions within the Italian left, the PSI founded its own national recreational association, Aics (*Associazione italiana cultura e sport*), whose membership, by 1977, had increased more than threefold.

Following the crisis of *centrismo*, the PSI officially entered the government coalition in 1962 and governed with the DC in a center-left coalition until the late 1960s. During those same years, the radio and television broadcaster, strictly under DC's control, began to open up to the moderate left, and various members of the Socialist Party obtained positions of responsibility within RAI. In the second half of the 1970s, the PSI was allocated the second national television channel, RAI2.

The Liberal Forces

A brief last note on the Liberal Party, which had once played a central role in the pre-Fascist government led by Giovanni Giolitti. At the end of World War II, the party was pervaded by internal tensions between monarchists and republicans, and between those who wanted to emulate the Western democracies' model and those who pushed for a return to the pre-Fascist political and institutional scheme. Schisms and internal contrasts reduced the Italian Liberal Party (PLI) to a marginal position, from which it never recovered. The PLI often joined the DC-led government coalitions; its presence within the public broadcaster was usually marginal.

A Blocked Democracy

The constitution and the triparty coalition in the immediate postwar years (1946-1947) were expressions of the previously united anti-Fascist front. But in the winter of 1947, as the situation normalized and both the United States and the Vatican tried to circumscribe the power and influence of the Italian Communist Party, Prime Minister Alcide De Gasperi expelled the PCI from the government. In the spring of 1948, he inaugurated a new four-party alliance (known as *centrismo*) comprising the Social-Democratic Party (PSDI), the Republican Party (PRI), and the Liberal Party. The Communist Party was excluded from joining any government coalition according to a formula known as *conventio ad excludendum*. Many argued that this exclusion indicated a significant regression in the democratization process. Certainly, it frustrated the postwar democratic expectations of many:

> The period between '47 and '48 represented the moment when the potentials for effective political and social innovations received their harshest counterblow. The "historical opportunity" for a radical change of the Italian political class, . . . [and for an] anti-Fascist and democratic [development], was fading away.[24]

The PCI's exclusion was the main cause for the evolution of a *sistema incompiuto*, an incomplete system or a blocked democracy, one in which governments could not alternate. Indeed, the DC, either alone or together with other parties, ruled the country from 1947 until 1992. Because the Christian Democrats had so much power, the Italian democracy was also defined as a democracy with an authoritarian face.[25]

Contrasting Visions

The consolidation of democratic practices was further complicated by deep-seated political and philosophical controversies centering on the meaning of democracy itself. Indeed, the two main cultural groups, Catholics and Marxists, lacked a common background of experiences and values. The only common ground shared by them was their anti-Fascist struggle, but that experience seemed to vanish with fascism itself. A few crucial factors must be taken into account if one is to fully understand the postwar situation:

> a fundamental uncertainty among the anti-Fascist political class about the idea itself of democracy, linked to different ideological premises and different readings of history; an even more profound uncertainty regarding the democratic status of political parties themselves; and lastly, the complex and contradictory experiences of common people.[26]

A clear understanding of what the Italian democracy should look like was missing: democracy was not a "well-defined category, neither was it a plethora of common values."[27] Instead of being a unifying principle, democracy became the locus for a bitter conflict, doomed to develop even further in the years ahead:

> [R]evolutionary hopes (on the part of the Marxist parties) on one hand and the faith in an objective truth and divine justice (on the part of the Catholic party) on the other introduced strong utopian tensions in the making of the new democracy. This colored Italian postwar political life and induced average citizens to commit themselves strongly to either one or the other party (the DC or the PCI).... Italian democracy was therefore born in an unbalanced condition in which its utopian element [the democratic ideal] was the strongest and central one, to the disadvantage of more functional and instrumental elements [concrete democratic institutions].[28]

The Communists' idea of democracy was based on the revolutionary potentials that, according to the PCI, appeared to be alive and active in certain social strata at the end of the war, but for years the party was torn between its Bolshevik dream of leading the country toward a socialist revolution and the necessity of following a more realistic strategy of social-democratic reforms. The kind of democracy that the PCI envisioned was defined as a progressive democracy, one in which liberal-democratic principles, such as civil guarantees, political pluralism, and parliamentary institutions, should be married to the classic ideas of socialist reforms, such as higher salaries and the redistribution of wealth, and social guarantees like free health care, affordable housing, and free education. However, in order to achieve such goals and in order to deepen its roots among different regional cultures and social realities, the party adopted different strategies, often in open contradiction between them. Progressive in the advanced north, more conservative and traditional in the impoverished south, the PCI was "an advocate of those who were keen to make radical changes in the state structures in the north and the center. . . . [But in] the south . . . it supported the reconstruction of the old state and its authority."[29]

The democratic aspirations of the Catholic political culture were also problematic because of the long history of Church opposition to the philosophical foundations of democracy and liberalism. According to Catholic doctrine, history was the actualization of God's will on earth, and truth was to be considered as an objective and transcendental value. In such a context, democracy was condemned as subjective, and with it such classic libertarian freedoms as freedom of expression and freedom of the press. Even the more socially oriented Catholic doctrine of Pius XII, so aware of the mechanisms of modernity and the importance of not undermining them, was imbued with an antimodern culture, and a fundamentally suspicious attitude toward the process of secularization.

The Party System (*Partitocrazia*)

> *Partitocrazia* . . . characterized the activities of all major parties. . . . [The term] describes a series of practices aimed at conquering positions of power, portions of the public and state territory. In so doing, public resources were transformed into private ones, as they were colonized and shared among [the party's] secretariats and their oligarchies.[30]

As long as the parties were able to maintain their role as mediators among the citizens, the state, and political institutions, they remained vital and central to democratization. As society evolved and parties began to lose such centrality, however, the connection between parties and their members became progressively weaker. *Partitocrazia*, which means government of the parties, refers to this gradual detachment of the party system from its initial purpose and its growing influence and power within state institutions and public administration.

This phenomenon, which became particularly evident during the 1980s, was technically made possible by the proportional system of electoral legislation. The proportional system, which was supported by both the Socialist and Catholic forces, was first introduced at the end of the First World War in an effort to extend representative power to vast strata of society. Through the years, however, such a system encouraged the development of disciplined mass parties, and vilified the electoral and political process by increasing the influence of the party machinery over nominations. Indeed, in the absence of primary elections, candidates for parliament were chosen by the party leadership, usually among full-time party employees: as a result, party secretariats became the "*eminences grises* of the Italian political system."[31] Politicians' moral standards declined because of the lack of alternate government and many of them became professional politicians,[32] seeking office mainly for material and personal gain. The lack of alternation in the government and the proportional electoral system both represented fundamental steps toward *partitocrazia*, but the roots of *partitocrazia* are to be found in the weakness of state institutions and in the typical Italian conception of a political party as a substitute for the state.

Occupation of power and bureaucratization of the party structure were key ingredients of *partitocrazia*. Instead of citizens being the subjects determining political changes and the parties being their instrument, the parties had become, as Scoppola put it, "the actual political subjects while citizens' consensus was reduced to mere instrument."[33] During the 1980s, the increasing detachment of parties from citizens and the underlying assumption that citizens' consensus was of use to politicians, were also reflected in the shift in television programming. Partly due to the advent of the new commercial channels, television began to foster image making and emotional persuasion, squeezing the forums for rational debate.

The growing influence of political parties within the public administration and the state structures is important for understanding *lottizzazione* in the public administration in general, and particularly in RAI. During the years of *centrismo*, from 1947 through the early 1960s, the DC governed the public broadcaster by itself. In the 1960s, when the PSI joined the center-left coalition, the Socialists became increasingly present within RAI, and after the 1975 reform of RAI, the DC and the PSI, and later the PCI, shared positions of power inside the public broadcaster.

Party Factionalism (*Correntocrazia*)

Party factionalism, another important phenomenon to understand how parties' control evolved inside the broadcaster, refers to the formation of factions (*correnti*) within political parties. Historically, *correntocrazia* was an effect of the bureaucratization of the parties' structures, of the DC first and the PSI later, and gained momentum in the 1960s. As Eugenio Scalfari wrote:

> Once the channels of communication between the base [of the party] and the leadership of that party, and between the party as an institution and society at large, started to fade away, a double phenomenon became inevitable. On one side, a ferocious centralization of power occurred, i.e., participatory rights were almost totally taken away from the voters by the sclerotic leading party elite to its own advantage; on the other side, power itself within the party underwent a process of feudalization. A complex system of *vassalage* was established that implied a reciprocal "respect" among the different factions' leaders, each the chair of his own "province" [or fief], one that he could administer arbitrarily.[34]

Other explanations for the existence of factions inside the parties can be found in the shape of government coalitions. The lack of constitutional alternatives to government coalitions centered on only one party and the rigidity of alliances among parties were some of the main reasons for the existence of factions. Indeed, factionalism can be explained as an attempt to encourage political alternatives to be articulated through different alliances of groups inside the coalition parties.

Factions were usually formed on the basis of ideological, personal, and geographical, or geopolitical, interests. Ideological factions were most likely to be found within the PCI, personal-interest factions could be found within the PSI, and all sorts of factions divided the DC from the end of the 1950s. In the 1950s and 1960s a powerful faction within the DC was the *Fanfaniani*, from the name of a famous DC leader, Amintore Fanfani. This faction had a major influence over RAI. Indeed, one of

RAI's most powerful director-generals, Ettore Bernabei (in RAI from 1961 to 1974), was close to the *Fanfaniani*.

The PSI experienced internal divisions from the end of the 1960s. In contrast, the highly centralized structure of the PCI served for a long time as an antidote to any internal division. By the mid- to late 1980s, however, factions based on ideological differences emerged also within the Communist Party as a symptom of the loosening up of the party's apparatus.

There are both technical and political explanations for *correntocrazia*. Technically, higher centralization of a party's structure was inversely related to the number of factions inside that party. For instance, a structurally unified party like the PCI had fewer *correnti* than the DC, which had a decentralized structure and, consequently, many internal factions. The broad range of the party's electorate brought along with it a vast spectrum of different political and ideological positions that contributed to factionalism. *Correntocrazia* was also cause and effect of the proportional electoral system and the bureaucratization of the party system. Public administration and state/public institutions came to be affected by the existence of these factions as various sectors of the public administration were transformed into centers of power. Indeed, nominations in the public administration and in other institutions, including RAI, were often made on the basis of the particular faction to which a given candidate belonged. For instance, according to a mechanism known as *lottizzazione nella lottizzazione* (*lottizzazione* within *lottizzazione*), power sharing inside the broadcaster did not happen just among parties, but also among the various factions within each party. There was a tendency to inflate jobs, especially in the news departments, where vice directorate positions multiplied to create space for representatives of various parties and factions. In a similar fashion, each minister had at least two vice ministers, each being chosen as the representative of a certain faction and/or a certain party. Scalfari wrote,

> [Each] minister's main concern was . . . to reinforce his own personal role as a "great feudatarian." Since his own power derived . . . from his party and his faction, his main focus was to strengthen, with all his might, his own faction. . . . [His] "full-time job" [as a minister] consisted in offering . . . major favors to create consensus around his own party and his own faction. Major favors consisted in nominating this or that friend for this or that board of directors, in obtaining certain tax breaks for this or that public corporation, etc.[35]

The Industrial Reconstruction: Italian State Capitalism

As the political scene was evolving in a complicated and somehow anomalous fashion, the private industrial sector was also developing in a rather peculiar manner. Indeed, already by the time of the Fascist dictatorship, Italian capitalism had been characterized by an intricate relationship between private capital and state industry. This relationship continued during the industrial reconstruction (1945-1952), and represented one more sign of the persistence of old inheritances. Notwithstanding constitutional dictates and pressures from the Allies to adopt more liberal economic models, the corporate state, as the practice of state intervention in private enterprises was defined, emerged early on in the life of the new democracy.[36]

Indeed, according to economist Ernesto Rossi,[37] one of the main tasks of the moderate center in power was to

> ensure private capital's continuous influence on the government, the press, the banks, the holdings, the economic ministries, the boards of directors of big industry, and the party secretariats. The industrial elites received guaranteed treasury loans, the concession of public services, financial assistance, and considerable tax exemptions.[38]

The Italian postbellum political economy followed a complex route, one in which liberal political economic models, sanctioned by the new constitution, developed together with a politics of state intervention and the formation of the welfare state. If the mix of public and private interests were at the core of Italian political economy, only timid attempts were made to establish a more liberal model of government nonintervention in the economy.

Even though the constitution sanctioned state financial assistance only for small and medium industries, already by 1947 large influxes of capital were flowing from the state treasuries to major industrial sectors, and a network of intermediate state structures was established to control state special funds, such as the funds for the underdeveloped south. Within this network, the DC created its own space for exercising political influence and fostering clientelist practices: of this network of public intervention in the private sector, IRI, the Institute for Industrial Reconstruction, was a central institution. The institute, founded in 1933 to administer public and state financing for the private sector in an attempt to strengthen the domestic financial market, was another inheritance of the

Fascist era. The autarchic politics inaugurated by Mussolini in the mid-1930s—also in response to the economic sanctions imposed by the League of Nations, the bank reforms of 1936 and 1938, and the world war—reinforced even further the presence of the state in the economy and thereby the role of IRI. The institution survived the fall of Fascism, was reintegrated into the new democratic state, and contributed to the reconstruction of the industrial apparatus.

IRI was restructured as a state holding company, an association in between public and private interests, financed by private as well as by public capital but still dependent on the minister of the treasury. In this mixture of private and public capital, RAI was conceived as a hybrid entity, as a private corporation (*società per azioni*) financed by advertising revenues and license fees, and controlled by IRI, which owned about 95 percent of its shares. Such an original corporatist enterprise model, by mixing public and private capital and by financing "public" television partly through advertising revenue, in effect set itself up for an eventual invasion of its "sphere" by private broadcasting companies. It became harder and harder to defend RAI's monopoly given that the broadcaster was not completely noncommercial.

The state presence in the industrial sector included corporations directly controlled by the state administration, like the post, the telegraph, the telephone, and the railway system; public bodies that operated in economic sectors; and private corporations, whose capital was underwritten by the state. In total, more than half of Italian corporations were controlled by the state or by public bodies, and often state control of the corporations went beyond normal administrative practices. Soon after the end of the war, the DC imposed its control over IRI, which became a haven for insatiable politicians, with thousands of jobs and enormous flux of capital. Appointments of managers and directors became increasingly determined by parties' *lottizzazione*, clientelism, and nepotism. Understandably, the media sector also became a natural environment for *partitocrazia* to flourish. Indeed, the distribution of jobs in the public broadcaster could be easily rationalized not as mere monetary favors but rather as a way of making sure that all factions were properly represented and had a chance to make their case in the formation of public discourse.

The Ministry of State Participation

A political-technocratic network was created to control the growing economic and cultural power of these public/state industries. This political network, crucial for understanding the role that the DC played inside the public broadcaster, was the Ministry for State Participation, founded in 1956 to monitor and facilitate the relations among the state, various ministries, industry, and the financial sector. Through this network of ministries and other public institutions such as the Southern Fund, instituted in 1950 to support the financial and industrial development of the south, political control over large sectors of the economy was secured in the hands of the Christian Democrats:

> [T]he system of public/state-run companies, of which the DC became the owner, was not organized nor created with any organic strategy of public intervention in the economy in mind. It was, more than anything else, a way to ensure to the DC clientelist power deriving from the control of such giants.[39]

State interference in the industry further intensified after the elections of 1948, when the DC was confirmed as the country's political and social hegemonic force. Preexisting interests and agreements between state and private capital grew stronger, and the Christian Democratic Party was dexterous in mediating between the two opposed political economic models, liberal versus state managed. These two opposing tendencies, rather than representing an impediment, were instruments in the hands of the powerful economic groups and the political elite:

> [S]tate intervention in the economy was resumed once the DC had consolidated its position as the fulcrum of the country's financial interests . . . and once state intervention was securely channeled so as to guarantee . . . the development of the northern industrial pole. . . . The question of which theoretical model to follow [the liberal versus the statist] during the reconstruction was not so much a question of theoretical preferences as it was a question of power. The question was: which social stratum and economic group would benefit most from any chosen model? For the Italian postwar political economy, the question was a political one, not just a technical one.[40]

The classic liberal opposition between public and private sectors and between state and private industry was addressed in a peculiar fashion and reinterpreted by letting the public sector be administered by the private one, and by "multipl[ying] the intermediate agencies subject to political pressures."[41] In a parallel fashion to the inflation of intermediate agencies in the corporatist structure, levels of management in RAI were also multiplied in the attempt to please various factions.

It is in this context that the relationship between the governing party and the public broadcaster, in the first decades of its life, must be understood. To expand its electoral base, the DC needed not only clients but also a site to establish cultural and political consensus, and RAI was conceived as a government property. Not only had the Christian Democratic Party inherited from the Fascists a public apparatus whose functioning and structures it did not substantially modify, but it also occupied this apparatus.

Opening to the Left

During the first years of the DC leadership, the economic conditions of the country improved. Some important innovations were made, such as the beginning of television broadcasting in 1954; the development of a highway system across the country in 1955; and the institution of the Credit Bank (*Medio Credito Centrale*) in 1959 to sustain the industrial development of the northeast regions.

The social costs of rapid industrialization, known as the economic miracle, were high. Low salaries, determined by the necessity of maximizing profits and increasing production, and by the influx of an indigent workforce due to immigration from the impoverished south, created social tensions, especially in the overpopulated cities of the industrialized triangle (Genoa, Milan, and Bologna). The government responded by increasing political control, by giving more power to the police, and by forming a center-right government with the MSI (*Movimento Sociale Italiano*, the heir to the Fascist Party) in the spring of 1960, known as the "Tambroni government" from the name of the prime minister. Riots and strikes exploded in major northern cities in July 1960 in protest against low salaries and the right-wing government.

The Tambroni government fell shortly thereafter and the DC, in search of social legitimation and of stronger and more stable governing alliances, looked to the left for potential allies. That was the beginning of a long era known as the center-left period, or *centro-sinistra*, which lasted almost ten years. The PSI, led by Pietro Nenni, joined the government in the summer of 1960 as an external supporter, and by 1963 had become part of the ruling coalition. During the earlier years of *centro-sinistra,* 1962-1964, important reforms were passed, including the institution of public middle schools and the nationalization of the electric energy industry. Crucial changes happened also inside RAI: between the early 1960s and 1974, when Bernabei was director-general, the public broadcaster, strictly controlled and staffed by the DC and the Vatican during the 1950s, slowly opened the doors to members of other parties. Giorgio Vecchietti (Socialist Party) was appointed director of the news program in 1963; Italo De Feo (Social Democratic Party) became a member of the RAI board of directors and vice president of the corporation; Gianni Granzotto was appointed managing director with the blessings of socialists, social democrats, and republicans; in 1965, Giuseppe Antonelli (another socialist) was appointed vice-central director of radio; and in 1966 Enrico Manca (Socialist Party) was appointed managing editor of the newscast (*telegiornale*).

But a series of domestic and international events contributed to the collapse of the center-left experiment: the student protest in 1968; the internal crisis of labor wages; the U.S. currency devaluation and the monetary crisis in 1971; and the oil crisis in 1973. In Italy, the student protest was soon joined by extreme fringes of the organized working class and the extraparliamentary organizations. The first episode of terrorism was the 1969 bombing of Piazza Fontana in Milan, carried out by neo-Fascist groups, which initiated a decade of terrorism, the so-called *anni di piombo* (years of lead).

Terrorism and the Media

The years of lead had important repercussions on Italian journalism as many questioned where to draw the line between the necessity to inform citizens and the need to protect certain kinds of information, how much space the journalists had for voicing dissent against the government's decisions, and their independence in such a difficult phase in the life of the republic. How much coverage should be given to terrorists' activities? How were journalists supposed to report terrorist attacks, given that the majority of accessible sources were only government sources? Government control, especially on RAI's newscasts, intensified. As Maria Grazia Bruzzone writes, "a sense of 'imperial power' was reflected more than anywhere else in the telegiornale, where all illusions of journalistic autonomy . . . had disappeared."[42] No longer did the news programs attempt to understand or explain reality; they mostly silenced dissent. With some noticeable exceptions, government pressure was also exercised on the major national newspapers, like *Corriere della Sera*.

The reaction of the journalists was immediate. Giorgio Bocca describes the situation:

> [M]any journalists had soon realized that the state authorities were not reliable. We had proofs that some state persecutors and local heads of public security were intentionally sidetracking the persecution and hiding the evidences. We touched with our hands that there was this imperial power. We realized that it was up to us to do something to create some kind of democratic information.[43]

Ferment among journalists, including those from the Catholic zone, signaled the crisis of the DC's political equilibrium inside the public broadcaster, and the overall crisis of the postwar social and cultural order. As a result of internal tensions within the DC and the crisis of the center-left, in 1969, major changes occurred within the public broadcaster indicating that the Bernabei era, the time of a powerful director-general, was coming to an end. A sign of the diminishing centrality of the director-general's role was the appointment, which was contrary to Bernabei's decisions, of the conservative Willy De Luca as director of the news program.

A phenomenon known as the "politicization of journalists" occurred not only in RAI, but also in the press. At the end of 1969, more than one hundred journalists founded the Committee for Freedom of the Press and Struggle against Oppression in Milan; in Rome, in the early winter of 1970, almost five hundred journalists, including RAI journalists, founded the Movement for Democratic Journalists. In the midst of the critique against the widespread paternalist culture and the formation of new social movements (youth, women, community organizations, teachers, etc.), public service television came under intense fire.

New Progressive Legislation

The results of the May 1968 elections—when the government parties, especially the Socialists (joined by the Social Democrats), suffered the worst defeat of their history by receiving only 14.4 percent of the vote—

were symptoms of a growing fracture between society and the party system. According to Norberto Bobbio, this electoral loss was an expression of social unrest, a symptom of the bureaucratization of the party system, and the result of inequalities created by the economic growth of the previous decade (workers' agitation reached an unprecedented intensity during the so-called *autunno caldo* of 1968).

At the 1968 elections, the Communist Party clamorously advanced, thereby making its exclusion from the government even more problematic. The victory of the PCI further undermined the center-left coalition, opening up a season that would be characterized by weak governments, with an average of one government per year. The political system showed further signs of crisis when, in 1972, 1976, 1979, 1983, and 1987, five legislative sessions all ended prematurely, revealing a "fragility ... that led, at the end of the 1970s, to the first proposal for sweeping reforms."[44]

Because of internal disputes over such issues as the proper relationship to entertain with both the PCI and the DC, the Socialist Party split in 1969. The difficulties within the PSI, the diminishing consensus around the DC, and the threat of domestic terrorism determined a change in the government coalition. The new cabinet, which followed closely the model of the centrist governments of the 1950s, consisted of the DC and three minor lay parties, the Liberal Party (PLI), the Republican Party (PRI), and the Social-Democratic Party (PSDI).

The new government coalition had to face the question of the relationship with the PCI at the national and the local administration levels. The Communist Party was growing in influence and popular support, and its relevance for any future government stability could no longer be underestimated. Indeed, even though the Communists were not allowed to enter government coalitions at the national level, they had been governing for years at the local level, gaining wide consensus. Awareness of the PCI's political and electoral strength, and the social unrest of the late 1960s and 1970s, prompted the new centrist coalition to consider, and eventually implement, new reforms. In 1970, local governments (*Regioni*), foreseen by the constitution but never realized up to this point, were instituted and became effective in 1972. In 1974, unprecedented legislation, the *Decreti Delegati*, established the accountability of public schools at all levels of administration through the institution of controlling bodies, promoting participation of parents, community members, and representatives of civil society in the school's activities through ad hoc committees.

In mass media regulation, major changes were also implemented. In 1974, two sentences of the Constitutional Court, no. 225 and no. 226, provided some criteria for the impending reform of the public service broadcaster: more power should be given to the parliament, the professional autonomy of journalists and programmers had to be ensured, the right of access on the part of social movements had to be guaranteed, and advertising revenues on television ought to be limited in an effort to protect the financial support for the printing press. Both sentences stated the constitutionality of the state monopoly over broadcasting.

A new reform of the broadcasting system, and of RAI in particular, was advocated by many of those who believed in the necessity to realize more democratic information, especially the Communists, interested in giving more control to the parliament, and the Socialists, whose main goal was to decentralize television production. In 1975 a new law was passed that established a closer relationship between the public broadcaster and the parliament through the *Commissione Parlamentare di Vigilanza*, the Parliamentary Committee founded in 1947. The committee, whose forty members were appointed by the two presidents of the houses (the Senate and the Chamber of Deputies) and chosen among the representatives of all parliamentary groups, was given major powers, including the power to supervise RAI's programming and its financial resources. The law expanded party influence on the public broadcaster in an attempt to liberate RAI from the control of the DC and, ultimately, from its dependence on the government. But as the power of the Christian Democrats was questioned and other political parties—many of which had interests in opening up the airwaves to independent and commercial broadcasters—became more visible and influential, the monopoly status of RAI began to crumble. Not only did RAI need to become more independent from the government and the DC, but new social movements also demanded a more liberalized broadcasting context. Financial and industrial groups lobbied in the name of "freedom of antenna," while exponents of the Socialist Party and the Christian Democratic Party, although unofficially, encouraged the birth of foreign TV stations in the Italian language and cable televisions across the country, including Teleroma-cavo, Telepiombino, Telealessandria, Telediffusione Italiana (the only cable experiment in the southern city of Naples), and Telebiella, which began its cable operations in 1973. In 1976, for the first time in the history of Italian broadcasting legislation, the Constitutional Court (sentence no. 202), ruled in favor of local commercial broadcasters, formally questioning RAI's monopoly over local radio and television broadcasting.

In the sector of private law, progressive and democratizing laws were also passed. The divorce bill received unexpectedly wide popular support in the national referendum of 1974. In 1975 a new family code was established. In 1978 a bill was passed legitimating abortion almost on demand. Italian society was now moving away from the powerful hold that the Church had been able to exercise in the immediate postwar years and gradually becoming a lay society; citizens were emancipating themselves from religious and ideological constraints. Indeed, the fracture between citizens and the political party system was getting deeper, while the contradictory situation of the PCI, the second most powerful party, yet not allowed to govern, was becoming untenable. In this phase, civil society and social movements were gradually taking over the social and political space previously occupied by political parties: the success of progressive forces at the 1974 referendum in favor of the divorce bill was a clear symptom of the fact that the Catholic bloc was losing its hegemony over social, cultural, and moral norms. It was also a sign of the declining legitimacy of the voice of that bloc, the public broadcaster.

At the elections of 1976, the PCI gained an unprecedented 38 percent, the greatest electoral victory in its history. Support for the DC and the PSI dropped. Overall, the parties' traditional ability to "comprehend and generalize" was diminishing, as they were becoming instruments "to represent and mediate among competing interests"[45] in the context of an "autonomous politicization of society."[46]

The Historic Compromise

The idea of the historic compromise was elaborated by Enrico Berlinguer soon after the events that took place in Chile in 1973 (the coup d'etat of Pinochet and the murder of President Salvador Allende). The PCI's secretary general thought that it would be dangerous for a capitalist country like Italy, going through a social and economic crisis, to be governed by a party that had only 51 percent of the votes. It was necessary, Berlinguer argued, to encourage "a convergence of forces, historically important, like the Catholic, the Communist and the Socialist ones, that could lead the nation towards a historical compromise with the aim to ameliorate the economic conditions, to improve national solidarity, and to create a new civil ethic."[47] According to its leadership, the PCI was ready to sacrifice some international communist doctrines, like the Leninist theory on the destruction of capitalism and the Gramscian call for an alliance between workers and peasants, in order to promote a new alliance between the workers and the middle class. The result would be, Berlinguer thought, a "democratic alternative" rather than a left alternative, namely, a practice of actual collaboration with the bourgeois party. Aldo Moro, president of the DC national council, was fond of the PCI's proposal, which also received the support of the DC left wing after the 1976 election results.[48] However, the notion of the Communist Party formally entering the government zone was obviously feared and opposed by many. Extreme left groups and some fringes of the Communist Party itself considered the PCI attempts to join the government a betrayal of class struggle; on the other side, the DC right wing perceived any collaboration with the PCI as a dangerous concession. Furthermore, Italy's most influential ally, the United States, also opposed the historic compromise, and the Carter administration publicly declared its position against including the PCI in any new government.

At the end, the revolutionary idea of a compromise between the Communists and the governing party was never realized, and its failure was marked by a very tragic event. On March 16, 1978, when the Chamber of Deputies was scheduled to vote on a new government coalition that was going to be directly supported, for the first time in history, by the PCI, Moro was kidnapped by a Red Brigade command in downtown Rome, and fifty-five days later he was murdered.[49] A series of other terrorist events escalated through the early 1980s, reinvigorating citizens and politicians' fear of the "red menace." The state and the constitutional parties grouped together against terrorist attacks and in defense of republican institutions.

The following elections of 1979 obviously resonated from the political and social turmoil or international and domestic events, such as the crisis of the Soviet Union, the menace of red terrorism, and the PCI's failed attempts to realize the historical compromise and offer a viable alliance between the working class and the bourgeoisie. The results of the elections were dense with important novelties. The Communist Party dramatically lost electoral support, which dropped from 34.4 percent at previous elections to 30.4 percent; the DC stagnated at 34 percent.

But the demise of the communist question would prove to be a major cause of the tectonic movement that, during the next decade, would shake the party system to its foundations, eventually leading to its collapse in the early 1990s. Indeed, with the end of the communist question, which had represented a major concern of postwar political life, the role and function of the DC also became questionable. The end of the reciprocal siege, which had ensured dynamism, pluralism, and political conflict during the first decades of the republic, would lead both parties to a condition of isolation. Over the next decade the political system would become more sclerotic, autoreferential, and rigid, while the process of detachment from the citizens and the voters continued. As a consequence, the political significance of elections also began to fade away as parties increasingly became mere "containers of interests,"[50] less antagonistic, and more similar to one another.

The 1980s

The stagnation of productivity, high inflation (21.1 percent in 1980), growing public debt, permanent political instability, and continuing terrorist events were signs of the international and domestic crisis continuing through the early 1980s. The crisis affected both the main governing party and the opposition: at the elections of June 1983, the DC obtained the worst results since the end of the war.

Among the main parties, only the PSI reported a considerable success (+12 percent). Meanwhile, at the local/regional level, new political formations, like the *Liga Veneta* (the Venetian League, the "mother of all leagues," of which the most famous would be the *Lega Nord*), were making their first appearance. Because of the crisis of the two most powerful political formations, the PCI and the DC, the Socialist Party found itself, once again, in a strategic position as a hinge of the party system. Indeed, in 1981, after more than thirty years of DC hegemony, the leadership of the government went to a Republican Party member, Giovanni Spadolini. Successively, Bettino Craxi, secretary-general of the PSI since 1976, led two of the longest governments in the republic's history, from 1983 to 1987.

Some of the most important pieces of legislation during Craxi's governments established new relations between workers and corporations, and laid foundations for unprecedented innovations in the broadcasting sector. On February 14, 1984, the decree abolishing wage indexing passed, indicating a major setback for the working class, the Communist Party, and the workers' unions. The abolition of wage indexing inaugurated a new course in the PSI's strategy: the definite severing of any residual tie with the Marxist tradition, and a new mission to represent the aggressive middle class of the 1980s. At the end of 1984, the so-called Berlusconi decree conveniently allowed the commercial broadcaster Fininvest, owned by Silvio Berlusconi, a builder contractor turned media mogul based in Milan and Craxi's personal friend, to continue its national broadcasts. This decree contravened the Constitutional Court sentence no. 202 of 1976, which forbade commercial entities to broadcast nationally. (However, in that same ruling, the Constitutional Court had already recognized the legitimacy of radio and television broadcasting at the local level, supporting its decision with the notion that there were no risks of monopoly or oligopoly at the local level.)

The Socialists were expanding their consensus among the middle class, and the decree ad hoc for Berlusconi can be interpreted as part of their plan to please voters—indeed, Fininvest channels were already very popular by the mid-1980s. On the other side, the abolition of wage indexing was designed to please the industrial sectors: small and middle industrialists, the core of the Italian economic force, constituted a new pool of voters for the Socialists. Overall, Craxi's politics were clearly animated by the intent to cancel much of the PSI tradition of progressive politics. Privatization of politics, the search for personal gains, the abuse of public office for private benefits, and the generalized reflux into private affairs characterized the 1980s. Of this general tendency, the secretary-general of the PSI was an interpreter. During his leadership, indeed,

> political participation was compressed and replaced by the search for personal success. The government's efficiency was beneficial only to industry [represented by the *Confindustria*, the union of industrialists], Agnelli [owner of FIAT, the automobile industry], and Berlusconi. Under Craxi's government . . . the state became "strong against the disenfranchised classes and weak vis-à-vis the powerful ones."[51]

The Socialists permeated every sector of public administration and state structures to a point where degeneration of the party, and political corruption, became "inevitable consequences, cynically accepted when not deliberately pursued."[52] In this context the fracture between the political party system and the citizens deepened. The mass media, which were often subservient to the parties and to politicians' will, became their most wanted, and often only, interlocutors.

Analyzing those years, Norberto Bobbio argued that the democratization of the nation seemed to have failed to take place.[53] According to him, the reflux into private concern, which so heavily characterized the 1980s (the so-called *anni del riflusso*), and the ideology of pluralism that ensued from the diminishing importance of meta social philosophies and political ideologies, were giving voice only to particularistic and corporativist interests rather than fostering broader political representation:

> Years of democracy, years of opportunities for confronting ideas, years of mass communicated information, had failed to produce a greater and better political education for citizens. Quite to the contrary, many signs indicated that citizens were poorly educated. . . . [I]t was also possible to notice a persistence of oligarchies, of elites that were "imposing," rather than "proposing," themselves.[54]

A feudalization of the political system was already occurring as the five parties in power, the *pentapartito*, were becoming increasingly more pervasive and invasive. The political sphere was gradually relapsing into a prepolitical, private condition, where the parties', and their leaders', private interests were being pursued. The parties were taking over the political scene in a context in which citizens were either becoming instrumental to the parties' own goals, or losing interest in political participation altogether:

> Once ideologies had ceased to be the glue around which consensus was created . . . parties tried to obtain consensus using the institutions they controlled. They now . . . possessed and controlled the entire system. From here, a kind of prosaic politics originated, one that was unable to satisfy the requests coming from society.[55]

The heavy diet of imported soap operas and television series on the Fininvest channels soon became very popular, inducing also the public broadcaster to rely on mostly imported products to compete with the private networks. While Italians were watching, after decades of monopoly, *Dallas* and *Beautiful* (from the United States), and *Dancing Days* (from Brazil), the struggle over the control of television on the part of the political parties continued. In this critical context, the Communist Party was presented with the opportunity to be part of the government zone. The PCI endured an identity crisis and was internally divided,

> torn between the aspirations to radically adapt its political methods and strategies in order to be accepted within the normal democratic dialectic and the will not to compromise with the corrupted politics of the party system.[56]

But because of international events (the collapsing Soviet Union) and domestic pressures (diminishing votes and a collapsing party system), the PCI finally entered the government under the formula of *consociativismo*. Formally, the Communist Party was still excluded from powerful positions, but was able to accept some kind of partial involvement with the government parties: at times it seemed inflexible, at other times it joined the system to demonstrate to its electorate its strength and bargaining power. One of the major effects of the party's entrance into the country's "normal democratic dialectic" came when RAI3, the third channel of the public broadcaster, became the Communists' channel in 1987. By the end of the 1980s, the PCI officially declared its ideological distance from the Soviet Union. And at the end of 1990, its then secretary-general Achille Occhetto declared the end of the Communist Party and the birth of a new party in line with other Western social-democratic parties, the Democratic Party of the Left (*Partito Democratico della Sinistra*, PDS).

The Privatization of Politics

During the 1980s, and increasingly toward the end of the decade, broadcasting and printing became strategic centers where political and economic interests converged in the absence of an appropriate and up-to-date legislation that would regulate competition and provide antitrust measures. The 1975 Reform Law had only provided regulations for the public broadcaster in a condition of monopoly, while the Berlusconi decree had allowed the commercial Fininvest channels to broadcast nationally in an unregulated sector. Although more was needed to prevent concentration in the media sector, proposals to regulate commercial broadcasting were met by intense opposition, especially from the DC right wing and the PSI. The resulting situation, often described as the far west of the airwaves, allowed Berlusconi's channels to expand and consolidate. By 1984, Berlusconi's group, Fininvest, owned three national television channels (Canale5, Rete4, and Italia1), which, by the second half of the decade, competed directly with the three national public channels. By 1987, RAI and Fininvest controlled approximately 95 percent of total advertising revenues for television and had an audience share of 85 percent.[57] Not only did Berlusconi's channels receive favors from the party system thanks to the Berlusconi decree, but Fininvest also received favors from the CAF, an acronym indicating the political bloc in power from 1989 to 1992, consisting of an alliance among Bettino Craxi (who, after the end of his government in 1987, became PSI's secretary-general), Giulio Andreotti (DC and, for the seventh time, prime minister from 1989 to 1992), and Arnaldo Forlani (DC secretary-general). A new broadcasting law, passed in August 1990, was indeed another government concession to Berlusconi. The bill was initially proposed in 1989 during the De Mita government (from the name of the prime minister, Ciriaco De Mita, DC left wing), and in its original intent was supposed to regulate the commercial broadcasting sector. The DC left wing, other minor parties of the *pentapartito* (like the Republican Party), and the PCI looked at this bill as an opportunity to reduce the concentration of television channels, newspapers, and magazine ownership in the hands of Berlusconi, who had also acquired, and by 1990 become president of, Mondadori Publishers, a prestigious and lucrative publishing house that controlled such influential newspapers as *La Repubblica* and weekly magazines like *Panorama* and *L'Espresso*.[58] The PCI and the left DC also wanted to limit the amount of advertising on commercial television. The PSI and the DC right wing instead proposed looser definitions of what constituted concentration and supported only minimum regulation over advertising.

The Mammì Law, as the 1990s law was called after Minister of Posts and Telecommunications Oscar Mammì, was the result of climaxing struggles among the party secretariats, and the epitome of party influence over parliamentary activities. Whereas in its initial intentions the law was supposed to encourage participation of multiple subjects in a regulated free-market broadcasting environment, in the end what came out of the parliament reflected the intentions of those who supported Fininvest predominance in the commercial broadcasting sector and merely confirmed the existing duopoly of RAI and Fininvest. Indeed, following the PSI and the DC right wing's interests, the final version of the law sanctioned the predominance of Fininvest in the broadcasting sector, its power, and its monopoly. Commenting on the results of parliamentary confrontation over the law, Gianni Rocca wrote, "It was a nightmare. . . . Never in the long history of the postwar republic had we witnessed such an open defense of particular, private interests."[59]

The Crisis of the Party System

By the end of the 1980s public debt was high, and public services and the public administration were in disarray as a result of decades of expenditures aimed at ensuring clientelism and illegally financing parties. The crisis of the postwar political establishment had reached its apex with the disappearance of the communist question, whose presence had kept together the parties in a sort of reciprocal siege. The crisis affected all parties, the governing ones as well as the one in opposition. Indeed, especially during the 1980s, governing the country had meant administering power according to the metaphor of "concentric circles," a formula indicating that all parties, including the opposition, would share power and privileges. Through the years those circles had become

> more and more numerous to the point that each party had been brought inside the government at one point or another, therefore leaving the opposition empty. For this reason, it cannot be said that corruption, partition, and scandals . . . were only the DC's business. Each party, to different degrees and at different times, shared the blame because through *consociativismo* each party had co-administered the *res publica*.[60]

The PSI still hoped that the final outcome of the PDS/PCI crisis would be beneficial to the Socialists, and indeed at the 1990 regional elections Craxi's party obtained 15.2 percent of the vote while the PCI lost 6 percentage points.[61] By the 1992 general elections, however, the picture was very different. The DC and the PDS failed miserably, while the PSI made no advances. The crisis was clear: the vote share of the three largest parties dropped from 75.2 percent in 1987 to 59.4 percent in 1992. A four-party coalition led the country from 1992 to the next general elections of 1994. During this time, the party system suffered from the ongoing anticorruption drive initiated by a group of magistrates in Milan in February 1992 investigating the illegal financing of parties. The Clean Hands bribery scandal, as the investigation was called, exposed corruption at the highest levels of politics, bringing to the surface the decades-old practice of illegal financing of parties and politicians' connections with the Mafia and big business.

The scandals had echoes inside the public service broadcaster. The dominant discourse was now filled with calls for more objectivity in reporting, an end to political interference, and in general, more transparency in public administration, greater efficiency, and a new customer-oriented ethos in sectors that had previously enjoyed decades of monopoly status (e.g., the postmaster, the public school system, and the national health care system). Whereas the practice of sharing out positions of power within the broadcaster among ideologically different groups had earlier been an accepted notion, now Italian public opinion seemed more ready to condemn it, demanding a new level of objectivity and balance in reporting.

The results of a referendum on the electoral system, held in April 1993, paved the way for a new electoral law introduced in August 1993. The new law replaced the "old party list system of proportional representation with a hybrid system whereby 3/4 of the members of both houses [were to be] elected by the single-member, simple plurality method, with the remaining quarter of the slots being distributed proportionately."[62] The end of the proportional electoral system marked another major blow to the postwar political establishment.

As parties became dismembered, a political void occurred and a technocratic government, led by former governor of the Bank of Italy Carlo Azeglio Ciampi (who, in 1999, became the tenth president of the republic), was appointed in 1993. In that same year, law no. 206 was approved to liberate RAI from its dependence on political parties, and defined new criteria for the appointment of the members of the board of directors. In the summer of 1993, a technocratic leadership, the "council of five sages," was appointed to take over the broadcasting network. Its main mission was to eradicate *lottizzazione* and to sever the deep-seated relationships between the broadcaster and the parties.

The mass parties that had created the postwar republic had by then all disappeared. The former neo-Fascist party, the *Movimento Sociale Italiano* (MSI), had changed its name and become *Alleanza Nazionale*. The *Lega Nord*, a separatist party born in the northwest region of the country in the early 1980s, was the only party that gained votes at the 1992 elections. At the end of 1993 the Fininvest party, *Forza Italia*, was founded by Berlusconi, who was planning to launch his own candidacy at the spring 1994 elections. Critics suggested that Berlusconi entered the political scene not only, as he proposed, to offer himself as a viable alternative to the left, but also because Fininvest was overwhelmed by financial difficulties. The center-right alliance, comprising *Forza Italia*, Umberto Bossi's *Lega Nord*, and Gianfranco Fini's post-Fascist right party, *Alleanza Nazionale*, won the elections. The vote determined a new geopolitical configuration: *Forza Italia* won in the north and Sicily, the left gained votes in the center, and *Alleanza Nazionale* triumphed in the south. Berlusconi was elected prime minister, and a new board of directors, packed with government nominees, was chosen to lead the public service broadcasting entity. The elections of 1994 marked the definite end of the DC, which split into a variety of small parties, and the collapse of the PSI, from which only a few small groups survived. Bettino Craxi, faced with corruption charges for the illegal financing of his party, fled to Hammamet in Tunisia to escape the trial. He died in exile in January 2000.

Conflict of Interest and the Second Berlusconi Government

The question of conflict of interest between Berlusconi, owner of the commercial media monopoly, and Berlusconi, prime minister, was timidly addressed by the leader of *Forza Italia* in 1994 but never resolved. In the fall of 1994, conflict of interest and clashes with important institutions, such as the presidency of the republic, RAI and its journalists, the Bank of Italy, and the magistrature, together with the government's inability to deliver the promised institutional reforms and "one million more jobs," brought down the first Berlusconi government.

A government of technocrats led the country until the national elections of 1996, when the center-left *Ulivo* coalition (led by the PDS) won. Romano Prodi was appointed prime minister, and then Massimo D'Alema (PDS secretary-general) formed two new governments, one in 1998 and one in 1999. In 2000, D'Alema resigned and Giuliano Amato led the next government until the national elections of spring 2001.

The center-left government fully adhered to the philosophies and practices of neoliberalism. In line with other center-left governments in Europe and the United States, the center-left government embraced a notion of liberal democracy only slightly tempered by some sense of social responsibility and proceeded to privatize previously state-controlled services: the *Poste Italiane* (Italian Postal Service), the National Energy Company (ENEL), the *Ferrovie dello Stato* (the State Railway Service), and the telephone company SIP (now Telecom Italia). Finally, the IRI was dismantled in 2000, putting an end to the practice of state-subsidized industries and services.

In the field of broadcasting legislation, Law no. 249 of 1997 established the Communications Authority with the task of defining and implementing antitrust measures. It also established that advertising revenues for each operator should not exceed 30 percent of the total advertising resources in the TV sector. In an attempt to weaken the dominant positions of RAI and Mediaset and open the market to multiple operators to ensure pluralism, the law also set provisions to restructure the public broadcaster, with one channel (probably RAI3) to become an advertising-free channel. The law established that no single operator could own more than two terrestrial television channels, and that by January 1, 1998, any additional channel would be transferred on satellite. However, none of these provisions was ever realized. As time went by and the switch to digital television (by 2010, Italians should have digital television) became more imminent, the necessity to reduce the number of broadcasting channels lost its urgency.

In April 2000 the results of regional elections were favorable to the right, foreshadowing the success at the national elections of May 2001 of the center-right coalition led by Berlusconi, the so-called *Polo delle Libertà* (led by *Forza Italia* and including *Alleanza Nazionale* and *Lega Nord*). Berlusconi was appointed prime minister once again, this time counting on a strong consensus and a solid government alliance. A law regulating the prime minister's conflict of interest, first proposed by the ruling coalition in February 2002, established that there is incompatibility between administration positions in any corporation and government positions. However, according to this law, ownership of corporations is not incompatible with holding a position as prime minister, or any other government position.

Conclusion

The blocked democracy, *partitocrazia*, the role of factions inside each main party, and the intricate relationship of public and private interests, state and capitalism, were fertile soil from which *lottizzazione* sprung forth. But, even if the blocked democracy and the old party system were necessary conditions for the birth of *lottizzazione*, the collapse of the old system in the early 1990s did not necessarily put an end to political interference inside the public broadcaster. Indeed, as we will notice in the next chapter, those "old" practices continued.

The notion of democracy has been a highly contested one throughout the history of postwar Italy. The DC embodied for forty-five years the idea of a monoparty democracy (authoritarian democracy) to the point that in Italy democracy was almost synonymous with "Christian" democracy. In the immediate postwar period, both the PCI and the PSI fought for a democracy based on social justice and social rights, and traces of their initial efforts can be found in the constitution of 1948. However, the left parties were unable to offer alternatives to the system that was being established by the DC. Once the PSI joined the government coalition in the early 1960s, the Socialists soon learned the Christian Democratic art of government. Social reforms were an important part of their plans to govern the country; occupation of public administration and sharing of positions of power became, however, their most practiced activities. *Forza Italia* and its allies also advocated a renewed democracy and the end of corruption and *partitocrazia* as main goals of their governments. Their defense of democracy and freedom, however, meant the defense of private interests (Berlusconi's first of all), representing the epitome of that process known as the "privatization of politics."

The definition and the practice of public service broadcasting have also been contested since the beginning of television. RAI was never conceived as a place for fostering critical reasoning as in the public sphere, but rather was perceived as a political entity and an instrument of government. The governing Christian Democrats, followed by the Socialists, and, in the 1980s, by the Italian Communist Party, often considered RAI's public role as one in which each party could establish its own cultural and political influence. In this context, *pluralism of information*, the concept informing the 1975 Reform Law's effort to democratize RAI by opening it to the influence of parties other than the DC, actually translated into a *pluralism of viewpoints* based on each party's orientation.

RAI's public service mission was to "educate while entertaining or entertain while educating," a pedagogical mission that was used to justify, through the years, the practice of parties' interference. During the decades when political parties were still the representatives of the majority of Italians, their influence on the public broadcaster was interpreted as a source of pluralism, an additional element of democracy, rather than a corruption of an ideal pristine public sphere. But as social, cultural, and political conditions changed, ideological affiliation lost its pungency, and *lottizzazione* abandoned, as Giovanni Cesareo put it, its "noble" character:[63]

> party pressures became more "vulgar," much less inspired by ideological commitment and cultural purposes. To the point that now they tend to be based more on "interests" than "ideas" and political commitment.[64]

Notes

1. "Blocked democracy" refers to the lack of alternate government that characterized the Italian political system from 1947 to 1992.

2. Universal male suffrage was introduced in 1912; in 1945, legislation allowing women to vote was passed.

3. No author, *Costituzione italiana*, 1947, 3.

4. In the Kingdom's Constitution before the unification of Italy, *Statuto fondamentale del Regno di Sardegna* (1848), the king granted individual freedom (art. 26), the inviolability of one's residence (art. 27), the right to own private property (art. 29), and freedom of the press (art. 28). Regarding this last right, the statute stated that "a law will repress any abuse." Such provision was, of course, used to implement political censorship, as when, during a parliamentary crisis, the decree of June 22, 1899, no. 227, imposed limitations on freedom of the press.

5. Dante Germino and Stefano Passigli, *The Government and Politics of Contemporary Italy* (New York: Harper & Row Publishers, 1968), 48.

6. A decree signed at the end of May 1946 had already abrogated the administrative preventive sequester of publications introduced by the Fascist laws, stating that such a severe measure had to be authorized by judicial order and justified by a formal sentence. See Paolo Murialdi, *La stampa italiana dalla liberazione alla crisi di fine secolo* (Bari: Laterza, 1995), 60.

7. Art. 49, title IV, no author, *Costituzione italiana*, 14.

8. See Pietro Scoppola, *La repubblica dei partiti. Profilo storico della democrazia in Italia (1945-1990)* (Bologna: Il Mulino, 1991).

9. Germino and Passigli, *The Government and Politics*, 118.

10. A famous case was that of two journalists (Guido Aristarco and Renzo Renzi of the magazine *Cinema nuovo* [New Cinema]) arrested on charges of vilipend against the armed forces for publishing information about a film on the conduct of Italian soldiers in the 1941-1943 period. See Murialdi, *La stampa italiana*, 113-116.

11. Scoppola, *La repubblica dei partiti*, 72.

12. The regime used the cinema as an opportunity to educate and influence the emerging mass public. Fascist organizations promoting social and community events, like the *Opera Nazionale Dopolavoro*, competed with the Church in providing citizens with opportunities to go to the movies. By 1937, the majority of movie theaters were run by associations of the PNF.

13. In the mid-1800s the illiteracy rate of Italy was between 75 and 80 percent (similar to that in Spain and lower than that in the Russian Empire); in France the percentage of people who could not read and write was 40-45 percent; in the U.K., it was 30-33 percent; in Sweden, only 10 percent. By the early 1900s, 18 percent of the French population was illiterate, as compared to 48 percent in Italy. In 1901, only 4 percent of Parisians were illiterate compared to 8 percent of *Torinesi* (inhabitants of Turin, the capital of the Italian kingdom),

22 percent of *Romani* (from Rome), and 43 percent of *Napoletani* (inhabitants of Naples, former capital of the southern Kingdom of the Borbons). In 1901, when the French illiteracy rate was 18 percent, the illiteracy rate in Italy was 45 percent. By the early 1980s, Italy's illiteracy rate (2.5 percent) was comparable to that of Spain and higher than the illiteracy rate of Poland and Hungary (0.7 percent). Elaborations from table 7, *Analfabetismo. 1861-1991*, in the "Demografia e movimenti di popolazione" section, from table 29, *Tasso stimato di analfabetismo. Paesi Europei. Metà ottocento*, in the "Scuola e istruzione" section of the Data Bank Compact Disc included with *Guida all'Italia contemporanea*, ed. Massimo Firpo, Nicola Tranfaglia, and Pier Giorgio Zunino (Milan: Garzanti, 1998).

14. Still in the early 1980s, the percentage of illiterate people in the north was 1 percent compared to 2.3 percent in the center, and 6.3 percent in the south (data from table 28, *Popolazione italiana oltre i 6 anni per livelli di istruzione. Aree geografiche italiane. 1981, 1991*, in the "Scuola e istruzione" section of the Data Bank Compact Disc included with *Guida all'Italia contemporanea*, 1998).

15. Mariuccia Salvati, "Amministrazione pubblica e partiti," in *Storia dell'Italia Repubblicana*, vol. 1, *La costruzione della democrazia*, ed. Barbagallo et al. (Turin: Giulio Einaudi, 1994), 416.

16. Giovanni De Luna, "Partiti e società negli anni della ricostruzione," in *Storia dell'Italia Repubblicana*, vol. 1 (Turin: Giulio Einaudi, 1994), 758.

17. Salvati, "Amministrazione pubblica e partiti," 416.

18. Giuliano Amato, quoted by Sebastiano Messina in "Così la partitocrazia uccide la repubblica," *La Repubblica* (Rome), July 10, 1991.

19. "The Church's main challenge—writes Lanaro—consisted in the attempt to stand up in front of the modern, to capture it and offer it to the eternal, and that was achieved through the attempt to domesticate the emerging visual civilization" Silvio Lanaro, *Storia dell'Italia Repubblicana* (Venice: Marsilio, 1992), 100. First the cinema, and later television, were the main media in which the Church concentrated its efforts.

20. De Luna, "Partiti e società," 758.

21. Lanaro, quoted in De Luna, "Partiti e società," 760.

22. Data from table 7.2, *Analfabeti sulla popolazione con più di 6 anni*, in the "Demografia e movimenti di popolazione" section of the Data Bank Compact Disc included with *Guida all'Italia Contemporanea*, 1998.

23. Umberto Eco, *Apocalittici e integrati* (Bologna: Bompiani, 1954).

24. Enzo Santarelli, *Storia critica della repubblica* (Milan: Feltrinelli, 1996), 38.

25. Some of the most comprehensive works on the history of postwar Italian democracy are: Lanaro, *Storia dell'Italia Repubblicana*; Ennio Di Nolfo, *La repubblica delle speranze e degli inganni* (Florence: Ponte alle Grazie, 1996); Alberto De Bernardi and Luigi Canapini, *Storia d'Italia 1860-1995* (Milan: Bruno Mondadori, 1996); Santarelli, *Storia critica della repubblica*; and Scoppola, *La repubblica dei partiti*.

26. Scoppola, *La repubblica dei partiti*, 45.
27. Scoppola, *La repubblica dei partiti*, 51.
28. Scoppola, *La repubblica dei partiti*, 28.
29. Manlio Rossi-Doria, quoted in Francesco Barbagallo, "La formazione dell'Italia democratica," in *Storia dell'Italia Repubblicana*, vol. 1, *La costruzione della democrazia*, ed. Barbagallo et al. (Turin: Giulio Einaudi, 1994), 63.
30. Paolo Flores D'Arcais, "La riforma dei partiti," *La Repubblica* (Rome), April 3, 1990.
31. According to a definition by Germino and Passigli, *The Government and Politics*, 63.
32. *I professionisti della politica* is a phrase often used by the press to indicate the fame-oriented careers of many politicians.
33. Pietro Scoppola, quoted in Messina, "Così la partitocrazia."
34. Eugenio Scalfari, *L'autunno della repubblica: La mappa del potere in Italia* (Milan: Etas Kompass, 1969), 145.
35. Scalfari, *L'autunno della repubblica*, 151.
36. The corporate state referred initially to a phenomenon of the Fascist state in which "social control was steered closely by organizations created and licensed by the state. In contemporary analyses of 'liberal corporatism,' the corporate state is typified by a tripartite relation among state, capital, and labor." Cinzia Padovani and Andrew Calabrese, "Berlusconi, RAI, and the Modernisation of Italian Feudalism," *Javnost/The Public* 3, no. 2 (1996): 118.
37. Ernesto Rossi, *I padroni del vapore* (Bari: Laterza, 1957).
38. Ernesto Rossi, *I padroni del vapore*, 4-5.
39. De Bernardi and Canapini, *Storia d'Italia 1860-1995*, 477.
40. Salvati, *Stato e industria*, 9.
41. Salvati, *Stato e industria*, 280.
42. Maria Grazia Bruzzone, *L'avventurosa storia del TG in Italia dall'avvento della televisione a oggi* (Milan: RCS Libri S.p.A., 2002), 169.
43. Giorgio Bocca quoted in Bruzzone, *L'avventurosa storia del TG*, 168-169.
44. Norberto Bobbio (trans. Lydia G. Cochrane), *Ideological Profile of 21st-Century Italy* (Princeton, N.J.: Princeton University Press, 1995), 169.
45. Franco De Felice, "Nazione e crisi: le linee di frattura," in *Storia dell'Italia Repubblicana*, vol. 3.1, *L'Italia nella crisi mondiale. L'ultimo ventennio*, ed. Barbagallo et al., 37.
46. De Felice, "Nazione e crisi," 40.
47. Luigi Parente, *I partiti politici nell'Italia repubblicana (1943-1992)* (Naples: Edizioni scientifiche italiane, 1996), 240.
48. See Stephen Hellman, *Italian Communism in Transition: The Rise and Fall of the Historic Compromise in Turin, 1975-1980* (New York: Oxford University Press, 1988).
49. For a complete account in English of Aldo Moro's kidnapping, see Robin Erica Wagner-Pacifici, *The Moro Morality Play: Terrorism as Social*

Drama (Chicago: University of Chicago Press, 1986); see also Bob Lumley and Philip Schlesinger, "The Press, the State and Its Enemies: The Italian Case," *Sociological Review* 30, no. 4 (November 1982): 603-626.

50. According to De Felice, "Nazione e crisi."

51. Gianfranco Pasquino, quoting a very famous phrase ("the state strong with the disenfranchised classes and weak vis-à-vis the powerful ones") by a Socialist partisan and founding father of the republic, Pietro Nenni. Pasquino, "Politica e ideologia," in *La cultura italiana del Novecento*, ed. Corrado Stajano (Bari: Laterza, 1996), 507.

52. Pasquino, "Politica e ideologia," 508.

53. Norberto Bobbio, *Il futuro della democrazia* (Turin: Einaudi, 1984).

54. Pasquino, "Politica e ideologia," 507.

55. Scoppola, quoted by Messina, "Così la partitocrazia uccide la repubblica."

56. De Bernardi and Canapini, *Storia d'Italia 1860-1995*, 504.

57. For the years 1987-1990, RAI's annual average audience share for the entire day was 47.54 percent, whereas Fininvest's audience share was 37.94 percent (elaboration from data by RAI Annual Report, 1990/1991, p. 15).

58. The struggle for the control of the Mondadori group went on for years and was finally resolved in 1992. At the end of the so-called *Guerra di Segrate* (named after the location where the Mondadori Publishers is based), Berlusconi stepped down as president of Mondadori while retaining control over book publishing and various weekly magazines, including the most popular, *Panorama*. The weekly *L'Espresso*, the daily *La Repubblica*, and half of the advertising collecting agency Manzoni were retained by Carlo De Benedetti, former managing director of Olivetti.

59. Gianni Rocca, "Tutto nel nome di Sua Emittenza," *La Repubblica* (Rome), July 27, 1990.

60. Alberto Cavallari, "La dinastia democristiana che regna da 45 anni," *La Repubblica* (Rome), December 10, 1990.

61. In the previous elections of 1987, the DC had obtained 34.3 percent of the votes, the PSI had gained some points (up to 26.6 percent of the votes), and the PCI had lost 3 percent of its points.

62. James L. Newell, *Parties and Democracy in Italy* (Aldershot, UK: Ashgate, 2000), 28-29.

63. Giovanni Cesareo, "Tesi," personal correspondence via e-mail, March 28, 1999.

64. Giovanni Cesareo, "Tesi," personal correspondence via e-mail, April 7, 1999.

Chapter 2

RAI and the Party System (Part I)

> *In Italy there is freedom, but one is not used to it. Before writing their pieces, most journalists ask for permission from the censor. Which censor? The one that has been inside themselves for centuries and without which they could not survive.*[1]

Through the years *lottizzazione*[2] became deeply rooted in the journalists' professional culture: almost second nature, certainly, for many of them, a normal condition. How did that happen? What kind of intellectual and professional tradition allowed that to occur? Since Italian broadcasting journalism derives from press journalism, the following section briefly introduces the main characteristics of the journalist tradition from its origin in the sixteenth century until the end of the Second World War.[3] I then draw a history of the relation between the party system and the public broadcaster, which I divide in four main periods: (1) the prehistory of *lottizzazione*, from 1954 until 1975; (2) "classical" *lottizzazione*, from 1976 through 1986; (3) "complete" *lottizzazione*, or "iron" *lottizzazione*, from 1987 through 1992; and (4) "late" *lottizzazione*, which began in 1993. Chapter 2 covers the period until 1975; chapter 3 covers the time from 1976 to 2003.

The Tradition of Italian Journalism

The Origins

The origins of journalism in Italy can be traced back to the sixteenth century when the first papers (quasi-newsletters, or gazzettes), containing news and information were published in Venice and Rome, first, and then in Florence, Genoa, and Milan. Given the many foreign dominations and internal divisions that characterized the history of the peninsula, the conditions of the print media differed substantially from region to region. By the end of the century, however, all governments had realized the importance of the gazettes and some of them were promoting the publication of official papers.[4] The internal divisions, the domination of various kingdoms, and the overall power of censorship of the Catholic Church set the foundation for a kind of journalism that was meant to spread the official views of the prince or the pope and create consensus around the ruler, first among the aristocracy and later among the upper bourgeoisie. Under those circumstances, the journalist's role was not much different from that of a court official: the reporter was a *"marchand de papier . . .* who follow[ed] closely the norms established by princes and inquisitors: he was certainly not a man of culture, one who could make conscious political choices."[5] The conditions of the press in Italy were thus rather different from those in the rest of Europe, where the Protestant Reformation and the creation of the first nation-states saw the decline of the Church's authority, the birth of some initial forms of religious tolerance, and the first individual freedoms.

In the second half of the eighteenth century, the enlightenment and the experience of the *Encyclopédie* in France echoed throughout the country, especially in Venice, Milan, and Lucca (in Tuscany). The new ideas coming from Europe sparked much enthusiasm and kindled publishers' interest: over eighty-one new papers were published during those years. However, there were structural impediments to the development of a lucrative press. The level of illiteracy was very high, and the periodical circulation was still extremely low: most of the gazettes sold only two or three hundred copies, reaching a little over one thousand copies only in the major cities. This situation made it impossible for journalists and reporters to make a living out of their profession, making them particularly vulnerable to the desires and interests of those in power. Although conditions were changing during the last decades of the ancient regime, there were also profound geographical differences: the enlightened monarchies in the north and center-north of Lombardia and Tuscany, able to counter the power of the Church, began to grant some press freedoms, whereas the absolutist kingdoms of Turin, Rome, and Naples maintained an extremely tight grip on the press. Literary papers were flourishing in various parts of the country, including the *Giornale de' Litterati d'Italia* (1710) in Venice, the *Gran Giornale de' Litterati* (1701) from Forlì, the *Novelle Letterarie* (1740) in Florence, the *Notizie Letterarie Oltramontane* (1742) from Rome, and the *Gazzette Letterarie* (1722) in Milan.[6] Opinion papers like *Il Caffè* (1764) from Forlì can be considered the antecessor of political journalism.

Information coming from France and North America on the revolutionary struggles for freedom and independence had great impact in Italy, where the gazettes began discussing political events and dedicating more space to contemporary issues and international events. That marked the birth of political journalism in various cities across the peninsula, including Milan, Venice, Rome, Turin, and Palermo. This was also a phase of relative freedom for the gazettes, a phase that ended at the time of the war between France and the Austro-Prussian Empire, when, in an effort to control the information coming from the other side of the Alps, foreign papers, popular among literate people since the seventeenth century, were closely monitored, and the kings reserved the right to shut down any publication.

At the time of Napoleon's domination, in the late eighteenth century and early nineteenth century, many new publications came out, and for some time, press freedoms were reestablished in parts of the peninsula. Timid examples of political journalism provided the readers with domestic information and debates about what was happening in France and the rest of Europe. The problem of low circulation, however, continued to constrict journalists' prospects. In the early eighteen hundreds, the average circulation of papers such as the *Corriere Milanese* and *Giornale Italiano* was around three thousand copies; for other papers, the circulation was approximately one thousand copies.[7]

After the fall of Napoleon and the Vienna congress (1814-1815), which led to a restoration of the Austrian domination of the northern regions of the peninsula, political journalism came under threat while tight control again stimulated the growth of literary journalism. But nationalistic sentiments and aspirations for the unification of Italy ran high among various strata of the population. Even though the circulation of papers was still low compared to other European countries, the reading public was expanding beyond the aristocratic elites into the middle and low bourgeoisie, interested in the liberalization of commerce and the ideals of equality. New papers addressed the needs for innovation and more freedom; between 1830 and 1840 there was also a growth of the popular press, which, however, never took off as it did in the United Kingdom and Germany.[8]

The struggles for a unified Italy and the growth of political movements brought along with them a new awareness of the importance of a free press. One by one, various states, like the Vatican, the Grand Duchy of Tuscany, and the Sicilian Kingdom relaxed, while the Piedmont Kingdom abolished, their censorship regulations. On March 26, 1848, in the Piedmont Kingdom, article 28 of the *Statuto Albertino* established norms concerning the printing press: the press was finally proclaimed free, even though a law was to "regulate any abuses." Papers multiplied, and each political group—the moderates, the democrats, and the conservatives—aspired to have its own. According to Paolo Murialdi, in 1858, 117 papers were published in the Sardinian Kingdom (the only state where there was freedom of the press), 68 in the Lombardo-Veneto, 27 in Tuscany, 50 in the south, and only 16 in Rome.[9] Illiteracy rates were still very high, with an estimated 75 to 80 percent of the population unable to read and write in the mid-1800s.[10] The average circulation of papers was 2,000 copies. Advertising revenues continued to be scarce, and papers had to rely on funds from the government and from various political groups in order to survive. The majority of the papers were still literary and cultural papers, though a certain number of publications specialized in scientific and technical matters.

As a result of the politicization of important strata of the bourgeoisie and of intellectual elites, Italian journalism acquired a strong political orientation during the *Risorgimento* (1815-1861), when it was mostly practiced as a political activity. One could easily argue that the new press freedoms, or at least the diminishing censorship, had created an environment in which political papers flourished around the peninsula. One of the most representative papers of this period was *Il Conciliatore*, founded in Milan in 1818 by Federico Confalonieri and Luigi Porro Lambertenghi, of which Silvio Pellico, one of the forefathers of the movement for the liberation and unification of Italy, became managing editor. Certainly not conceived in the Anglo-American tradition as the fourth estate, journalism was conceived as an activity where political loyalty surpassed any sense of commitment to the profession as papers were, after all, "instruments of political struggle for the formation of consensus."[11] It was a political pedagogical mission that remained a constant thread of Italian journalism through the centuries, "openly aiming—as Raymond Williams wrote in a different context—at the establishment of ethical and cultural hegemony, one which [tended to leave] the function of informing the public in the background."[12]

Illiteracy rates were still high during the first half of the eighteenth century, when 50 to 90 percent of the population could not read and write. The highest number of illiterates was in the south, where public schools were fewer, and fewer were the pupils attending them.[13] Instead, in the northern regions of Lombardo-Veneto under Austrian domination, the public elementary school system was well organized and funded, and attendance was much higher. Whereas by 1859 in the southern region of Campania there was only 1 pupil for every 90 inhabitants, in Veneto the ratio was 1 pupil per 24 inhabitants, and in Lombardia there was 1 pupil per 14 inhabitants. In the second half of the century, when the unification of Italy was finally accomplished, illiteracy was also slowly dropping. In 1871, it sank to 68.8 percent; in 1881, it was only 42-45 percent in the most advanced northern regions. Although these percentages were still high compared to other European countries (40 to 45 percent in France and 30 to 33 percent in the United Kingdom), they certainly indicated a considerable improvement from previous decades.[14]

Political journalism played a crucial role during the preunification years (1840-1861) by giving voice to the struggles for independence, even though only political and intellectual elites were able to read the papers. The traditional gap between intellectual elites and the masses of peasants, the "nation," as Gramsci defined it, continued to result in low circulation figures and the absence of a popular press. According to Gramsci's analysis, this was due to the fact that Italian intellectuals were traditionally removed from the nation and its people, as they were the expression of elites with traditionally cosmopolitan, rather than national, aspirations.[15]

The government financially supported friendly papers through the publication of government announcements and later through secret funds from the Interior Ministry. Journalists' salaries continued to be low; up until the end of the nineteenth and the beginning of the twentieth century, journalism was not even considered a profession in itself, and those who practiced it continued to come from other professions, usually intellectuals and men of letters, and often lawyers interested in getting into politics.[16] They lacked autonomy and were, as Alberto Asor Rosa says, "appendices . . . of the political game."[17]

Political Journalism and Opinion Journalism

The introduction of new printing technologies (1862), rising advertising and subscription revenues, and an improved railway system, which made it easier to deliver newspapers around the country, created a more stimulating environment for the daily press, and indeed many newspapers were established in the years immediately following the unification of Italy. According to some estimates, in 1880 there were 216 papers in Milan, 155 papers in Turin, 147 in Rome, 114 papers in Naples, and 101 in Florence.[18] Among them, there were major national newspapers. In 1861, the triweekly publication of the Holy Sea, *L'Osservatore Romano*, became a daily paper. In 1866, *Il Secolo*, voice of the political opposition, with Giuseppe Garibaldi as one of its main contributors, was founded in Milan; in 1867, *La Gazzetta Piemontese* (which later became *La Stampa*) began publication in Turin. *Corriere della Sera*, which by the early twentieth century would become the country's most important newspaper, was founded in Milan in 1876. Still, Italy failed to develop either the objective journalism of newspapers like the *New York Times*, which started publication in 1851, and the *Times* of London, which by the late 1800s had established its hegemony in England, or the level of circulation of French newspapers, which in 1870 sold a total of 1 million copies. Instead, Italian journalism continued to be political and partisan, and "subordination to . . . politics and [literary] culture remained one of its long-time traits."[19] But this peculiarity should not be necessarily conceived as a negative aspect of the Italian tradition: for intellectuals like Antonio Gramsci, for instance,

> Italian newspapers [were] much better than those of the French. That was because our papers have a double function—to inform and to offer a general political direction, on one hand, and to provide for a political, literary, artistic, scientific culture, on the other. In France, instead, even the first function gives birth to two kinds of newspapers: the ones that inform, and the ones directing public opinion.[20]

Gramsci also recognized the political value of newspapers: at a time when political organizations were not very efficient and parties were not yet well organized, it was the task of newspapers to "constitute the real parties."[21] This role became particularly significant during the first two decades of the twentieth century, even though the gap between the intellectuals and the lower strata of the population continued.

During the last decades of the nineteenth century, political journalism found its venues in various antigovernment publications, like the magazine *Critica sociale*, founded in 1891 by Filippo Turati and Anna Kulisgcioff, the weekly *Lotta di Classe Giornale dei Lavoratori Italiani*, established one year later and directed by Camillo Prampolini, and the Socialist Party's official newspaper *L'Avanti!*, founded in 1896, which was well received even from the more conservative intellectual elites of the time. Other newspapers, like *L'Unità Cattolica* (1863, Turin), the Socialist *La Plebe* (1868), and *Fede e Avvenire* (1863, Milan), reflected the social commitment of political commentators after the unification. The Catholic press, perhaps the only true example of a popular press, also developed during those years, with a strong network of local publications close to the peasants and the artisans. Besides the already cited *Osservatore Romano*, other Catholic papers were the conservative *L'Unità Cattolica* from Turin and the progressive, socially oriented *L'Avvenire* from Bologna.

By early 1900s, the conditions for an increase of publication and distribution were maturing: cities were growing at a stable rate (around a half million people in the major centers, like Rome, Milan, and Naples), by 1901 the national illiteracy rate had dropped to 48.7 percent, and the use of the telegraph was enabling news to circulate faster. Between 1902 and 1903 long-distance telephone services between Rome and Milan, and Milan and Paris were established. Local and long-distance telephone service, privately owned until 1907, were rapidly expanding (fivefold from 1885 to 1905), making it easier for journalists and newspaper editors to exchange information.[22] Voting rights were still limited but expanding: in 1861, only 1.9 percent of the population could vote, in 1909, 8.3 percent of males could, and finally, in 1912 the suffrage was extended to all males over 30 years of age and the electoral body rose from 3,300,000 to 8,443,205. Circulation of newspapers was also growing. Between 1900 and 1909, the sales of *Corriere della Sera* more than doubled (from 70,000 to 150,000 copies) while expanding its readership into the lower strata of the bourgeoisie and even the working class. *Il Secolo* and *La Tribuna* reached circulations of about 100,000 copies in those same years and those of the Venetian *Gazzettino* went up sixfold from the beginning of the century to 1922.[23] These newspapers were important opinion makers, committed to trends of public opinion and participating in the political, social, and economic struggles of those years.

The economic conditions of journalists, especially of those working for major newspapers, were slowly but steadily improving thanks to rising advertising and subscription revenues, but government attempts to financially control papers were still a major reason for doubting many papers' ability to act independently. Political journalism was still prevalent as the First World War loomed and public opinion was becoming polarized in pro- versus antiwar positions. At the dawn of Italy's entrance into the war, measures to control the press were established: news of military relevance could be censored for any reason at any time, and no information other than official news, not even reports on casualties, could be distributed from the war front. *Corriere della Sera* and *La Stampa* reached circulations respectively of 500,000 and 200,000 copies; from the beginning of the First World War until 1922, the average circulation of *Gazzettino* (Venice), *Gazzetta del Popolo* (Turin), and *Giornale d'Italia* (Rome) was 187,000 copies.[24] The Catholic press was also becoming more popular in the political and industrial centers of Rome, Milan, and Turin.

Political journalism was still predominant between the end of the war and the first years of the Fascist era in the early 1920s. In 1918 Amadeo Bordiga founded the revolutionary weekly paper *Il Soviet*; one year later, Antonio Gramsci, Palmiro Togliatti, and Angelo Tasca cofounded a weekly review of Socialist commentaries, *Ordine Nuovo*, which in 1922 became a daily paper. In 1921, *La Voce Repubblicana*, official paper of the center-left Republican Party, was founded; in 1922, the antifascist satirical publication *Il Becco Giallo* was established in Rome.

During the early days of the dictatorship, control of the press was accomplished through the intimidation of journalists and a tightening censorship. Nevertheless, antigovernment dailies managed to be published: in 1923 Giuseppe Donati founded the Catholic, anti-Fascist daily *Il Popolo*, organ of the Popular Party. One year later, Antonio Gramsci founded the Communist daily *L'Unità*. But after the official proclamation of the dictatorship on January 3, 1925, *il duce* proceeded to ensure stricter political control over the major newspapers, and all major non-Fascist political newspapers were closed down. At first control focused primarily on newspapers' political section with the expectations that the press would perform its role as an integral element of the dictatorship. Only later, at the time of the Africa campaign (1935-1936), did the regime demand that newspapers' publishers and their ownership be in line with Fascism and newspapers were put under the direct control of the state and of the Fascist National Party (PNF). The news agency Stefani, founded in 1853, became the official and only press agency under the leadership of a devote Fascist, Manlio Morgagni, who led the agency from 1924 to 1943. Stefani, which was the fourth news agency in Europe after the French Agence Havas, the German Continental Telegraphen Compagnie, and the British Reuter Telegram Company, enjoyed the financial support of the regime even during the years of sanctions and autarchy. The agency, a crucial instrument to ensure control over political news in both newspapers and news programs on the radio, disappeared with the fall of Mussolini.

Radio Broadcasting

Radio broadcasting in Italy developed slowly compared to other Western nations. The first legislation on wireless communication dates back to 1910, when radio broadcasting was declared a public service and its operations were granted to private corporations and regulated under state control.[25] During the First World War, radio was used predominantly for military purposes, and after the war its use remained circumscribed among a very small group of amateurs.

The effective birth of radio as a medium of mass communication coincided with the first years of the Fascist regime. The first piece of legislation on radio broadcasting, the decree law of May 1, 1924, no. 655, established the revenue source of radio bulletins—advertising and the license fee paid by all radio owners—and indicated the kind of programs that could be aired: mainly concerts, theater plays, political speeches, and sermons. News could only be broadcast according to specific norms to be established by the concession agreement between the state and the broadcaster. Initially, news broadcasts represented only a small portion of the total output and were technically and qualitatively below the standards of other European radio broadcasts. The daily bulletins consisted of short reports about government activities and other information coming from the Stefani news agency; not until 1926 was the radio broadcaster allowed to use the newspapers as news sources—as long, the government stated, as they were not under judicial seizure.

On August 27, 1924, the three major national broadcasters, Radio Araldo, Radiofono, and S.I.R.A.C. (Società Italiana Radio Audizioni Circolari), formed URI (Unione Radiofonica Italiana), which was granted the monopoly of radio broadcasting by the decree law of December 14, 1924. In exchange, URI agreed to air six hours of programs per day and to build new radio stations in Naples, Milan, and Palermo. The decree law also established norms for the appointment of the president and the managing director of the corporation, who had to be welcomed by the government. The government was given two hours of airtime daily for its communiqués.[26]

During the first years of radio broadcasting, Mussolini, a former press journalist himself and director of the Socialist newspaper *L'Avanti!*, showed little interest in the new medium, perhaps still unaware of its immense potential. Indeed, the state monopoly over radio broadcasting was mostly dictated by the lack of private capital rather than imposed by propagandistic plans.[27] Radio stations were first limited to only the major cities, and those in Milan and Rome were the best in terms of quality of their broadcasts. But as the regime consolidated consensus around itself and industrial groups showed much interest in the radio business, the importance of the radio grew. By 1926, a new station was built in Florence and a second one in Milan. Increasing subscriptions, more advertising revenues, and additional revenues from other sources (shares of property taxes paid by owners of public places, and city taxes) were used to improve the infrastructures and build new stations in Turin, Genoa, Trieste, and Palermo. In 1928, broadcasting from Naples began. Four years later, the Palermo radio station started its operations. By 1933 the national radio network was almost completed.

By 1926 all major newspapers had been secured under the control of the regime; in 1927 the Fascist Union of Journalists was founded to ensure political control over journalists; in 1928 a national List of Italian Journalists (*Albo dei giornalisti*) was instituted. The function of the Italian press, which, according to Mussolini was the only free press in the world because it was not subjected to industrial interests nor to the interests of political parties, was to educate readers, and to do that according to Fascist ideals and the Fascist mission. Meanwhile, political control over the radio broadcaster was reinforced through a new piece of legislation. In 1927, the decree law no. 2207 of November 17 reformed the broadcasting sector: the government refinanced the private groups constituting URI and founded EIAR (Ente Italiano Audizioni Radiofoniche), which soon obtained the concession for radio broadcasting for the next twenty-five years. The law also established that the government should elect four members of the EIAR board of directors and that other members elected by the government sit in the *Comitato Superiore di Vigilanza*, a committee created to control EIAR's programming.

The broadcaster continued to develop at a fast pace reflecting the growing popularity of the new medium. In 1927, EIAR had forty thousand subscribers; one year later, there were more than sixty thousand.

Despite its growth, EIAR's subscription rates were still below those in Germany and the United Kingdom, respectively 2 million and 2.5 million subscribers.

Programming

Religious programs were still rare during the 1920s. Indeed, Pope Pius XI waited until 1931 to present his encyclical *Urbi et orbi* on the radio. However, over the next decade, the Church became increasingly aware of the medium's enormous potential. By 1940, indulgences were being granted to those who listened to the Sunday mass on the radio. In the meantime, Mussolini's earlier mistrust for the new medium was also ending: by the mid-1930s, radio had become an essential element of the regime's propaganda machine as representatives of the government regularly used the medium to convey their programs "of high internal and global relevance."[28]

Press journalists, critics, exponents of the cultural organizations of the regime, men of letters, and writers, went to work for EIAR or became regular hosts of various programs. The new medium was acquiring prestige among intellectual and political elites, and playing a significant role in the linguistic unification of the country. Training courses for EIAR technical personnel were instituted in 1933 by the Marconi Radio Experimental Center Foundation, and in 1936 a school for radio professionals was founded with the mission to form a class of professional radio journalists. But the project was never completed and radio journalists continued to come from other media, especially from political and literary journalism, and from upper- and middle-class backgrounds.

Daily radio programming included theater, conferences, speeches, lessons, sermons, government news, sports news, and children's news, but most of all, opera and concerts. Starting in 1939, more attention was dedicated to topics of social relevance: a new program for workers (*Radio Sociale*) began in April of that year with popular music, unions' information, and sports; programs for the series *Radio Igea* offered information on social events sponsored by the regime; female listeners living in rural areas were also a target audience of the new program, *L'ora dell'agricoltore e della massaia rurale*. In line with the colonial aspirations of the regime in northern Africa, in the second half of the 1930s news bulletins in Arabic, conversations with Arab sheiks, the recitation of the Koran, and folk songs from Libya became a popular feature. EIAR extended its services (news and communiqués) to North and South

America, Asia, and the Mediterranean. Although the quality of broadcasting and the variety of genres improved, news bulletins remained below average compared to those of other European broadcasters. By the mid-1930s, more news was broadcast from Naples, Turin, Genoa, Palermo, and Trieste; during the Africa campaign the time allocated to news programs rose to more than 20 percent of total programming. Public affair programs, such as *Cronache dal regime* and *Commento ai fatti del giorno*, became the voice of Fascist propaganda. A new ministry for the press and propaganda was instituted in 1935, replaced a couple of years later with the Ministry for Popular Culture in an effort to downplay the strict propaganda function and reinforce the idea of a regime close to the people and their culture.

Between 1937 and 1939 political propaganda occupied almost one-third of radio programming. Most news bulletins consisted of information on political and military events overseas; domestic news was also mostly political. Listening to foreign broadcasts was forbidden by a decree in 1938, which established severe sanctions for those who contravened. When Benito Mussolini decided to join Germany and Japan in the Second World War, control over the press and radio intensified, and the overall tone of radio programs reinforced the country's sense of mission and pride in the rebirth of the Italian empire. The number and variety of news programs grew, with more daily editions of the news bulletin *Giornale radio*, more special programs from the war front, and more news from the armed forces headquarters.

Meanwhile, EIAR was expanding its structures: broadcasting stations were established in all cities throughout the peninsula, and subscription rates were also growing. By 1938 there were 997,295 subscriptions to the radio (compared to 13 million in Germany and 9 million in the United Kingdom). Sixty percent of subscriptions were from the northern regions, 33 percent from the center and the south, and very few (approximately 3 percent) from the islands. In an attempt to reach more listeners among lower socioeconomic strata, between 1934 and 1938 the government destined a large number of radio sets for public use (in 1934, 1,405 radio sets were provided to PNF's organizations for collective listening; in 1938, 16,000 sets were donated for that use; in 1934, 2,000 loudspeakers were placed in public schools and other public places; in 1938 that number went up to more than 23,000).[29] This notwithstanding, the majority of listeners still belonged to the upper and middle bourgeoisie.[30] By the end of 1939, EIAR counted about 2,000 employees and produced a total of 10,178 hours of broadcasting. At that time there were more than 1 million subscribers.

The End of the War

By 1941, the credibility of EIAR and of its news programs had diminished considerably. News about German and Italian defeats were delayed and misrepresented. After the landing of the Anglo-American troops in Sicily and Calabria in the spring and summer of 1943, and the fall of fascism on July 25, 1943, EIAR continued its activities with the same leadership, in concert with the Ministry for Popular Culture. By then, Italians had begun to rely on other sources, of which the most credible was Radio Londra, the BBC broadcasts in Italian conducted by Italian and British journalists. During the *Resistenza* (1942-1945), underground publications by antifascist groups, political parties, and partisan organizations resumed, also with the support of the Anglo-Americans and their Psychological Warfare Branch. After their landing in Sicily, the Allies gained control of all radio stations in the south and the islands, including those in Palermo, Bari, and Naples; they also controlled the press by supervising political and parties' activities and managing the flow of information through the various press agencies, like Reuters, Associated Press, United Press, and the International News Service.

In October 1943, *Il Popolo* resumed its underground publication, and so did *L'Unità*. After the liberation of Rome, in the late spring of 1944, most party newspapers were legally published. Only a few years after the end of the war, all the pre-Fascist party newspapers had come back to life, including *La Voce Repubblicana*. This and other party newspapers, as well as the journalists working for them, were welcome as a tangible expression of the new democratic freedoms. Young journalists with no, or very little, previous experience worked for those papers with a well-defined mission: to educate the masses about democratic life. Generally speaking, in the independent newspapers, access to the profession did not require any specific professional training: as it was usually said, one was born a journalist, and journalism was seen as a mission, a vocation. In fact, for the most part, journalists were the children of the upper middle class, as access to the profession happened mostly through family connections and friendships. In the newly reborn party press, instead, access was determined by party affiliation. This was a clear sign of the democratizing function of the party press: those who did not possess the social capital to enter the profession could still do so through political and party connections. The difference was net: the majority of those working for the independent newspapers had been involved with fascism and most of them were senior journalists; in the party press, instead, a large number of reporters were young people with lofty and democratic ideals. One thing was certain: in postwar Italy, independence was not synonymous with impartiality. As a media scholar wrote, "The idea that impartiality was the condition for independence was at those times ludicrous. Quite the contrary: the identifiable political affiliation of each party newspaper and of the single journalist was seen as a criterion and a guarantee of pluralism."[31] Perhaps paradoxically from an Anglo-American perspective, according to which a free press is an independent and impartial press, the return of the party press was saluted as a sign of the new freedom and a prelude to the democratizing role that political parties were going to play in the period ahead.

The Birth of RAI

The Allies' support for the party press lasted only a short period of time. Fear of the advancement of the left in the political arena, and the need for a moderate center, were reasons for supporting the independent, nonparty newspapers, such as *Il Tempo*, *Il Messaggero*, and *Corriere della Sera*. Their leaders compromised with fascism were replaced, but the newspapers continued to be published; both the *Federazione Nazionale della Stampa* (founded in 1908) and *Albo dei Giornalisti* (founded in 1928) remained. All political parties agreed to continue the state concession for radio broadcasting, but convened that the old EIAR should be closed down and a new corporation should be granted the broadcasting license.

On October 26, 1944, decree no. 457 changed the name of the national radio broadcaster from EIAR to RAI, a private corporation (*società per azioni*). For a few years, from 1945 to 1948, journalists and officials previously involved with fascism were marginalized, and the public broadcaster hired new people; among the journalists, many came from the party press. The hopes and expectations for innovation and for a truly open and democratizing radio were high, but lasted only for a brief period. When, in 1946 the high commissioner in charge of eliminating from the public administration top-level officials who had been involved with the regime was withdrawn, and the Communist Party was formally excluded from government coalitions (1947), the centrist government, together with the Vatican, established tight control over radio broadcasting. Any alternative leftist perspective inside RAI was marginalized. For reasons connected to the restructuring of order and power in all sectors of political, administrative, and social life, and because of the long-standing tradition of the broadcaster's institutional, ideological, and political dependence on the government, it was fairly easy for the Allies and the government party to promote conformity in programming and news reporting, and overall subservancy to the hegemonic bloc.

Indeed, soon after the 1948 elections, RAI's leadership was already in the hands of the government party, while the leftist forces appeared unable to elaborate their own mass media political culture, or even to realize the importance of radio for the new democracy. Even though there were a few programs such as *Voce dei partiti* (the Voice of the Parties), *La voce dei lavoratori* (the Workers' Voice), *Conversazioni* (Conversations), where political parties—including the Socialist Party of Proletarian Union and the Liberal Party—as well as workers' unions (including the *Camera Generale Italiana del Lavoro*—C.G.I.L., a leftist workers' union), could present their ideas, for the most part radio remained a business in the hands of the groups in power as a tool to educate the public. News programs, indeed, were still under government control and subjected to severe self-discipline. Programs of religious character abounded, including Sunday masses, *Notiziario Cattolico* (the Catholic Bulletin), and other programs from Radio Vaticana. News from the United States and the United Kingdom were reported with reviews of the French and the British press, while programs from Radio Londra and Voice of America became regular features on RAI's schedules. Instead of the *Lezioni di tedesco* (German lessons) of the 1930s, now lessons of French and English filled the airwaves in the afternoon hours. Music (opera, operetta, classical music, popular music, modern Italian songs) remained a main element of daily programming (American music also became popular), as did children's and educational programs (in concert with elementary public schools), and programs for women. As a whole, RAI's three radio channels were improving their broadcast quality and diversifying their genres, with the usual strong emphasis on light entertainment. Overall, radio remained a tool to educate, to elevate the public's taste while entertaining. That role was well expressed by the following words of a commentator:

> Culture can and must be imposed. . . . Try to present to a worker authors such as Tolstoi [sic] . . . Balzac, Dickens, Verga, Nievo. . . . [He]

will soon become joyous and a faithful admirer of those giants. Not only do we have the right to do so, it is our duty to do so; and R.A.I. [sic] will only benefit from it.[32]

Radio was fast expanding its audience, and media consumption in general was increasing: radio subscribers reached 2.611 million in 1949, newspaper circulation also rose, and cinema, especially American movies, became very popular.

The Postwar Model: Top-Down Political Control

In 1952, RAI obtained the rights for television broadcasting, which was at an experimental stage. The agreement between the state and RAI established that IRI (the Institute for Industrial Reconstruction) would obtain an absolute majority of the corporation's shares;[33] through IRI, which depended on the Ministry of the Treasury, the government ensured its control over RAI. The public broadcaster was, from the beginning, a hybrid entity, a legacy of the private-public mix established during fascism. As Peppino Ortoleva underlines,[34] Mussolini placed all major media, including telephone and radio, under the supervision of formally and judicially private corporations that in reality were fully in the hands of the government. The result was a peculiar public-private system, controlled by the state through ownership rather than through norms and regulations. This ownership structure remained almost unchanged during the transition from EIAR to RAI and from the regime to the new democracy. Paradoxically, such an inheritance made government control over the broadcaster even "more invasive than it had been during the previous fascist era."[35]

The 1952 concession decreed that the government would nominate six out of the sixteen members of the RAI board of directors (four members were already government nominees and represented the Foreign Ministry, the Interior Ministry, the Finances and the Post Ministries—the two additional members introduced by the new agreement were appointed by the presidency of the Council of Ministries and the Ministry of Treasury).[36] The remaining members of the board were appointed by IRI. Complete government control was guaranteed as all appointments were, informally and de facto, negotiated among the various currents of the Christian Democratic Party (DC), later joined by the Italian Socialist Party (PSI) and the Italian Republican Party (PRI). The government parties negotiated among themselves also the appointment of RAI's president, managing director, and director general, which had to be approved by the Ministry of Post and the Council of Ministries.

Unlike the leftist parties, which, strong in their tradition of critical thinking and the Frankfurt school, assumed a rather elitist attitude toward the mass media, the DC and the Vatican fully understood the ideological importance of the new medium. According to Pope Pius XII, the public authority in charge of supervising radio broadcasting not only had to make sure that the nation's political interests would always be defended, but it also had a moral obligation to "watch over public morals, which descend directly from the natural law that is written in every heart."[37] This attention to the moral and pedagogical duties of the medium was the foundation of the DC's political culture in RAI, especially that of its left wing, traditionally more involved in socially oriented activities.

For the Catholic bloc, television was an important tool of social intervention, an occasion not to be wasted to make Catholic culture appealing to the masses. For many, the new medium ought to be used as an instrument of cultural promotion. Filiberto Guala, RAI's managing director from 1954 to 1956, embodied those ideals. Close to the DC left wing of Amintore Fanfani (DC secretary-general at the time), he was also welcome by the Vatican. Guala soon adopted an internal code of self-discipline in line with the dictates of Pope Pius XII who supported a stricter moral control over broadcasting. The provision included a detailed list of topics that could not be discussed on television: divorce and extramarital affairs (divorce could be represented only if the story took place in a country where divorce was legal—in Italy it was not), crimes, sex and sex-related events, antigovernment strikes, and any negative reports from the United States that could impinge upon the good relationship between Italy and its most important ally.

One of Guala's main tasks was to get rid of, or marginalize, the so-called *aziendalisti*, the group of the old guard, the middle and top managers who had passed almost unchanged from EIAR to RAI. They embodied the culture of techno-administrative power, seemingly less concerned with ideological and political control, the *piemontese* tradition of rigorous and parsimonious administration from Turin, the initial capital of broadcasting. In opposition to this tradition, Guala centralized political control over programming and moved the direction of program content from Turin to Rome, where he placed it under his direct supervision. The news (*telegiornale*), initially broadcast from Milan, was also moved to Rome, where an independent department for the production of news was created in order to make it easier for the Vatican and the political world to monitor its content. The corporation ceased to be a mere technical instrument in the hands of the government, and became "in itself a body of major relevance for the cultural politics of the DC."[38]

Guala's leadership was inspired by a moral commitment and by an awareness of the almost messianic role of television. And even if it was brief, his administration was very incisive. He talked to journalists about "contents and values," and that was a novelty. In a society as static as the Italian one at the time, his first challenge was to "bring to full fruition the intellectual talents within RAI, and to recruit new blood."[39] Indeed, recruitment and training were Guala's main legacy. The men he hired during his tenure were those who then became the true assets of public broadcasting in Italy. Guala accomplished this goal through the valorization of existing journalists, but also through the in-house training of new hires.

This was done at the expense of the *aziendalisti*, many of whom were moved from positions of power to less important roles, while others received incentives for retirement. In the effort to marginalize the old group, Guala hired new people from the DC and the Catholic communist faction (socially conscious leftist intellectuals close to the progressive Catholic area), and trained them through internship programs. RAI's *Centro Didattico Interno* (Center of In-House Didactic), directed by the social Catholic Pier Emilio Gennarini, provided the training for the new hires, who then became top officials in RAI: famous journalists and academicians like Fabiano Fabiani, Emmanuele Milano, Alessandro Guglielmi, Umberto Eco, Gianni Vattimo, and Fausto Colombo.[40] The corporation continued to grow: at the end of Guala's tenure, RAI had 5,668 employees, an increase of 25 percent compared to the beginning of his leadership in 1954. In the same period (1954-1956), broadcast hours on television increased 36 percent or 540 more hours.[41]

If political control over programming was the most important goal of the new administration, it was a difficult task to achieve given the continuous internal struggles among the various factions within the DC. The government party was already by then not a monolithic entity, but rather a party that was divided in groups representing different interests and conflicting ideologies. In RAI, those interests had to be represented according to their relative weight and hegemony within the party. In the words of one senior Italian journalist, Paolo Murialdi, things in RAI looked like this:

One day, somewhere in the early 1950s, I was visiting an old friend of mine, a journalist, at RAI's old headquarter in Rome. While I was chatting with him, another colleague, a Christian Democrat, joined us. He told me something that I'll never forget: "in RAI each one of us should wear a T-shirt with his sponsor's name on it, as bikers do during *il giro d'Italia*. The names on our T-shirts should be the names of our political referees within the DC, of people such as Mariano Rumor or Flaminio Piccoli."[42]

Murialdi's colleague was referring to one of the DC's most powerful factions. Indeed, Mariano Rumor was the founder and a leader of the *dorotei*, of which Flaminio Piccoli was also a member.[43] This faction and the *fanfaniani* group were both very influential inside RAI during the 1950s and 1960s. Both of them contrasted the *aziendalisti*, which in turn could count on the support of the DC right wing.

Finally, however, it was the struggle among factions and internal power groups that contributed to the end of Guala's tenure. Too extremist in his moral views for the progressive wing of the DC, too drastic in the changes he imposed inside the broadcaster, Guala lost his allies. Perhaps he went too far in his zeal to introduce reforms, and the DC's right wing and some of the factions within the broadcaster still linked to the *aziendalisti* resented him. The overall political context was also changing: the DC left wing was moving away from what came to be considered as Fanfani's extreme moral views on the use of television and his centrist politics, and was opening to more moderate ideas. As the lay parties allied with the DC began questioning Guala's interference in programming, his intolerant views on Catholic morals and the mass media became, somehow, out of fashion. Nor had IRI appreciated Guala's restructuring of the broadcaster. In particular, the owner of RAI was not happy with the new people that were promoted too soon in places of responsibility with the overall focus on programming and disdain for administrative business. Guala finally resigned in 1956 and became a Trappist monk.

Meanwhile, the popularity of television was growing fast. In 1954, broadcasting stations in Rome, Milan, and Turin began regular programming. Weekly output was 24 hours in the last months of 1953, 28 hours in 1954, and 35 hours in 1955.[44] It was a rather impressive development, if we consider that the French public service broadcaster produced 35 hours per week in the ninth year of operation (which started in 1944); and that the German television, which began its broadcasts in 1950, produced only 22 hours per week by 1954.

News, information, and public affairs programs represented 18.3 percent of total broadcasting output in the last months of 1953, up to 28 percent in 1954, and up to 29.4 percent in 1955.[45] There was one prime-time edition of the news program, or *telegiornale*, at 8:30 at night, and an additional edition at the end of the day. In 1954 there were 516 broadcasts of *telegiornale*, 623 in 1955.

In line with EIAR tradition, genres varied and centered on entertainment. The early television genres included scripts for television, opera and ballets, light entertainment (of which the first example was the program *Un, due, tre*), quiz shows (like *Attenti al fiasco* and the famous *Lascia o raddoppia?*), cultural programs, programs for children, and current and public affairs programs. Meanwhile, the popularity of the mass media, both radio and television, continued to rise: radio subscribers went from a little over 4 million in 1953 to almost 6 million by 1955. In 1956, they numbered well over 6 million, 50 percent of whom were from the north, the rest from the center and the south, with only five hundred radio subscribers from the islands. According to RAI's estimates, the number of people listening to the radio in their own homes went up from 16 million in 1955, to 18 million in 1956.[46]

Television subscribers—88,118 in 1954, 178,793 one year later, and 366,151 in 1956—were also geographically determined. In 1955, approximately two-thirds were from the north, one-third from the center and the south. Only in 1956 did a few households in the islands begin to pay their license fee for television.[47] By 1955, 400,000 people watched television on a regular basis at home, 800,000 at friends' houses, and 3,000,000 at local coffee places. The percentage of those who watched TV in the evening hours in public places decreased from 50 percent to 15 percent between 1956 and 1963.

Technological Developments

Guala's successor was Rodolfo Arata, former director of the DC newspaper *Il Popolo*, whose appointment was supported by the DC conservative wing. Marcello Rodinò, also close to the DC right wing, was appointed RAI's managing director. Increasing revenues from the license fee and advertising allowed RAI to expand its infrastructures and improve its technological capabilities. The corporation was growing very rapidly: new buildings were being acquired and new headquarters were being opened. RAI's broadcasting network expanded to satisfy the universal service required by the 1952 agreement with the state: by the end of 1956 the national television network was completed, and almost 95 percent of Italian households were potentially able to receive the signal. The division between creative and production processes, established by Guala, intensified and radio and television news services were unified in a central directorate (*Direzione centrale servizi giornalistici*) under strict political control. A Catholic journalist close to the DC right wing became director of the radio news program (*giornale radio*) and another DC journalist became head of the television news program (*telegiornale*), strengthening the DC hegemony over the information sector. The *aziendalisti* were given control over the administrative structure, with the appointment of Marcello Severati as head of the personnel directorate, which was moved from Turin to Rome. The model of political control adopted by Arata and Rodinò was straightforward: the "medium was conceived as a simple and rigid variable dependent on the government forces, which were the real 'brain' of the entire productive apparatus and the only real referents of the entire television production."[48] News programs were conceived simply as "resonance chambers for the initiatives of the center parties."[49] Indeed, the newscasts were rather monotonous and included communiqués from various ministries, inaugurations and other formal events of various kinds, and information on the platforms of the government parties. The result was a program that was scarcely informative and purely propagandistic. Overall, most of the information on political events came from government sources, which meant a superabundance of images and information about DC politicians.[50]

Meanwhile, Italian society was gradually evolving. The Catholic postwar model in dealing with mass media soon became insufficient. It was time to replace the straightforward, top-down political control over television, with a more dialectic model, one that could embrace opposition and show some openness to different viewpoints and instances present in the society. For that, a more articulated and ideological—rather than simply political or propagandistic—use of television was required. The medium had to emancipate from its position of almost passive dependence on the government parties to one of autonomy and "independence." Timid steps in this direction were taken toward the end of Arata's leadership, while the DC was definitely moving away from the disastrous center-right government of the summer of 1960 toward a new alliance with the lay leftist parties, which did not approve of the political culture of the DC. Meanwhile, some news and public affairs programs were becoming more open to society and to alternative viewpoints. An important novelty of 1960 was *Tribuna elettorale*, a current affairs program where ministers and parties' secretaries, even the secretary-general of the Communist Party, had the opportunity to present their political programs on video, and after a brief introduction, were invited to answer the questions of various journalists from an opposite party. This was a rather innovative format: traditionally, leaders of the opposition parties were not shown on video, and if they were, their comments would be preceded and followed by the comments of a representative of the government. However, the political jargon used during those interviews by both politicians and journalists was detrimental to the overall clarity of the discussions. Once again, it seemed that not even this program was actually designed to foster rational debate and give citizens an opportunity to understand the issues at stake, but rather to promote polemic arguments among just them, the politicians and the journalists. Furthermore, Guala's code of prohibited words and topics were still in force, considerably limiting the range of items that could be discussed.

The Bernabei Model: An Enlightened Monarchy

After the collapse of the center-right Tambroni government in the summer of 1960, Amintore Fanfani inaugurated what came to be known as the "center-left experiment." Echoes reverberated inside RAI: after a decade of *centrismo* and center-right governments, after Guala's era of Catholic extremism and Arata's techno-administrative rigorism, the public broadcaster was now ready for a more dynamic leadership at a time of profound changes. The opposition, finally aware of the power of television in orienting voting preferences (electoral outcomes favorable to the governing parties gave the impression that the overwhelming victory of the DC was due to its influence over *telegiornali*), was mobilizing for new legislation. Furthermore, news programs, because of the pervasive pro-government bias, were losing credibility among certain strata of the population, certainly among leftist voters.

The monopoly over radio and television broadcasting was being challenged by private entrepreneurs attempting to start their own television business in Milan and Rome. Even though the Constitutional Court ruling no. 53 of 1960 asserted the legitimacy of state monopoly over radio and television broadcasting, the sentence underlined that the foundations for the legitimacy of that monopoly were objectivity of information and guaranteed access to the airwaves for those groups who wanted to use the public broadcaster to express their ideas.

In this context, where domesticated information continued to represent the core of news on RAI, while the pressures from the opposition and various consumers' groups demanding the implementation of the 1960 ruling were growing, drastic changes were needed. Ettore Bernabei, former director of the DC newspaper *Il Popolo*, was the right man at the right time. He became director general in 1961. His administration is often remembered as a time of innovation, as the expression of the center-left coalition that dominated the 1960s. With Bernabei, the broadcaster emancipated itself from a condition of dependence and became, through the years, less identifiable as a docile instrument in the hands of the government party.

Important innovations followed in programming. Political talk shows, such as *Tribuna politica*, which ensued the 1960 edition of *Tribuna elettorale*, and in-depth news reporting, such as *TV7*, the first in-depth news magazine of its kind on Italian television, offered some opportunity for alternative voices:

> Information and public affairs programs were the mirror of the evolution of political life in the country. Actually, we might say that news and public affairs slightly foreran the changes in society. It is certainly true that news reporting was always careful not to openly criticize the powers that be, especially those powers that were in line with RAI's leadership.... However, there was the will to present non-homogenous elements and to illustrate topics from different perspectives. For the first time, people from the center-left and the left were being asked to participate in the news specials, even before the Left took power in the government. An example of this was in-depth, alternative news program such as *TV7*. This was a way to educate the public to develop a more critical approach.[51]

But others argued that the innovative character of *TV7* and *Tribuna politica* was only an attempt to gain hegemony over cultural and political life, to embrace the opposition in order to neutralize it. According to Giovanni Cesareo, the author of various seminal works on RAI, Bernabei's innovative programs were dictated by a pure logic of power, rather than a coherent political culture. Well-balanced programming was created so the viewer had the impression that television was impartial; at the same time, however, opposite views would neutralize themselves reciprocally. In fact, "every aspect of Italian political and social life was presented as if each aspect were equally important, as if problems existed and were inevitable."[52] In other words, television was not being used to initiate changes in society nor to challenge problems, or to attempt to resolve them. Indeed, alternative public affairs programs such as *TV7* were never broadcast in prime time, and critics observed that new spaces for in-depth coverage were created mainly to please political opposition: the politics of "impartiality" boiled down to an implied centrism.

In 1961, the second television channel was born. In 1963, the two channels were restructured and programming was unified under a centralized *Comitato programmi* (programming committee). Scheduling became the crucial element of Bernabei's editorial and programming policy. Alternative programs were realized and broadcast. But they were scheduled as to receive the least possible exposure. As another television historian, Franco Chiarenza, put it, Bernabei was very clever in "obtaining the double effect of showing that RAI was open to the new political trend, while scheduling the programs not in line with the DC in such a way that only a very few people could actually watch them."[53] Others agree: the opening to the center-left and the innovative character of some programs ought to be interpreted as a very articulated strategy to achieve the same old objective, namely, the confirmation of the DC supremacy in the public broadcaster. Opposition was not to be avoided, but rather embraced; contradictions had to be reduced to "dialectical instances within the larger project of strengthening Catholic hegemony."[54] RAI was becoming more autonomous from the government parties, not to promote a truly independent broadcaster, but rather to gain credibility and prestige, and to establish consent and legitimacy around itself, especially in the delicate sector of information. Creating spaces for center-left representatives to voice their points of view meant also that now "all center left parties . . . and the DC itself, were put in the condition where they *had to negotiate* with RAI to guarantee their own presence in the information sector."[55]

Nevertheless, the new programs were commendable in giving a voice to the opposition, other parliamentary parties, and journalists not in line with the DC. Besides *TV7* and *Tribuna elettorale*, other relevant programs of those years were *Cronache dai partiti* (parties' chronicles); *Tribuna sindacale* (a forum featuring unions' leaders); *Zoom* and *Cronache dal XX secolo* (Chronicle of the Twentieth century), both edited by an excellent journalist, Andrea Barbato; and public affairs programs such as *Prima pagina* (Front Page), edited by Furio Colombo with the collaboration of Andrea Barbato, Alberto Ronchey (a journalist from the lay area), and Roberto Morrione (a member of the PCI). Morrione's reports on apartheid in South Africa, those of Sergio Zavoli and Furio Colombo on the Vietnam War, and the reports from Cuba, Greece, Sudan, and Ethiopia are examples of the quality and breadth of public affairs programs during the 1960s.

The production of fiction also improved under Bernabei. This too was another difference with the previous Piedmont style of administration, which instead promoted the bourgeois, highbrow theater but hardly any fiction for the middle. Bernabei encouraged big productions, the kind of fiction for television that everybody could enjoy, like the literary masterpieces *L'Odissea* (*The Odyssey*), *Gli atti degli apostoli* (The Apostles' Acts), *Delitto e castigo* (*Crime and Punishment*, the first production of this kind realized in the new production facilities of Naples), *Mastro don Gesualdo* (from Giovanni Verga's masterpiece), *I promessi sposi* (Alessandro Manzoni's novel), and *I miserabili* (*Les Misérables*). Nothing controversial, just good quality entertainment for the middle class. Other famous programs included popularizations of art and science (such as *Almanacco*, a sort of popular encyclopedia).

Administrative Problems

But if programming was in some respects innovative, administration was problematic. Bernabei inflated the broadcaster's techno-structure: during his tenure the central administration grew from 4 to 8 directorates, and the overall number of directorates grew from 13 to 47. In 1961, there were 112 directors; by 1966, there were 156, and 285 in 1973.[56] Full-time personnel in news and public affairs departments went from 2,798 units in 1962 to 3,177 in 1966; technical personnel went from 2,690 in 1962, to 2,971 in 1966; administrative personnel increased from 1,869 to 2,093 in the same period; and the total number of journalists grew from 308 in 1961 to 800 in 1974.[57] At the end of Bernabei's tenure, RAI counted 12,000 employees, three times more than in 1960. Moreover, full-time employees were only a part of the immense network of collaborators that were on RAI's payroll. In 1970, according to various estimates, RAI had more than 21,000 external collaborators.[58] At the end of 1974, 20 billion lire, out of a total of 26 billion lire of RAI's revenues, was spent on salaries and other personnel-related expenses, leaving only 6 billion for production of programs and investments in technology.[59]

The overall geographical distribution of personnel was also indicative of the centralization and "romanization" process: by 1966, the majority (48 percent) of RAI's full-time workforce was based in various headquarters in the capital and other locations in central Italy (Florence, Perugia, Ancona);[60] 40 percent of the workforce was in the north (mostly in Milan and Turin); and only a few hundred employees (12 percent of the workforce) in the south and islands.

The growth of the broadcaster was due only in part to the growth of hours of programming. Although a new channel had been born, and in 1968 afternoon programming was added, the expansion of the internal structure was due primarily to clientelistic politics (after all "political profit" was Bernabei's main guideline), inspired by the need to create new positions (often without any real power or function) to please the various parties and the various power groups inside RAI, and to control the opposition. In 1961, when Bernabei took over, RAI produced thirty-one minutes of TV broadcast time per employee; by the end of his tenure, in 1974, RAI's output was only twenty-seven minutes per employee. In striking contrast, during the following thirteen years (1974-1987), production efficiency went up more than 2.5-fold, to sixty-eight minutes per employee.[61] Given the overall improvements of technology and infrastructures, the dropping efficiency during Bernabei's leadership is even more noticeable.

Meanwhile, the popularity of television was soaring. By 1969, 22 million people watched it, with an average viewing of one hour and twenty minutes per day; by 1972, RAI offered 5,912 hours of programming and could count on almost 11 million subscribers (they were growing at an unprecedented rate: almost 700,000 new subscribers per year, between 1961 and 1974). Ninety-eight percent of the population received the signal of the first channel, Rete 1; 91 percent received the signal of the second channel, Rete 2. Italians were also consuming more television compared to other wealthier European countries. For instance, in 1963, 6.8 percent of Italian households had a TV set, compared to 5.2 percent in Austria and 4.8 percent in Switzerland (whose per capita incomes were, respectively, 25.6 percent and 155 percent higher than the per capita income in Italy).[62]

Personnel

Hiring personnel was a business that Bernabei enjoyed taking care of personally. He received about 20,000 letters of inquiry and recommendation per year and had a staff of two people, very loyal to him, do the initial selection. Letters of recommendation, in Italy, are usually not considered an honest means of getting a position (contrarily to what happens in the Anglo-American world): they are generally seen as a way of conducting business "under the table" that tends to undermine the legal way to get a job, which often occurs through public national examinations. Technically, public examinations were also a way of hiring new personnel during those years. Theoretically, those examinations were supposed to minimize the interference of personal networking, privileges, and recommendations. Obviously, Bernabei had ways to get around things and make sure that even the more impersonal route of public examinations would still be controlled by himself, so that only trustworthy people would finally enter. Criteria for selecting candidates were strict: prospective employees needed to have credible recommendations, be bright, and, most of all, most of the time, be cleared by the main parties (including the PCI) in agreement with the Vatican. Certainly this method did not guarantee that the best journalist would get in; Bernabei himself recalls that "in order to get somebody good, I had to hire somebody who was not very good: that was the price to pay."[63]

Bernabei's Vision

Somehow in contradiction with a disingenuous clientelistic politics, Bernabei's leadership was animated by a powerful, almost religious commitment to the educational role of public broadcasting, of which he continued to be a supporter even after his tenure at RAI. For him, hiring people of proven "faith" was a way to ensure that the mission of the public broadcaster would be fulfilled. The former director general, a fervent Catholic, is passionate about the values of television and the negative effects of commercialization: "It is absolutely necessary," he affirmed, "to destroy commercial television and go back to public television. . . . Because of commercial television, there is now a soft narcosis, which does not require one to use higher and noble human qualities, only the sensual ones. By doing that, advertising is transforming the public into an automatic consumer."[64]

A consumer was certainly not his ideal viewer, but neither was a citizen in full command of his or her own rational abilities. Bernabei's conception of "his" public, at the time when he was the most powerful person in Italian television, was of viewers in need of guidance, according to a mix of paternalistic instincts and political calculations. Viewers needed to be cared for, even protected from harmful information; therefore, television could convey only information that was considered appropriate by the broadcaster's leadership. This desire to use television as an educational tool, as a means to entertain people with quality programs, while creating consensus around the Christian Democratic Party, was defined as the "party/pedagogical hypothesis."[65] Bernabei is still very proud of the ideals informing his leadership, whose aim was to enlighten and entertain all viewers. And since almost half of RAI's viewers were Communists, that meant that he had to please even them. If RAI could not afford to produce programs taking the part of the Communists, at least it had to make sure that even communist citizens would be protected:

> My leadership was characterized by a profound respect for the viewers, whatever their political affiliation was. Take for instance President Kennedy's assassination. We received the news around 7:40 p.m. After only a few minutes, at 20:05, when the Tg was already on the air, a note from the Associated Press said that Lee Oswald had been in Moscow for six months. There were some allegations suggesting that the USSR might be involved in the assassination, and that was why we decided not to release that piece of information. We did not want our viewers, who loved Kennedy, to start harassing the Communists. In the little towns and villages of the "red belt" regions everybody knew who the Communists were, and we worried that something bad could happen to them. Before airing the news about Lee Oswald, we wanted to make sure that the Soviet Union had nothing to do with Kennedy's death.[66]

The Restructuring of 1969

In 1965 Gianni Granzotto was appointed RAI's managing director. His appointment was supported by a variety of groups: the *dorotei*, whose intention was to limit Bernabei's power, while the left parties, like the Socialists, the Social Democrats, and the Republicans, welcomed the appointment of a man who was a well-known and respected journalist, and not a direct emanation of the DC. But those who believed that Bernabei's influence within RAI could be somehow circumscribed were soon to be proven wrong. After the death of Sergio Pugliese, director of television programming, Bernabei appointed Luigi Beretta as head of that department. Beretta, as well as his closest collaborators, came from the old Guala integralist group, and were chosen with the precise aim to "impose an ideological turn to programming."[67] The directorate of *telegiornali* was given to Fabiano Fabiani, a man close to the *fanfaniani* current; Vittorio Chesi, former director of the Milan edition of *Il Popolo*, became director of *Giornale radio*, the radio news. The directorate of general affairs went in the hands of Gregorio Pozzilli, another *uomo di fiducia* of the DC. The plan, first designed by Guala, to eliminate the old guard of *aziendalisti*, and replace them with men of proven Christian Democratic faith, was almost completed. By the mid-1960s the *aziendalisti* controlled only the administrative sector and the personnel division. But the administrative problems, the overwhelming power of the director-general, his overtly clientelistic practices, the partiality of the majority of the programs, and the inefficiency of the corporation were gradually coming to the surface. Unable to contrast Bernabei's plans, Granzotto resigned from his position as managing director in 1969.

A new leadership was appointed by the center-left government. The Italian Socialist Party (PSI) and the Italian Social Democratic Party (PSDI), together with the DC, negotiated their respective zones of influence inside the broadcaster; among the center-left parties, appointments were discussed as if "radio and television were family matters, and no politician seemed to be concerned about accountability to the government."[68] Christian Democrats, Socialists, and Social Democrats were appointed in various positions as vice presidents, members of the board of directors, and as managing director. Aldo Sandulli, former head of the Constitutional Court, became president of RAI. The appointment was proposed by the Republican Party, with the mandate to guarantee objectivity and pluralism. Ettore Bernabei was confirmed director-general.

Major changes occurred in the following months. More emphasis was placed on entertainment and educational programming, and most important, the corporation was centralized even further under the hands of the director general. He became the absolute arbiter of RAI, the one who assured its "functioning, the definition and realization of its production . . . the one who [would] plan, organize, and control the activities of all sectors of the corporation."[69] In redefining the various leaderships in the different sectors, Bernabei opened up more spaces for the PSI, while confirming the hegemony of the DC. New appointments were made that reflected the new balances of power inside the government coalition. While the directorate of radio programming was given to the Socialists; the directorate of television programming was divided in two sections: the cultural programs division under Fabiano Fabiani (who was removed from the direction of the news programs), and the entertainment division under Angelo Romanò, another DC. Children's and educational programming were left in the hands of the DC; Vittorio Chesi remained director of *Giornale radio*, with two vice-directors, a DC and a Social Democrat. Willy De Luca—closely linked to the DC, and somehow considered more docile than Fabiani to the will of the party—became director of the news department.

But once again, the pervasive role of the parties did not indicate that the public broadcaster was in their hands. In fact, the corporation gained even more autonomy, ensured by the greater power that Bernabei had centered in his hands. The concessions he made to party factions and to the government coalition were in line with his strategy: they were expedients to embrace and neutralize conflicts and opposition, and to create an even stronger center of power independent from political power. He was able to achieve this, some observers notice, thanks to the caliber of his management. Even though appointments were rigorously checked and negotiated with the parties, the quality was, in general, excellent:

> That was a period when RAI enjoyed a great deal of autonomy because the management, of excellent quality, was unconditionally respected by the main party, the DC. When there were things to deal with everybody knew that, yes, Bernabei was a Christian Democrat; however, he did not take orders from the DC. He was the DC, and a very important piece of it. Because of this, the public broadcaster started to enjoy its own autonomous power and this power was recognized in a non-conflicting manner by the government party.[70]

Lottizzazione in Its Blood

The restructuring of the public broadcaster in 1969 and the appointments of PSI and PSDI members were defined by Alberto Ronchey as "RAI's first *lottizzazione*." He wrote:

> [T]he parties have pursued a pure power game at the expense of a delicate public broadcasting service. . . . [T]he principle according to which Christian Democrats and Socialists, without consulting anybody else,

agree between themselves on how to divide RAI up is unacceptable. It is not acceptable that each department, invariably, must have a director designated by the DC and a vice-director appointed by the PSI. But this has been happening everywhere in RAI, in the news department as well as in the cultural-education department.[71]

Indeed, the "first *lottizzazione*" found a structure that was predisposed to facilitate the sharing of power. Bernabei had created an elephantine structure, inflated with directorates and departments, and that allowed the DC left and right wings, the PSI, and the PSDI to carve out seats for their representatives. After all, this was nothing new. Since the beginning, the apparatus of public service broadcasting was established with the specific function to create consensus around the hegemonic bloc surrounding the DC. As Renato Parascandolo, vice head of RAI Educational, illustrates,

> One main historical reason explaining RAI's dependence on the political elites is that at the foundation of the public broadcaster's relationship with the political system there was indeed little familiarity with the institutions of liberal democracy. In other words, *lottizzazione* was not an abnormality of the system. . . . [I]t was ingrained in the institutional relationship that linked, from its conception, RAI to the political elites.[72]

Managerial positions skyrocketed. After the restructuring of 1969 there were two vice-directors general, 14 central directors, 30 central codirectors, 53 vice central directors, and more than 200 service managers. In the news department, there were 3 codirectors, 9 vice-directors, 17 central managing editors, 32 managing editors, and 24 vice managing editors.

Preparing the Reform

Things were changing in the social and political realm. Italian society was growing apart from the political and party system, Fanfani's power inside his party as well as inside the government coalition was also in crisis, and Bernabei's "party-pedagogical hypothesis" was losing its legitimacy. Progressive forces asking for a reform of the broadcaster and promarket interests supporting private broadcasting were gaining momentum. Various right-wing groups and parties, including the Italian

Social Movement (MSI) together with conservative liberalist forces and the Italian Liberal Party (PLI), fringes of the Socialist Party, and the Republican Party (PRI)—supported by the telephone industry (SIP), which was interested in the opportunities for cable television represented by the emerging private stations—were working to undermine RAI's monopoly and supported the birth of the first private cable television, Telebiella, in 1973. Other cable television stations started their operations in those years, including Teleivrea, Telealessandria, and Televercelli.

It would be a mistake, however, to assume that the left parties were the ones protecting the monopoly, and the right parties were those open to private entrepreneurship. Members of the PSI encouraged local initiatives of television broadcasting; certain exponents of the DC itself, albeit unofficially, were aware of the problems inside RAI, and showed a certain openness to the idea of putting an end to the monopoly. Overall, within the pro-reform movement there was disagreement between those who sustained the need for a reform of the broadcaster while maintaining the state monopoly, and those who campaigned for an end of the monopoly and the liberalization of the airwaves.

The attitude of the various parties toward commercial broadcasting varied but was, in general, rather contradictory. At the beginning, the Socialist Party was mostly interested in affirming its own power within RAI. Only after its control over RAI was secured at the end of the 1970s did the party begin to support independent/commercial broadcasters. The PSI encouraged liberalization and independence from the state in the commercial broadcasting sector, while continuing to exercise its control over the public broadcaster. The DC had a history of uninterrupted support of RAI and its monopoly. Catholic fervor and parties' interests were the foundation of the Christian Democrats', especially of its left wing, strenuous defense of public service broadcasting. But, as mentioned above, that did not preclude some members from supporting, although unofficially, the liberalization of the airwaves. The PCI, which in the 1950s had failed to understand the potential of television, in the 1970s supported the rise of independent stations. In 1980, the NET (*Nuova Emittenza Televisiva*), a chain of eighteen local television stations close to the Communists, was established under the presidency of Walter Veltroni, a leader of the Communist Party. The Communist Party was also a supporter of decentralization of RAI structures and programming, and an advocate for local and community access to the means of media production.

A battle for more diversity in the media, for political independence, and a struggle for a decentralized RAI in order to promote local production and more participation of the newborn regional institutions were behind the citizens' strong demand for participatory tools in political and social relations and the proreform front. Debates at all levels were conducted in a variety of forums revealing the unprecedented interest among citizens and consumer groups to reform the broadcaster. In RAI, too, the atmosphere became incandescent, especially after the restructuring of 1969, when workers, including journalists and programmers, went on strike to protest against the DC monopoly inside the broadcaster. The movement requested a reform of the broadcaster and advocated that RAI operators, as well as social and community formations, participate in programming decisions to "connect the central apparatus to social forces and places where people lived their social experience."[73] The pro-liberalization front also demanded that a reform of the broadcaster take into account a policy of decentralization of RAI's structures and programming.

If RAI had become, in the eyes of large strata of public opinion, the elephantine bureaucracy of a state-controlled monopoly, private broadcasters represented, for many, freedom from government influences and a source for alternative information. A public opinion movement, fostered by national newspapers such as *Corriere della Sera* and weekly magazines such as *L'Espresso* and *Panorama*, rallied in favor of independent broadcasters. As Giuseppe Richeri noted, "Private stations were portrayed as dynamic and innovative, [whereas] RAI was shown as carved up among the parties and incapable of any innovation."[74]

Citizens and social/political activist groups were advocating independence from the party system, and for many of them, local and independent broadcasting stations represented the new heralds of civic and democratic freedoms, the examples of true decentralization, the symbol of liberty. They joined in the so-called freedom of antenna movement, advocating independence from state and government control. Many who led this movement held strong political and social commitments to the left. Radio Antenna Rossa, Radio Città Futura, and Radio Alice were some of the most famous independent radio stations of the early and mid-1970s. But the game was getting out of hand and the revolution of the hundred flowers, as the emergence of independent radio and television stations was also called, soon came to an end. Paradoxically, the leftists who were advocating the importance of independent stations as an expression of freedom and democracy were the very people who "paved the way for private capital to play an increasingly active role in the ownership and control of broadcasting in Italy."[75] *Libertà d'antenna* (freedom of antenna) continued to be the motivating slogan of this movement, and among the ranks of those who chanted it was Silvio Berlusconi, owner of Fininvest. *Libertà d'antenna* came to signify freedom from RAI and from the state monopoly, and this quest ultimately came to mean freedom for commercial broadcasters to expand. The leftist movement advocating independent broadcasting ended up legitimating the existence of private/commercial broadcasters as the only alternative to party control. Entrepreneurs like the publisher Mondadori, initially, and later, Berlusconi, reaped the fruits of the freedom of antenna movement.

The citizens' strong support for independent broadcasters was certainly a sign that in a country where the DC and the Catholic bloc had imposed their values for decades in all sectors of the cultural industry, including of course, entertainment and news on television, viewers were eager for novelties, for more information, for a diversity of sources, and also for more light programs. Certainly Bernabei's party/pedagogical hypothesis was also in crisis because of its moral seriousness. For example, data from RAI's research department show that interest for news and public affairs programs was growing, and also viewers' predilection for TV series and films was considerably increasing.[76] The television audience was changing: the new viewers were now richer and better educated than their parents, with more free time available, and with a thirst for diverse sources of information and entertainment. Not only had the DC imposed on the quality and breadth of entertainment that Italians could enjoy, but the government parties also had purposefully delayed the introduction of color transmission until 1977 in an attempt to discourage consumerism during the economic crisis of the early 1970s.[77] One could argue that foreign programs in color played a role in importing new values and a less monolithic culture, which in turn resulted in more interest among ample strata of the population in the events surrounding the liberalization of the airwaves.

The Sentences of the Constitutional Court

In July 1974, two very innovative sentences of the Constitutional Court (225 and 226) echoed and interpreted the widespread concern, and provided directions for a future reform.

Sentence no. 225 of July 10, 1974, elaborated on the legitimacy of state monopoly over television broadcasting. Ruling with regard to a few cases concerning private citizens accused of the illegal installation of receivers for television programs broadcast from Switzerland and Yugoslavia, the court articulated some fundamental guidelines for state monopoly. First of all, given technological innovations, the court warned that the legitimacy of state monopoly over television broadcasting should not be considered a given anymore. Furthermore, according to the court, by sanctioning the installation and the operation of receivers, whose only purpose was to rebroadcast foreign television programs, the state would de facto force its citizens to "receive information only from national radio and television services . . . thereby precluding their opportunity to access other sources"[78]—a sort of "information autarchy," as the court called it. In other words, the court continued, "the need to guarantee objectivity and impartiality—which only legitimates the state monopoly over national broadcasting—are not disrupted by the presence of those receivers. [In fact] those receivers can only amplify . . . the number of accessible sources and the free circulation . . . of news and ideas."[79]

On that same occasion, the high court reflected on the conditions of the public monopoly over national television and radio broadcasting, and arrived at the following conclusions: the public monopolist should be

> conceived mainly as a necessary instrument to enlarge the area of effective manifestation of pluralism of the voices that are present in our society—as such, the court continued—its operations should follow two fundamental objectives: programs should offer the public a variety of services characterized by objectivity and complete information, by ample openness to all cultural trends, and by impartial representation of ideas; the broadcaster should [also] favor, make it possible, and guarantee the right of access.[80]

Without a reform law that would follow these two main directives (more pluralism in programming and guaranteed access), the court argued, the radio and television broadcaster, left to the initiative of those who administered it, risked being more damaging than if it were in the hands of a restricted number of private entrepreneurs. Indeed, as it was, the public monopoly "risked to be a powerful tool at the service of a few, rather than the collectivity. . . . Once free from any rule that correctly and efficiently disciplines it, the public broadcaster could sway in a direction diametrically opposite to the dictate of the constitution."[81] This was a major blow to Bernabei's model.

Ruling about recent developments in the local cable television industry, sentence no. 226 affirmed that any attempt to claim state monopoly over local cable television was unconstitutional. The rationale of spectrum scarcity (a concept on which the state monopoly of national television broadcasting was instead reaffirmed) did not apply, according to the court, to cable television channels. Since cable television channels were not restricted by spectrum scarcity and their cost was considered "irrelevant," the court declared that the "provision of state monopoly [could] not be justified on the basis of a de facto monopoly due to technical reasons, as it applies to broadcasting television."[82] On this foundation, the court stated that there was no reason to "inhibit and compress private initiative, which could only further expand the freedom of speech sanctioned by the constitution,"[83] and that no "general interest" could be advocated in support of state monopoly on local cable television. Especially significant for future developments, the sentence articulated the difference between cable television on a national basis—which, given the high costs of operations, should require state monopoly—and cable television on a local basis, which had to be open for private initiatives.

With these groundbreaking sentences, private broadcasters were allowed to broadcast foreign programs and local cable stations to transmit locally. The monopoly of public broadcasting at the national level was reconfirmed, but only as long as it guaranteed and assured access to all groups present in society, and only as long as it provided ample, complete information, reflecting all ideas and perspectives. The message to the public broadcaster was clear: the time of the DC's monopoly was over, and RAI had to change.

The Regions

The court's attention to the regional and local dimensions of television and radio cable was also a reflection of the changes that were implemented at the level of state administration with the establishment, in 1970, of regional institutions. The newly founded institutions were an expression of the need for an alternative juridical, administrative, and territorial articulation of the central government. The regions revolutionized all aspects of the old conception of the state as they gave "voice and strength to social and cultural realities once submerged by the centralistic structures of the state."[84] Particularly important was their role in advocating changes in the highly centralized structures of the public school system and the information sector and in sectors of the welfare state like the social health care system and the pension system. The new regional institutions (especially those in Lombardia and Campania) were also at the forefront of the struggle to reform the broadcasting system pushing in the direction of decentralization of creative and production capabilities. The regions advocated a cultural and territorial pluralism, which, in line with the experience of other European countries (like the German and Belgian regional broadcasters, and, in some respects, the third channel F3 in France), was to be realized through a radical transformation of the public broadcaster by providing regional headquarters with the adequate structures and resources to fulfill all stages of programming, from ideation to production to broadcasting and scheduling. In their struggles, the regions were able to mobilize journalists' associations, political forces, and unions. There was disagreement, however, as to how decentralization should be realized. Should it be accomplished through the realization of a third channel, on the French model, or through a more radical decentralization of the entire structure? At the Naples conference, in the fall of 1972, agreement was reached among regions' representatives on the second option. For fear of local information and regional programs being marginalized in a sort of regional ghetto, the regions opted to have their representatives inside the board of directors, hoping that this would eventually bring local production and information into the national circuit.

The Crisis of the Party/Pedagogical Model

Bernabei's model of a Roman, Catholic broadcaster was clearly in crisis. Without the support of Amintore Fanfani, who was preoccupied with dissent in his own faction, Bernabei's confidence and, with it, RAI's sense of autonomy were also decreasing:

> [T]owards the end Bernabei was unable to say "no" to whatever politicians asked him. His mistake was that he was not willing to tell the two parties [DC and PSI] "listen, I agree with you, but let me do things my own way." Instead, he kept giving in, granting too much importance to what the politicians would say. At that time his close friend, Amintore Fanfani, was way too worried about his own political future and didn't have the time to support him. And at the end, a reform of the broadcasting system became a necessity.[85]

An era was clearly ending. Bernabei's mission to marginalize the old power groups of *aziendalisti*, renovating management, production, and the news department with people open to center-left ideas, had been completed. But his ability to mediate among opposing tendencies—the moderates, the centrists, the Socialists, the Communists, and the Vatican—had caused resentment on the part of most conservative groups, which took the opportunity to criticize Bernabei and RAI and coalesce public opinion against the monopoly of radio and television broadcasting. His leadership was attacked on all sides, from the left as well as from the right. Moreover, continuous conflicts within the DC had repercussions on Bernabei's own power: conservative factions opposed the opening to the left, and questioned the leadership of programming, which included various people from the PSI and the DC left wing. The treasury minister, Emilio Colombo, from the *dorotei* group, cut funds to the broadcaster and, even worse, denied its application to adjust the license fee for inflation. The agreement between RAI and the state was due for renewal in 1972, but was delayed waiting for a reform of the entire broadcasting system. In 1973, the DC briefly reunited under the leadership of Fanfani in a center-left alliance, but the overwhelming pro-divorce result of the 1974 referendum resulted in a powerful defeat for the DC and a major blow for the Church. Those results showed that control over television was no longer sufficient to ensure hegemonic control over morals and lifestyle choices. The supremacy of politics and of the postwar model of hegemony over cultural and social relations were becoming outdated. Other interests, rather than the struggles between the old guard and the new leadership inside RAI, were preoccupying the political elites. Other forces pushing for the liberalization of the airwaves were making the party/pedagogical model outdated. In September 1974, Bernabei ended his mandate and, once again thanks to Fanfani, became director-general of Italstat, another corporation of the IRI system; Willy De Luca replaced him as the new director-general of the public broadcaster.

Democratizing the Public Broadcaster

The broadcaster had to be restructured, more channels ought to offer a variety of cultural options, previous centralized structures of production should be decentralized, or new regional structures and a regional channel should be created. Units of production ought to replace the divisive system that Bernabei had purposefully put in place to separate the ideation phase from production and scheduling of programs; and access ought to be granted to the collectivity.

Intense debates were developing around the need to increase citizen participation in the national broadcaster, decentralize RAI's structures and programming, and incorporate pluralism of ideas and perspectives into RAI's political culture. Political parties, national unions, citizens' organizations, community organizations, the newly established regional institutions, RAI program makers, journalists, and intellectuals were all exercising enormous pressures for a reform of the broadcaster. Intellectuals, broadcast and print journalists and other media personnel, Communist and Socialist politicians, workers' unions, grassroots and social movements all participated in the struggle to promote a progressive reform in the broadcasting sector. Ideally, the new law was supposed to open the public broadcaster to alternative points of view and new models of television production, like decentralization of programming. Widespread was the agreement that the public monopoly over radio and television broadcasting should be subtracted from the control of the executive. Divergent, instead, were the opinions with regard to the nature and purpose of that monopoly. Was the state monopoly supposed to simply "protect" the collectivity from the formation of centers of power (public or private) in the broadcasting sector, or was its purpose to have a more "positive" function, namely, to educate the public, to shape opinions, and, at the political level, to "establish the norms and directions through which that would be done"?[86] Certainly, as I said, one thing was clear: the existing government monopoly, exercised through a highly centralized structure, was the common enemy to defeat. In order to do that, the monopoly had to shift from the executive to the parliament. But how much power was to be given to the parliament? And how was decentralization going to be actualized?

The so-called Reform Law no. 103, passed on April 14, 1975, was the first law reforming the broadcasting system after the war. The spirit of the new law was to free RAI from government pressures, creating a space for other parties to join in. Indeed, the lay parties, including the Socialist, Liberal, Republican, and Communist Parties, were claiming their roles within the broadcaster and voicing their discontent with a public broadcaster mainly under the control of the DC. The rationale was that for RAI to be a public service, it should represent the variety of political positions, and therefore pluralism, which meant party pluralism, ought to be adopted. For this reason, law 103 is usually considered to have initiated *lottizzazione*.

The new law formally established that "independence, objectivity, and openness to diverse political, social and cultural trends . . . [were] fundamental principles . . . for public service broadcasting."[87] The body designated to accomplish this goal was the Parliamentary Committee (*Commissione Parlamentare di Vigilanza RAI*). The committee, which had remained rather inactive since its establishment in 1947, was given major powers. It consisted of forty members appointed by the two presidents of the houses (the Senate and the House of Deputies), and its members were chosen among the representatives of all parliamentary groups. The intent of the legislation was to replace, through this committee, the government's control over RAI: now all parties, not just the DC, could finally get a foothold inside the public broadcaster.

In an effort to limit the power of the director-general and the managing director, and to dilute control among the representatives of political parties, the committee was required to nominate ten out of the sixteen members of the RAI board of directors, while the rest of the members were nominated directly by the parliament; the board of directors would then appoint the public broadcaster's president and director-general. The committee and the board of directors were also supposed to take over some of the tasks previously assigned to the director-general and president, including hiring and promoting journalists, news directors, and other top-level executives. The new law confirmed that advertising revenues, permitted ever since the 1924 Fascist decree law, would be "allowed . . . as an additional source . . . [and] should be compatible . . . with public interest objectives and [social] responsibilities of the public broadcasting service."[88] The Parliamentary Committee regulated how much time should be devoted to advertising and set the yearly maximum amount of commercial revenues. At a time when private broadcasting was becoming a real threat, and the government was starting to cut some of RAI's funds, none of those who cared for RAI's well-being ever questioned advertising revenues, even though such a source of income was inherently controversial. Symptomatic was the position of the Communist Party, which, a few years later, when Silvio Berlusconi was expanding his private television business, went so far as to propose to "abolish the advertising ceiling in order to give the RAI more of a fighting chance to compete."[89]

Cultural Pluralism or Political Pluralism?

The reform law mentioned in various places the importance to "favor the development of a [broadcasting] system that would respect the multiplicity of opinions also through the decentralization of production and ideation and by establishing an efficacious relationship with the reality of the country."[90] It established that four representatives of the regional councils be part of the board of directors (art. 8), and that each regional council elects a regional committee for radio and television broadcasting (art. 5). The task of the regional committee was to provide directions with regard to radio and television programs for regional broadcasts and to propose programs to the board of directors for national broadcasts. The law established that in order to favor pluralism of opinions, RAI's programming should be decentralized, and that local associations, national labor unions, religious organizations, political movements, and cultural associations should be granted access to national and regional broadcasts.[91]

However, even though the law seemed to conform quite closely to the needs for decentralization and "connection to the realities where people live their social lives," the implementation of the reform fell short of achieving a truly complete decentralization. What resulted was a "territorial decentralization," with regional productions aimed at a regional audience concentrated in the third channel, instead of the promised more complete and organic decentralization of all structures. Indeed, the kind of pluralism that was embraced with the reform law was political pluralism rather than the sort of cultural and territorial pluralism proposed by the regions. Political pluralism meant that the two national channels, RAI1 and RAI2, created by the new law as two autonomous structures able to project and realize their own radio and television programming (art. 13), had their own distinctive political and ideological identity, and were in competition with each other. Their political mission, critics argued, was their primary responsibility, and unless regional programming could show some kind of party affiliation, there was no space for "cultural pluralism" on either channel. Political parties were certainly eager to get rid of the DC (or at least to reduce its power), but not likewise eager to give up the opportunity to exercise their own political leadership inside a centralized, Rome-based broadcaster.

Contrarily to the expectations of the proreform movement, neither the right of access nor the full decentralization of creative and programming structures was implemented. After the Constitutional Court sentence no. 202 of 1976 declared the end of public monopoly over local radio and television broadcasting, there was a sense of urgency inside RAI to create the third channel, which was established in 1978, with a mission to be the regional channel. Needless to say, that sense of urgency was enhanced by the new competition of local stations.

In order to guarantee political pluralism, law 103 established two daily television news programs, one on RAI1 and one on RAI2 (called Tg1 and Tg2), and three radio news programs (Gr1, Gr2, and Gr3). News programs were granted greater autonomy, and indeed, the director of each Tg and Gr reported directly to the director-general, and not to the director of the channel, as was the case with all other programs. The director was responsible for the information and political structure of his or her program, and for its broadcasting.

The Effects of the Reform

The legislative effort to diminish the power of the director-general and give more responsibility to collegial bodies, like the board of directors and the Parliamentary Committee, aimed at making RAI more accountable and reducing the autonomy that the broadcaster had acquired during the years of Bernabei's administration. The presence of other political parties was also a means to support and control the broadcaster at a time of great changes and peril, as RAI was losing its monopoly status over local broadcasting. Commercial competition had to be challenged by a powerful RAI, fully supported by the entire party system. Indeed, a broadcaster representative of what most Italians still believed in might have a better chance to survive. In order to ensure pluralism and diversity, the three television and radio channels submitted to a first formal division of power. The first channel (RAI1) and its news program, Tg1, remained in DC hands, with Christian Democratic directors; the second channel was given to the PSI, and a Socialist was chosen as Tg2's director. A Socialist, Beniamino Finocchiaro, became RAI president; a Christian Democrat, Michele Principe, was elected director-general; Domenico Scarano, Christian Democrat, was appointed head of Channel 1; Massimo Fichera, Socialist, became the head of RAI2; Enzo Forcella, leftist intellectual, was appointed head of the third radio channel; Emilio Rossi, DC, became director of Tg1; Andrea Barbato, close to the PCI, was appointed director of Tg2.

Objectivity, Independence, and *Lottizzazione*

The sharing of television and radio channels among parties was facilitated by an established structural organization; indeed, the "strongest inheritance that Bernabei's pedagogical model transmitted to its successors was the norm of occupation to ensure party control."[92] RAI, in other words, was born as a child of the party system, and, as such, "could not help but depend on political power":[93]

> RAI was not born to fulfill a need for information and communication; it was born out of only one concrete fact, namely the need to ensure the powerful presence of parties, of one party at first. During the prereform years, the main question we asked ourselves [intellectuals and media professionals alike] was: How can we bring the country "inside" the public broadcaster? In the end, the most realistic idea prevailed, namely to expand, to enlarge the broadcaster, and subsequently share the power. But the authentic, true party occupation had already occurred with the DC. This was the original sin.[94]

If we take into consideration the history of the public broadcaster, its legislative and political inheritance, and the roots of journalists' political culture, it is easier to understand that the formal sharing of power among the most representative parties was meant to guarantee some sort of pluralism and should therefore be interpreted as a form of democratization. This kind of pluralism might be debatable, especially from the Anglo-American tradition of objective journalism, but it is much less controversial from an Italian standpoint, where the tradition of partisanship and advocacy journalism is well rooted. After all, objectivity and pluralism were fundamental concepts supported by the Constitutional Court—the legitimacy of state monopoly over broadcasting was based on those principles—and by the new law. But how could objectivity and pluralism ever go together? The debate among intellectuals was animated. But for Enzo Forcella, a journalist who took a leading role in those years, there can be no doubts:

> In fact, any information agency must have an editorial line. Pluralism can be horizontal across different agencies, but it is an illusion to think that one can reach internal pluralism, that is impossible. Certainly, a minimum degree of objectivity needs to be pursued. However, each agency gives its own interpretation. That is why the reform law proposed the creation of three channels with three news programs. They

did so to assure external pluralism, or as I call it, horizontal pluralism, the only pluralism that could ever be implemented.[95]

Sharing channels and news programs among parties and offering alternative interpretations of events was, then, a positive event. Political partition was the Italian way to achieve pluralism and whatever possible objectivity. But to embrace the enriching and democratizing role of partisan information and recognize the positive outcomes of the Reform Law, one needs to question the notion of journalists' autonomy and independence. After all, as Forcella points out,

> [O]bjectivity was always an illusion. Independence was another illusion. Journalists as such lack independence. This condition lies at the very core of what it means to be a journalist, of what information is. With this in mind, at the time of the Reform Law, the point was not to become independent from somebody, but to know who the referent was.[96]

After all, as Forcella wrote during the years preceding the reform, "where does objectivity of the public service end—an objectivity that as such should ensure to all trends of thought and to all cultural and political trends in the country the access to television, and where does the discretion of 'cultural politics' begin?"[97] As long as mass media and the information sector were recognized as "indispensable instruments of power, the problems are—insisted Forcella—the typical problems of power: those who have acquired control of it want to keep it, those who are outside of it, want to get in."[98]

For others, the problem was not political pluralism, but rather that pluralism was not open enough to other social realities. According to one of the pioneers of the reform, PCI-oriented RAI journalist and news director Alberto Severi, the new law brought profound transformations, but of course, as RAI opened itself to society, sometimes it did so in the "right way, sometimes in a way that was insufficient."[99] Others underlined that the kind of pluralism envisioned and favored by the new law brought new life into the broadcaster, at least initially, in particular because an element of competition among the two, and then three, channels was introduced, and people with different political perspectives participated more actively in the making of programs.

The Two Channels

Since the reform was also an inevitable compromise between the Catholic and the secular, lay culture, objectivity was to be conceived as confrontation between these two forces. That was the rationale for establishing the two channels. One, according to the reformists, had to remain in the hands of the Catholic culture; the second was going to be hegemonized by the lay culture. This was happening at a time in which it was economically possible and necessary to establish more channels to face the challenges of competition. Both cultural factions, the Catholic and the Marxist, felt energized by the change. Emilio Rossi, director of Tg1 at that time, recalls,

> This separation between the two newscasts brought not only a positive internal diversity, but also competition, which was a stimulus for everybody. The beginning of Tg1 was marked by a great commitment and a deep-felt desire to renovate our programs. The new technologies also came in handy. For instance, we inaugurated a new way to air party conventions. Before, party conventions were shown as static images in which only the face of the politician was shown. With the introduction of the Electronic News Gathering, we had mobile cameras able to pick up sounds and images and offer to the viewer more of a feeling of authenticity and truthfulness. As a result, viewers . . . got used to listening to more voices and to all parties.[100]

Francesco Mattioli, from the lay area, remembers that Tg2, the news on the second national channel, also encouraged experimentation and innovation:

> The news on the second channel was the true novelty, because that was not just the Socialist news but it represented the "lay" perspective. When people like me, and other foreign correspondents like myself, went to work for Tg2, we did so not because we were Socialists, but because Tg2 was the one that was doing new things.[101]

Television Programming after the Reform

These changes were possible also because the news departments and each channel gained more autonomy from the central directorate. Initially the news programs were articulated in three daily editions on

Channel 1 and on Channel 2; in the following years, as broadcasting hours increased, short editions of the news (*Tg flash*) were introduced. Programming and scheduling became crucial in defining the identity of each channel, in competition between them, and, by the late 1970s, in competition with the commercial broadcasters. New editions of Tg2 (like *Studio aperto* and the talk show *Tg2-ring*), and the new entertainment show on Channel 2 (*L'altra domenica*), represent some of the most important innovations of those postreform years. In *Tg2-ring* (which started in September 1976), politicians and other personalities were interviewed by the host, who asked pungent questions often without the customary prearrangements of previous years. *L'altra domenica*, starting in 1976 on RAI2, soon became a cult entertainment show for a new, Sunday afternoon, young, and leftist audience. During the first years after the reform the percentage of films on TV grew considerably (from 3.7 percent of total programming in 1975 to 5 percent in 1980). Some of the most famous films produced by RAI during those years included *Gesù di Nazareth*, by Franco Zeffirelli, *Padre Padrone* (1978), by the Taviani brothers, and *I clowns* (1981), by Federico Fellini.

All these novelties and creative programming were destined to soon end, as RAI, finally free from the grip of the DC monopoly, had to face new constraints imposed by the rules of competition. By the end of the 1970s, indeed, commercial television and radio broadcasters were consolidating their audiences and their operations in national networks, which drastically changed the quality of programming output on the public broadcaster, and the entire landscape of television in Italy.

Notes

1. Indro Montanelli, quoted in Paolo Murialdi, *Storia del giornalismo italiano. Dalle prime gazzette ai telegiornali* (Turin: Gutenberg 2000, 1986), 198.

2. *Lottizzazione* indicates the sharing of power among political parties within the broadcaster.

3. For this section, I am particularly indebted to Paolo Murialdi's seminal work on the history of the Italian press. See Paolo Murialdi, *Storia del giornalismo italiano. Dalle prime gazzette ai telegiornali*, and Murialdi, *La stampa italiana dalla liberazione alla crisi di fine secolo* (Bari: Laterza, 1998).

4. Giuseppe Farinelli, Ermanno Paccagnini, Giovanni Santambrogio, and Angela Ida Villa, *Storia del giornalismo italiano* (Turin: UTET, 1997), in particular see 13-15.

5. Valerio Castronovo, quoted in Paolo Murialdi, *Storia del giornalismo italiano* (Bologna: Il Mulino, 1996), 16.

6. For more information on the development of literary papers in those years, see Farinelli et al., *Storia del giornalismo italiano*, 24-43.

7. Murialdi, *Storia del giornalismo italiano. Dalle prime gazzette ai telegiornali*, 30-31.

8. See Murialdi, *Storia del giornalismo italiano. Dalle prime gazzette ai telegiornali*, 35-37.

9. Murialdi, *Storia del giornalismo italiano. Dalle prime gazzette ai telegiornali*, 51.

10. Data from table 29, *Tasso stimato di analfabetismo. Paesi Europei. Metà Ottocento*, in the "Scuola e Istruzione" section of the Data Bank Compact Disc included with *Guida all'Italia contemporanea*, ed. Massimo Firpo, Nicola Tranfaglia, and Pier Giorgio Zunino (Milan: Garzanti, 1998).

11. Murialdi, *Storia del giornalismo italiano. Dalle prime gazzette ai telegiornali*, 52.

12. Raymond Williams, quoted in Giovanni Gozzini, *Storia del giornalismo*, (Milan: Bruno Mondadori, 2000), 94.

13. In 1859 there were only 66,000 elementary school pupils in the Sicilian Kingdom, and only one-third of the southern cities had an elementary school. In the province of Salerno (south of Naples), with a population of 450,000 inhabitants, only 5,000 went to elementary school. In the Lombardo-Veneto, the northeast region under Austrian occupation, by the early eighteen hundreds attendance was mandatory for children from 6 to 12 years of age. In that part of the country, between 1832 and 1852 attendance doubled from 107,000 pupils to 216,000 (data from *Scuola ed istruzione* in the Risorgimento Italiano website at www.riccati.it/risorgi/1815-49.htm).

14. Data from table 7, *Analfabetismo. 1861-1991*, and from table 29, *Tasso stimato di analfabetismo. Paesi Europei. Metà Ottocento*, in the "Demografia e Movimenti di Popolazione" section of the Data Bank Compact Disc included with *Guida all'Italia contemporanea*, 1998.

15. See Antonio Gramsci, *Quaderni del carcere* 1, ed. Valentino Gerratana (Turin: Einaudi, 1975), 343-344.

16. See Murialdi, *Storia del giornalismo italiano. Dalle prime gazzette ai telegiornali*, 65.

17. Alberto Asor Rosa, "Il giornalismo: appunti sulla fisiologia di un mestiere difficile," in *Storia d'Italia*, ed. Ruggero Romano and Corrado Vivanti, vol. 4, *Intellettuali e potere*, ed. Corrado Vivanti (Turin: Giulio Einaudi, 1981), 1241.

18. Dario Papa, quoted in Alberto Asor Rosa, "Il giornalismo," 1229.

19. Gozzini, *Storia del giornalismo*, xvii.

20. Gramsci, *Quaderni del carcere*, 103.

21. Gramsci, *Quaderni del carcere*, 104.

22. Data on the development of telephone service are gathered from table 5, *Telefono: sviluppo del servizio urbano e interurbano. Italia. 1885-1925*, in the "Mezzi di comunicazione" section of the Data Bank Compact Disc included with *Guida all'Italia contemporanea*, 1998.

23. Data from table 31, *Tiratura di alcuni quotidiani. 1900-1924*, in the "Mezzi di comunicazione" section of the Data Bank Compact Disc included with *Guida all'Italia contemporanea*, 1998.

24. Elaborations of the author on various estimates.

25. Telephone service became a public service in 1907.

26. Antonio Papa, *Storia politica della radio in Italia*, vol. 1, *Dalle origini agli anni della crisi economica 1924-1934* (Naples: Guida ed., 1978), 21-22.

27. This thesis is detailed by Papa, *Storia politica della radio*.

28. Anonymous. "Radiofonia Italiana nel 1931," *Radiocorriere* 8, no. 1, (Turin: EIAR, January 2-9, 1932): 5.

29. Data from Franco Monteleone, quoted in *Apparecchi radiofonici presso scuole e organizzazioni del regime fascista. 1934-1938*, in the "Mezzi di comunicazione" section of the Data Bank Compact Disc included with *Guida all'Italia contemporanea*, 1998.

30. *Ente Italiano Audizioni Radiofoniche*, Referendum EIAR 1940-XVIII, quoted in Antonio Papa, *Storia politica della radio*, vol. 2, *Dalla guerra d'Etiopia al crollo del fascismo 1933-1943* (Naples: Guida ed., 1978), 81.

31. Milly Buonanno, "Degenerazione o mutamento?" in *Check up del giornalismo italiano*, ed. Jader Jacobelli (Bari: Laterza, 1995), 30.

32. Elio Talario, "Portiamo i grandi al microfono," in *Radiocorriere* 1, no. 1 (Rome: RAI, November 4-10, 1945): 5.

33. Art. 3 of the Concession of 1952, *Approvazione ed esecutoreità della Convenzione per la concessione alla Radio Audizioni Italia Societa per azioni del servizio di telediffusione su filo* (Concession of 1952 between the state and RAI for television and radio broadcasting services), approved by Presidential Decree no. 180 on January 26, 1952.

34. See Peppino Ortoleva, "Mezzi di comunicazione," in *Guida all'Italia contemporanea, 1861-1997*, vol. 4., ed. Massimo Firpo, Nicola Tranfaglia, and Pier Giorgio Zunino (Milan: Garzanti, 1998).

35. Ortoleva, "Mezzi di comunicazione," 310.

36. Concession of 1952, Art. 5.

37. Pope Pius XII, *Miranda Prorsus: circa la cinematografia, la radio e la televisione* (Rome: Tipografia Poliglotta Vaticana, 1957), 11.

38. Franco Monteleone, *Storia della RAI dagli alleati alla DC 1944-1954* (Rome: Laterza, 1980), 171.

39. Emilio Rossi, former director of Tg1 (RAI1 news program) at RAI since 1956, interview with author, *Centro Televisivo Vaticano* (the Vatican Television Center), Vatican City, January 4, 1997.

40. These new hires came to be known as *corsari*. The word *corsari*, as those who attend the courses or "corsi" in Italian, means "pirates," as those who overtook the ship from the hands of the *aziendalisti*.

41. Data from Paolo Dorfles, quoted in *Dipendenti RAI. 1953-1992* in the "Mezzi di comunicazione" section of the Data Bank Compact Disc included with *Guida all'Italia contemporanea*, 1998.

42. Paolo Murialdi, interview with author, tape recording, Milan, Italy, January 31, 1998.

43. The *dorotei* split in the mid-1970s, when Rumor was marginalized and Piccoli, with Antonio Basaglia, became the new leaders.

44. Data from RAI, Radio Televisione Italiana, *Annuario RAI 1954, 1955, 1956*, (Turin: Nuova ERI, 1958), xxiii.

45. Data from *Annuario RAI 1954, 1955, 1956*, xxxiii.

46. Data from *Annuario RAI 1954, 1955, 1956*, 272.

47. Data from *Annuario RAI 1954, 1955, 1956*, no page number available.

48. Francesco Pinto, *Il modello televisivo. Professionalità e politica da Bernabei alla Terza Rete* (Milan: Feltrinelli, 1980), 14.

49. Pinto, *Il modello televisivo*, 28.

50. For in-depth analyses of *telegiornali*, see Maria Grazia Bruzzone, *L'avventurosa storia del Tg in Italia dall'avvento della televisione ad oggi* (Milan: RCS Libri S.p.A., 2002), and Roberto Levi, *Le trasmissioni Tv che hanno fatto (o no) l'Italia da "Lascia o raddoppia" al "Grande fratello"* (Milan: Rizzoli, 2002), in particular pp. 197-204.

51. Rossi, interview cit.

52. Giovanni Cesareo, *Anatomia del potere televisivo* (Milan: Franco Angeli, 1970), 42.

53. Franco Chiarenza, *Il cavallo morente. Trent'anni di radiotelevisione italiana* (Milan: Bompiani, 1978), 120.

54. Pinto, *Il modello televisivo*, 23.

55. Pinto, *Il modello televisivo*, 31.

56. Data from *Annuario RAI 1967* (Rome: ERI, no publication date available), 83; *Annuario RAI 1962*, 454; and from *Annuario RAI 1972-1975* (Turin: ERI, 1977), 147.

57. Data from *Annuario RAI 1972-1975*, 147; from *Annuario RAI 1961*, 454; and from Ettore Bernabei and Giorgio Dell'Arti, *L'uomo di fiducia. I retroscena del potere raccontati da un testimone rimasto dietro le quinte per cinquant'anni* (Milan: Arnoldo Mondadori, 1999), 146.

58. Estimate by Minister Giacinto Bosco, quoted in Chiarenza, *Il cavallo morente*, 202; a similar estimate on the number of external collaborators was collected by the author from interviews.

59. Data from Chiarenza, *Il cavallo morente*, 201.

60. The number of employees of Rome's general directorate grew from 1,655 units in 1962 to well over 2,000 in 1966.

61. Elaborations on data from table 45, *Dipendenti RAI. 1953-1992*, and table 46, *Reti televisive RAI. Ore totali di trasmissione. 1953-1992*, in the "Mezzi di comunicazione" section of the Data Bank Compact Disc included with *Guida all'Italia contemporanea*, 1998.

62. The comparison with other European countries is an elaboration from data reported in Chiarenza, *Il cavallo morente*, 114.

63. Ettore Bernabei with Giorgio Dell'Arti, *L'uomo di fiducia*, 156.

64. Ettore Bernabei, interview with author, Rome, December 6, 1996.

65. Giovanni Cesareo, "Televisione," in *La cultura italiana del Novecento*, ed. Corrado Stajano (Bari: Laterza, 1997), 759.

66. Bernabei, interview cit.

67. Chiarenza, *Il cavallo morente*, 136.

68. Cesareo, *Anatomia del potere televisivo*, 59.

69. Act of the board of directors, April 23, 1969, reported in Chiarenza, *Il cavallo morente*, 159.

70. Piero De Chiara, responsible for the PCI mass communications division, interview with author, tape recording, Olivetti Foundation, Rome, April 3, 1998.

71. Alberto Ronchey, "La *'lottizzazione'*," in *La Repubblica* (Rome), October 12, 1980. In the fall of 1968, Ronchey was invited by the secretary-general of the Italian Republican Party to become a member of the RAI board of directors. He refused.

72. Renato Parascandolo, vice head of RAI Educational at time of interview, interview with author, tape recording, RAI headquarters, Rome, January 19, 1998.

73. Giovanni Cesareo, "Privatization: Some Questions and Paradoxes," paper presented at the Media in Transition Colloquium, Piran, Slovenia, October 17-21, 1992, 2.

74. Giuseppe Richeri, "Italy: Public Service and Private Interests," *Journal of Communication* (Summer 1978): 77.

75. Cesareo, quoted in Cinzia Padovani and Andrew Calabrese, "Berlusconi, RAI, and the Modernisation of Italian Feudalism," *Javnost/The Public* 3, no. 2 (1996): 115.

76. The "interest index," an indicator for the audience's preferences, shows an increase in "interest" on the part of the respondents for films on TV and TV series (64 in 1961 to 78 in 1973 for films; from 64 in 1961 to 73 in 1973 for TV series). The interest for other genres, including *telegiornali*, popular music, and sports programs remained rather consistent on average (for *telegiornali* the index of interest was 70 in 1961, went up to 76 in 1970, and down to 74 in 1973). *Annuario RAI 1972-1975*, 116.

77. Switzerland began color broadcasting in 1968; BBC1 began in 1969; in Finland color transmission began in 1970; in Luxemburg in 1972.

78. Constitutional Court, *Radiotelevisione e servizi radioelettrici-Radiodiffusione circolare per mezzo di onde elettromagnetiche-Questione fondata di costituzionalità* (Radio and television services-Radio broadcasting via

electromagnetic waves-Question of constitutionality). Sentence no. 225, July 10, 1974, Art. 4. Published in *Gazzetta Ufficiale* (Official Gazette of the Italian Republic), July 17, 1974, no. 187. Available at www.telestreet.it/telestreet/doc_legali/consulta225_74.htm.

79. Constitutional Court, Sentence no. 225, Art. 4.
80. Constitutional Court, Sentence no. 225, Art. 8.
81. Constitutional Court, Sentence no. 225, Art. 8.
82. Constitutional Court, *Radiotelevisione e servizi radioelettrici-Servizi di televisione via cavo-Questione fondata di costituzionalità* (Radio and television services-Cable television services-Question of constitutionality). Sentence July 10, 1974, no. 226, Art. 1, comma b. Published in *Gazzetta Ufficiale* (Official Gazette of the Italian Republic), July 17, 1974, no. 187. Available at www.telestreet.it/telestreet/doc_legali/consulta226_74.htm.

83. Constitutional Court, no. 226, art. 4, no page number available.
84. Sandro Fontana, "I nodi della riforma della RAI-TV," in *Il decentramento radiotelevisivo in Europa. La terza rete TV e la ristrutturazione della radiofonia pubblica in Italia*, ed. Franco Iseppi and Giuseppe Richeri (Milan: Franco Angeli Editore, 1980), 515.
85. Francesco Mattioli, president of the RAI International Relations directorate at time of interview, interview with author, tape recording, Borgo S. Angelo, Rome, March 1998.
86. Giuliano Amato, "RAI: La riforma interrotta," in *Informazione e potere* (Milan: Feltrinelli, 1979), 64.
87. Law 14 April 1975, no. 103, *Ordinamento del Servizio Pubblico Radiotelevisivo* (Ordinance on Public Service Broadcasting), title 1, art.1. Available at www.camera.it/_bicamerali/rai/norme/listitut.htm.
88. Law no. 103, art. 4.
89. David Forgacs, "The Italian Communist Party and Culture," in *Culture in Postwar Italy*, ed. Zygmunt G. Baranski and Robert Lumley (New York: St. Martin's Press, 1990), 109.
90. Law 14 April 1975, art. 13.
91. Law 14 April 1975, art. 6 and art. 13.
92. Cesareo, *La televisione sprecata* (Milan: Feltrinelli, 1974), 764-765.
93. Parascandolo, interview cit.
94. Alberto Severi, codirector of Tg3 at time of interview, interview with author, tape recording, RAI headquarters, Saxa Rubra, Rome, March 11, 1998.
95. Enzo Forcella, interview with author, December 8, 1996. Forcella was director of RAI Radio 3 from 1976 through 1986.
96. Forcella, interview cit.
97. Forcella, quoted in Chiarenza, *Il cavallo morente*, 167.
98. Forcella, quoted in Chiarenza, *Il cavallo morente*, 191.
99. Severi, interview cit.
100. Rossi, interview cit.
101. Mattioli, interview cit.

Chapter 3

RAI and the Party System (Part II)

Private Radio and Television Stations

Since the mid-1970s the number of private TV and radio stations skyrocketed: from zero in early 1974, to about 30 TV stations by the end of 1975; radio stations went from 70 to 120 in the same period.[1] After the Constitutional Court ruling no. 202 of 1976, those numbers grew even faster. From 68 TV stations in 1976, they became 244 one year later, and 434 in 1978;[2] 582 radio stations in 1976 grew to 1,176 stations in 1977 and 2,500 by 1978. The higher concentration of private television stations was in the central region of Lazio (53), followed by the northern regions of Lombardia (44) and Piedmont (38), Sicily (47), the southern region of Campania (42), and the center-north region of Emilia Romagna (36).[3] In 1981, according to the Ministry of Post and Telecommunications, there were a total of 800 private television stations.[4] They could count on a total share of approximately 35 percent of the average national audience.

The influx of private capital in the broadcasting sector and the consequent restructuring of the mass media industry completely modified the landscape that the 1975 Reform Law had envisioned. For instance, in

1977 private televisions shared only 2.4 percent of total advertising revenues; by 1983, that percentage had increased nearly twelvefold, to 27.59 percent. The growing market share of private TV also had enormous consequences on the press and, of course, on RAI. Whereas during the first half of the 1970s the share of the advertising market among the various sectors, including broadcasting and press, had remained constant (newspapers and magazines controlled 64.9 percent of total advertising revenues in 1970 and 64.47 percent in 1976; RAI controlled 12.4 percent in 1970 and 12.87 percent in 1976), that equilibrium had drastically changed in the following years. By 1983, the total share of advertising revenues for newspapers and magazines went down to only 46.74 percent, and not surprisingly, circulation numbers of newspapers diminished from 14 copies for every 100 inhabitants in 1970, to 9 copies in 1979.[5]

In 1980 a commercial channel, Antennanord, owned by the well-established publishing house Rusconi, began to broadcast across the north and northwest regions. At that time, Primarete Indipendente, a television station controlled by another famous publishing house, the Rizzoli family, broadcast its first national news program, conducted by popular journalist Maurizio Costanzo. In 1982 Canale5, the Fininvest television channel owned by entrepreneur Silvio Berlusconi, challenged the restrictions forbidding national broadcasting, managing to broadcast prerecorded tapes simultaneously by the large number of local stations owned by Fininvest, which covered almost the entire country. Two other main commercial broadcasters at that time were Italia1 (also owned by Rusconi) and Rete4 (owned by Mondadori, Editoriale Espresso, and the Perrone family). They began broadcasting only a few months after Canale5's first national broadcast. In January 1983 Fininvest acquired Italia1; in August 1984, Berlusconi bought Rete4.

Competition in the Early 1980s

As competition in the marketplace intensified, preoccupation with audience was informing programming and scheduling decisions inside the public broadcaster.

By 1980, broadcasting hours were extended to the afternoon hours and, on Sundays, broadcasting began at 10 a.m. By 1981, RAI counted more than 13 million subscribers and produced a total of 11,000 hours of output, an increase of 2.5-fold from 1975. In 1986, the public broadcaster began morning programming on RAI1, and offerings rose to more than 14,000 hours, a growth of 180 percent from 1975.

The composition of programming changed considerably. Across all channels, news was reduced from 15.3 percent of total output in 1975 to only 9 percent in 1986; the overall time dedicated to information (including public affairs and parliamentary services) dropped from 24.2 percent in 1975 to 22.9 percent in 1980, notwithstanding that all three channels were fully operating by the early 1980s. On the other hand, immediately after the reform, light entertainment rose sharply on RAI1, RAI's flagship channel, from the initial 4.9 percent in 1975 to 12.6 percent in 1977, to 16 percent in 1983 and to 21 percent in 1986.[6] In contrast, light entertainment on RAI2 declined from 11.1 percent in 1975 to 3 percent in 1986, as the channel struggled to establish its identity as a film and soap opera channel. On RAI2 all kinds of American imports, films for television and soap operas, could be found: the genre "films for television" went up from 5 percent in 1975 to 19 percent in the early 1980s. RAI3, which began its regular broadcasting on December 15, 1979, was also in the forefront of the competition war. After an initial emphasis on news, which grew from 7.9 percent in 1979 to 10.4 percent of the channel output in 1980, RAI3 changed direction sharply: following the 1984 consolidation of the commercial broadcasting sector in the hands of Fininvest, the amount of airtime dedicated to news programs (*telegiornali*) went down to 4.3 percent in 1986; light entertainment grew to represent, by 1985, almost 20 percent of RAI3's total offering; and sports, which accounted for 12.7 percent in 1979, went up to 19.8 percent of total output in 1986.

In general, from 1983 to 1986, imported programs on RAI channels increased to the disadvantage of internal production. Most of these imports were shown on prime time. Internal productions went down 3 percentage points on RAI1 and 7 percent on RAI2; imported programs rose 2 points on RAI1 and 8 points on RAI2. The total hours of imported programs went from 1,600 in 1983 (18 percent of total output) to 2,200 (23 percent) in 1986. By the early 1980s Italy had become one of the world's major importers of television programs.

Lottizzazione Intensifies

Another consequence of the competition war was an intensification of *lottizzazione*. More *lottizzazione* meant that hiring personnel in RAI became increasingly a matter of filling quotas. According to some, this had an impact on the new hires, whose quality decreased as parties, like the PSI and other small parties, began to bring inside the broadcaster only "loyal members, without considering very much whether they were good journalists or not."[7] If RAI2 and its news program had represented, at least in the first years after the reform, an innovative site for sharing lay perspectives, that soon changed in the early 1980s, when Tg2 lost its place as a commons amicably shared by various lay interests.

> The relationship among the lay parties [the PCI and the PSI] was becoming worse and worse during the 1980s, so that by a certain point the PSI said, "No, Tg2 is not the lay channel; it is the Socialist channel." This is what happened. Whereas at first the Tg2 and Channel 2 directors were Socialists but were also approved by the PCI, at one point the PSI began to encourage more homogeneity in Channel 2, inviting the DC to do the same with its own channel. At that point, a rigid logic of partition began: Tg2 became aligned with the Socialists and Tg1 became strictly DC.[8]

During the 1980s, indeed, party affiliation became a fundamental prerequisite to work in RAI. A motto popular among RAI journalists ran, "In RAI they get one DC, one PSI, one PRI, and then, finally, a good journalist!"

It was, however, a kind of *lottizzazione* that engaged only the government forces, with a primary role of the DC, a strong role of the PSI, and the crumbs to other government allies, such as the Republican Party. Because of the *conventio ad excludendum* (the agreement in place in the government since the end of World War II, according to which the PCI was not allowed to govern), the Communist Party was shut out, substantially excluded. Former PCI official De Chiara recalls:

> Only in the very first phase of the post-Reform era, when Channel 2 was still generally considered the lay channel, were there a few people close to the PCI around. But when *lottizzazione* became stricter, some of those people were given secondary positions. Like Angelo Guglielmi, a lay intellectual, who through the years had become closer to the PCI. He was widely recognized as one of the best in RAI, but he was given only positions of little importance, such as director of the RAI production center, a position without any real power.[9]

The Communist question had come to the fore since the time of the so-called historic compromise of the mid-1970s between the DC led by

Aldo Moro and the PCI led by Enrico Berlinguer. Even though a bloc of Catholic and Marxist forces never coalesced in a government formation, the attempts to create an alliance indicated how central the role of the PCI was becoming in the cultural and political life of the country. In the post-Reform era, the public service broadcaster could not be considered as such anymore as long as it continued to disregard the PCI, which represented a great part of the Italian electorate.

The exclusion of a powerful force like the Communist Party from the public broadcaster further undermined the spirit of the reform itself. Moreover, the *conventio ad excludendum* was becoming an obsolete formula, inside as well as outside RAI, destined not to survive much longer. Especially, it could not survive the challenges of commercial competition, when the full party system, even the opposition, needed to be called upon to support RAI. After all, ideological differences among the parties, which had previously been fierce enemies, were diminishing. Indeed, by the late 1980s, the PCI joined the government as an external supporter according to a process known as *consociativismo*. One of the consequences was that in 1987 RAI's third channel, RAI3, was finally given to the Communists.

Theories of *Lottizzazione*

Lottizzazione was so pervasively practiced that there was even a theory, a "philosophical elaboration," that legitimated it, at least in the eyes of the politicians and the journalists involved. Clearly, such legitimations were never publicly declared, but they existed, and were the guidelines for hiring and promoting people. Even though *lottizzazione* did not follow a written protocol, there was an exact procedure, as Piero De Chiara explains:

> Each party secretariat would have its own representative, who was supposed to find out information about a given member of the board of directors with whom he had to talk. The Reform Law had designed things in such a way that each member of the board was directly related to a given party. The conversations between the guy from the party secretariat and the member of RAI's board occurred in person. Then an informal meeting was called, prior to the formal board of directors' meeting. At that time the members of the board exchanged ideas and opinions among themselves. Finally they would agree on proposing a given can-

didate and the various "opinions" were brought to the board of directors.[10]

Very rarely did it happen that within a formal board meeting somebody would blatantly say, "Well, if you put this one, a DC, as director of news, then we want this other guy, a PSI, as vice-director." That was done before, during those informal premeetings. But even if those premeetings were informal, one should not think that *lottizzazione* was casually practiced. In fact, it was based on a set of well-established rules, a whole series of theories and derivations:

> One of these theories was the "zebra" theory (*teoria della zebratura*), which meant that for each director there had to be two vice-directors. One of them had to be a member of the same party [as the director's party] and the other one had to be a member of the second most powerful party. For example, if the news director of Tg1 was a Christian Democrat, then one vice-director would be from the DC, and possibly from another faction of the DC different from the director's faction, whereas the other vice-director would be a Socialist. Inside the newsroom this meant that there were always ways to boycott the director. Maybe not really boycott him, but some form of internal resistance was always possible.[11]

At the vertex of the corporation a similar dual system was also put in place. In 1986, after months of negotiations between Socialists and Christian Democrats, Sergio Zavoli, DC, president of RAI since 1980, was replaced by Enrico Manca, a Socialist. The director-general remained Biagio Agnes, DC, who had been in that position since 1982.

The Berlusconi Decree

Silvio Berlusconi, who by 1984 owned three television networks, challenged the Constitutional Court sentence of 1976 by broadcasting nationally. As a consequence, in the fall of 1984, a few judges in different regions of Italy shut down Fininvest's channels on the basis that national commercial broadcasting was illegal. A few days later, a decree was passed that overturned the judges' decisions and legitimated Fininvest's national broadcasting: it was signed by Prime Minister Bettino Craxi and became known as the "Berlusconi decree."[12] Contrary to previous pronouncements of the Constitutional Court (no. 202 of 1976 and no. 148 of

July 1981), which established that national broadcasting was reserved for the state, the decree approved the Fininvest network's broadcasting beyond regional borders. The decree also intervened to modify some aspects of RAI administration. Its board of directors was securely placed in the hands of the parties, as all its members were to be elected by the RAI Parliamentary Committee. The decree also confirmed that advertising on RAI had to be limited according to the guidelines established by the 1975 broadcasting law, and restated that the Parliamentary Committee was the body setting those limits. The limitation on advertising revenues, at a time of increasing competition, and the additional power granted to the Parliamentary Committee, had the effect of increasing the public broadcaster's dependence on the parliament, and this was probably something that the party system, as a whole, desired. Critics pointed out the self-evident pro-Berlusconi bias of the decree: indeed, while RAI was being subjected to further regulation and its advertising revenues were being circumscribed, Fininvest was left to thrive in an almost unregulated environment. The decree de facto accepted the mixed system of private and public broadcasting by acknowledging the existence of the already operating television stations and their nationwide operations; it blocked the authorization of new local stations, against the Constitutional Court's indications; and allowed the commercial stations to sell even more airtime to advertisers.[13]

Consequences

Various consequences came from the negotiations around the Berlusconi decree, and they were favorable to both the PSI and the DC. Craxi wanted to help Berlusconi, and indeed his party obtained the *nulla osta* for the commercial broadcaster to operate beyond regional borders. In exchange for setting Berlusconi free to do whatever he pleased with his television channels, the DC learned that more power was going to be given to RAI's director-general, who was going to be elected from now on by the assembly of shareholders rather than by the Parliamentary Committee. Clearly, more power to the director-general pleased the Christian Democrats, since the directorate-general was traditionally their fief. Of course, the Communists also got involved. As part of the negotiation, it was agreed that, if all major factions were going to have what they wanted, the PCI also would obtain, one day, its own channel. Piero

112   Chapter 3

De Chiara recalls the rationale beyond the choices that led, a few years down the road, to a communist presence within RAI:

> "Yes, we agree on the Berlusconi decree; we agree on giving more power to the director-general. However, in exchange for all this, we want the Communist management and journalists to be given more space inside the public broadcaster." This was the operation that led the PCI to obtain the third channel, which was a very successful business operation. We said: "Yes, Craxi is right in supporting the Fininvest channels; the DC is right in transforming RAI into a true corporation with a director-general who has to work hard to be efficient. But even the PCI is right because it wants to have a corporation where all the professional abilities that can make competition with Fininvest more difficult are going to be used."[14]

All of this happened in a political context that was already very compromised, amidst struggles among the parties in parliament and government crisis. But, in the end, the entire operation had its own logic and was a complete success.

1987-1992: The Years of "Complete" *Lottizzazione*

In 1987 another major restructuring of the public broadcaster occurred. RAI's news structures were strengthened and enlarged. The news department on the third channel was reorganized into two main divisions, one for regional news, the other for national news. RAI *Regione* became the DC's terrain of influence, and the national news, Tg3, was given to the PCI. In those times of competition,

> RAI could no longer enjoy the luxury of sacrificing Communist professionals inside the corporation and the potential audience represented by the electoral pool of the opposition. It was no longer affordable to alienate many excellent professionals only because they were Communists. Moreover, a third of the viewers who belonged to the lay area could not identify themselves any longer with the PSI. The objective need to open to the Communist pole was pursued out of fear of competition.[15]

Other observers confirm that competition with the private sector was an incentive for allowing the PCI to have a national news program:

RAI's leadership, and especially director-general Biagio Agnes, felt the need to stand up all together against Fininvest and involve also the opposition in this defense of the public broadcaster. RAI needed to get as much money as it could from the government, and therefore it needed all the protection it could get in parliament. Around RAI, as a compact wall, a defense line was created which consisted of Christian Democrats, Socialists, Social-Democrats, Republicans, and, finally, the Communists. This made RAI stronger, even though, from that point on, RAI lowered its standard by producing programs of less quality.[16]

But if it is true that RAI, especially its flagship channel RAI1, increased its offering of imported shows and soap operas, it is also true that, somehow, the public service mission was still powerfully felt by its leadership. Indeed, this sense of external threat and a powerful director-general contributed to the creation of an unprecedented internal cohesion within the public broadcaster:

> The internal bloc . . . at the time of the Berlusconi decree [1984] and at the time of the hemorrhage of anchors from RAI to Fininvest [1985-1987] was able to compact the corporation around a common goal. Biagio Agnes was able to bring all this together. He was able to use the pride of the old *aziendalisti*[17] and synchronize it with the interests of political power outside the corporation so that internal and external powers worked jointly together. The result was the victory of the public broadcaster, whereas a complete ruin had been predicted.[18]

According to many observers, that victory was due mostly to the director-general's determination to support the news department. Biagio Agnes devoted more funding to Tg1, while RAI president Enrico Manca supported the news on the second channel. After months of negotiations, Agnes and Manca agreed to offer the direction of Tg3 to Alessandro Curzi. Italo Moretti, PCI, and Guido Farolfi, DC, were appointed vice-directors of Tg3. Nuccio Fava, DC, became director of Tg1 with Ottavio Di Lorenzo, PLI (the Italian Liberal Party), and Ugo Guidi, PRI (Italian Republican Party), vice-directors. Luigi Locatelli, PSI, was appointed director of Tg2. Inside all newsrooms, the minor parties (PRI, PLI, and PSDI, the Italian Social Democratic Party) obtained what were called in *lottizzazione* jargon "crossed" vice-director positions.

Legitimating the Communists at RAI3

The PCI's role as the government's "external supporter" and the party's consequent gains inside the public broadcaster marked the end of the Communists' reformist potential. This meant that during the ongoing negotiations between the PSI and the DC on a new broadcasting law, the PCI was unable to credibly oppose the pro-Berlusconi lobby and stand up against government parties, its reformist potentials heavily compromised. As Murialdi noted, *lottizzazione*, now strong as iron, became handy even to Berlusconi and to the political power embodied by Andreotti, Craxi, and Forlani (the trio who governed Italy from 1989 to 1992) when a new law sanctioning the duopoly RAI/Fininvest passed in 1990.[19] Many, however, welcomed the new course, including Enzo Forcella, who wrote: "Throughout the entire history of radio and television broadcasting, it had never happened that a media person, be he a Communist or simply somebody close to the PCI, would be able to direct a news program, not to mention an entire channel!"[20] This marked the end of discrimination against the PCI. Forcella continued:

> By accepting the rules of the game, the PCI acknowledged that being different would not pay [as] one could not stay inside and outside the system simultaneously. . . . The entrance of the PCI into RAI marked the end of the phase when *lottizzazione* was imposed by the government parties, and the beginning of a new phase when *lottizzazione* became institutionalized.[21]

To the contrary, others accused the party leadership of betraying Communists' morals by becoming a member of the establishment. De Chiara, the PCI officer responsible for communication policies in those years, recalls:

> There were Communist journalists working in Tg1 who criticized us for accepting Channel 3, because, they said, "This way the PCI gets only a secondary channel that is worth nothing, and in doing so you leave to the DC the freedom to completely control Tg1, where a few of us have been trying hard to modify power relationships and represent the national interest." At that time, that thesis convinced me. I agreed with the idea that it was not fair to us to accept the third channel, and leave the other two, Channel 1 and 2, to our enemies. However, after a national PCI convention in which Walter Veltroni became the new strategist of the relationship between the party and the public broad-

caster, the alternative based on the hypothesis of the total separation among the three channels won.[22]

The option to give to each party its own channel became the most viable. This alternative was not really proposed by the PCI, nor by any other party. It was instead proposed by the RAI director-general himself. At that time, Tg3 was obviously not as solid as Tg1 and Tg2 with a low audience share, scarce funds, and limited technical equipment. Moreover, in 1987 Biagio Agnes had divided Tg3 into two parts, the national news and *RAI Regione*, with regional folklore and local news, a move that could have potentially further weakened the entire channel. It was certainly a risk, and the PCI leadership accepted it. De Chiara comments:

> Of course, director-general Agnes did not have a clue of how well things would go for Channel 3. But contrarily to everybody's expectations, that's what happened: RAI3 became a complete success, and even got to function with a sufficient degree of independence from the party.[23]

Others on the left embraced the solution, arguing that it would further promote partisan journalism. The fact that the PCI was finally granted its fair share of power was perceived as an event that would enhance fairness and pluralism. Celebrating the 1987 appointments, Enzo Forcella, once again, wrote: "Media professionals operate on the basis of their agreements with politicians; therefore, in the last instance, the referents of any media professional are always going to be the politicians. Only in the context of this logic is professionalism an important factor."[24] Piero De Chiara agreed: "You can be independent as much as you want, but good journalists have political ideas." Even the newly appointed head of Radio 1, Livio Zanetti, whose candidacy had been supported by the Republican Party, admitted that he was not "surprised at all that journalists in RAI had precise political opinions as this did not exclude that they could also be professionally qualified."[25] And Nuccio Fava, former Tg1 director, removed from his position by the DC right wing, admitted blatantly, "I had to go because of the internal dissent within the DC. I knew this was going to happen as soon as I heard about the decline of prime minister De Mita at the 1989 national convention of the DC."[26] Such comments on the inevitability of journalists' connection with political parties were for the Communist Party an important source of legitimation. Since professionalism could be appreciated only within a context of ideological affiliation, it was crucial not to lose the opportunity to ensure to Communist journalists key positions inside the broadcaster.

Iron *Lottizzazione*

Not only did the entrance of the PCI into RAI sanction the "iron" phase of *lottizzazione*, but it also further normalized public discourse on *lottizzazione*. In previous years critiques of *lottizzazione* had focused mainly on the exclusion of the Communist Party; after 1987 that ground for opposition was neutralized. *Lottizzazione* was now considered, at worst, the "typical sorrow and delight of the public broadcaster and the parties,"[27] a recurrence, a ritual practice to which everybody had, by now, got used to, inside as well as outside RAI.

Only rarely did somebody express astonishment and frustration against this process of normalization:

> What is really striking is the big picture. The sensational and tranquil, blatant and sincere confirmation of the fact that the corporation is owned by the party secretariats; and that these, and only they, are the ones who decide everything. . . . [T]hose of us who are scandalized by this reality are considered naive and laughable. It is bitter to realize that, for many, what we do is just an empty rhetorical exercise.[28]

The new appointments and the restructuring of 1987 brought to attention also the evolving dialectic relationship between the corporation and the party system. This kind of "iron" *lottizzazione* not only indicated the beginning of a new era, when all parties had their spot inside the broadcaster, but it also meant that the systems of power that had been created within RAI had gained some kind of independence from the party system itself. Indeed, the new appointments and the restructuring were decided at a time of government crisis (the winter of 1986-1987), when the external (political) equilibria of power were in a state of uncertainty, a time when, according to the stricter rules of *partitocrazia*, "not even a ball can roll, not even an usher can be appointed or removed."[29]

Theories and Corollaries

The post-1987 *lottizzazione* was more stable than ever before. The new phase had its own theories and corollaries:

[O]ne of the corollaries of the "zebra" theory, which had regulated the previous phase of *lottizzazione*, was the mechanism of the options. This meant that each journalist could choose whether to work for Tg1 or for Tg2, which caused a powerful homogenization inside each newsroom. In 1987, this mechanism was eliminated. As a consequence, the Tg3 newsroom was restructured ex novo and another theory emerged, i.e., the famous theory *"casella-casella"* [the box-to-box theory, a sort of quota mechanism]. This meant that at any time somebody (be he a top official or a simple reporter at any of the regional headquarters) left the corporation, or was sent away for any given reason, died or retired, he had to be replaced by somebody coming from exactly the same political zone, i.e., same party and same faction.[30]

"The *casella-casella* theory might seem ridiculous," De Chiara continues, "but it should be taken seriously." Indeed, it had a strong impact on the hiring procedures and career advancement of many journalists:

If you check the functioning of RAI during the post-1987 phase of *lottizzazione*, you'll find that this theory was followed almost one hundred percent of the time. Even in small regional headquarters such as the one in Ancona [in the center region of Marche], where there were only twenty journalists, if one of them retired or died, we had to search for clues to trace back his party affiliation, so that he could be replaced with somebody coming from exactly the same background.[31]

Decision-making power continued to be secured in the hands of a few. As De Chiara recalls, in the late 1980s there was an increasing marginalization of certain journalists inside the newsrooms. What happened was that "in case there was a nonhomogeneous vice-director in any given newsroom, he'd remain there, but he wouldn't be given any real decision-making power; neither would he have any influence on the final product." This marginalization was also a function of the *casella-casella* theory:

As an example of how the *casella-casella* theory worked during post-1987 *lottizzazione*, one should think about the candidates who won the national exam for fifty openings as journalists in 1989. The corporation hired the finalists only on the condition that their party affiliation be disclosed so that the new hires could be better located according to party affiliation. If there was a position left by a Socialist, that person could be easily replaced by another Socialist.[32]

This was done not only to please the parties, but also to ensure homogeneity inside the corporation: a direct connection to the parties' secretariats had become a sort of security blanket, as it would safeguard RAI from the "impure elements," those not in line with the culture of the corporation. Certainly, independence was not a value that the corporation cherished.[33]

Similar to the zebra theory was another corollary, defined as the "phone number" corollary. This began to be implemented in the immediate pre-1987 phase of *lottizzazione* and was refined during its iron phase. Rodolfo Brancoli, former director of Tg1, explains how it worked:

> Each newsroom was organized according to the following schema: 4-3-2-1-1-1. Tg1 was Christian Democrat; Tg2 was Socialist; and Tg3 was Communist. This meant that the directors were DC, PSI, PCI respectively. However, inside each newsroom there was a precise formula that had to be followed to hire journalists. For every four Christian Democrat journalists you needed three Socialists, two Communists, one Social-Democrat, one Liberal, and one Republican.[34]

This was a perfect *lottizzazione* formula because it reflected the equilibrium inside the government and in the parliament. Of course, the PCI was stronger than the PSI and therefore it should have had a higher number of representatives. But the PSI was a government party and the PCI still was at the opposition.

The State of the Industry

By 1986 there were in Italy 23 million TV sets for 18.5 million households and RAI counted more than 14 million subscribers; at the end of 1985, RAI2 broadcast past midnight, RAI1 began its daily broadcasts at 10:30 in the morning, while RAI3 began at 2 in the afternoon. In 1989, the public broadcaster offered a total of 24,300 hours of television, of which 6,642 were regional and local productions. Competition with the Fininvest channels was concentrated in the entertainment sector, which represented 90 percent of the commercial broadcaster's offer. In terms of audience share, after a difficult year, in 1988 RAI's average day share reached 47.4 percent, versus 37.4 percent of Fininvest. RAI1 consolidated its morning and early afternoon offerings and was the most watched channel among all national channels. The new third channel was the most successful with an audience that grew from 2 percent in January

1987 to 12 percent in January 1990; the audience of the news program on RAI3 (Tg3) also drastically increased from 3 percent in 1986 to more than 15 percent in 1989.[35]

Programming

Among the highlights of the late 1980s there was *Spot* (1986 on RAI1), a weekly public affairs program of interviews with a variety of political figures, including the controversial interview (which was never broadcast for political reasons) with Libyan President Mohammed Qaddafi during the April 1986 crises. *Il caso* (The Case) was another noteworthy public affairs program by Enzo Biagi, that, for fear of unwanted interference with political elections, was taken off the air in June 1987 shortly after its debut. RAI2 offered mostly fiction and news, but also some current affairs programs that were highly popular, like the program on immigration *Non solo nero* (Not Black Only).

A very successful channel was RAI3, directed by Angelo Guglielmi, with its offerings of public affairs programs, reality TV,[36] and with Tg3, the news directed by Alessandro Curzi. One of the highlights of RAI3's programming was *Samarcanda*, a left-wing talk show first aired in 1987, hosted by journalist Michele Santoro, who became famous for his unorthodox interviews with politicians and other personalities, and for his openly partisan approach. *Samarcanda* became such a popular talk show that in 1988 it moved to prime time. *Un giorno in pretura* (1988), a reality TV show on what happens during a court hearing, was also very popular on the third channel, as was *La TV delle ragazze* (1988), a satirical show realized exclusively by women, a novelty in its genre. The entertainment show *Indietro tutta* (1987-1988), a sort of postmodern cult show, soon became very popular among young urban audiences. By February 1988, new editions of regional news, *telegiornale regionale*, were also offered on RAI3 at 2 o'clock in the afternoon (nicely programmed right after the end of the national news, which is also lunchtime for many Italians); and a new edition of regional information was also scheduled at 7:20 in the morning on the third radio channel.

The Fininvest channels were also starting their first talk shows and news programs, even though they were not allowed live broadcasting yet. Their first news programs included *Parlamento in*, where politicians were showed in unusual settings, while cooking, getting a haircut at the barber, or a sunbath at the beach; *Elettorando* (1987) by Maurizio Costanzo, with high caliber journalists interviewing politicians during election campaigns; *Dentro la notizia* (1988), a news program without live reporting; and *Striscia la notizia* (1988), a quasi-satirical news program on Canale5, which soon became very popular.

Changes in the Government, Changes in RAI

The new government of 1989, led by Prime Minister Giulio Andreotti (DC, right wing) had immediate repercussions in RAI: director-general Biagio Agnes, left wing Christian Democrat, was replaced in December 1989 by Gianni Pasquarelli, loyal to Forlani, a DC right wing, secretary-general of the party, and ally of Andreotti. Bruno Vespa, a journalist from the DC right wing, was appointed Tg1's director. From *Federazione della Stampa* (the national press association), Bettino Craxi's protégée Giuliana Del Bufalo became vice director of Tg2. Luigi Locatelli (PSI) stepped down as RAI2 director because he was not in line with the party secretary-general; Giampaolo Sodano (PSI, closer to the PSI's leadership) took his place. Other Socialist journalists, such as Giovanni Minoli, were apparently denied promotion because they were not easily manipulated by the PSI. These changes in RAI were welcomed by the Fininvest's leadership: whereas the previous director-general Biagio Agnes had supported public service broadcasting at all costs and opposed any form of concession in favor of the private competitor, the new director-general was more open to the possibility of a *pax televisiva* between RAI and the Fininvest channels.

The New Law: Legitimating the Duopoly

By 1989 the double monopoly in the television market was well established with the commercial broadcaster collecting 61.8 percent of the country's advertising resources for the television market. Berlusconi's holdings were expanding also in other media sectors, in particular the print media: by 1988, Fininvest controlled the national daily *Il Giornale*, and by 1989, it had acquired a majority share in the publishing house Mondadori, thereby controlling 30 percent of weekly magazines and 16 percent of national dailies. Critics contested the concentration of ownership in Berlusconi's hands and his possession of three national channels. A tentative preliminary negotiation, achieved in 1988 by the DC government of Ciriaco De Mita, attempted to forbid newspaper/broadcasting cross-ownership; in exchange, Fininvest would be allowed to keep its three national channels and obtain the rights to live broadcasting. While waiting for the new law, Berlusconi relinquished the control of *Il Giornale*, which he passed to his brother Paolo. The De Mita government fell before being able to pass the broadcasting bill.

In the meantime, progressive forces, in particular the PCI and the DC left wing, were advocating stricter regulation over the private broadcaster in order to end its dominant position in the commercial sector. The PSI and the right wing of the DC, instead, supported an open, unregulated market. Together, the two parties backed Berlusconi's escalation, impeding an antitrust law and firmly opposing any enemy of Fininvest. The conservative bloc had also the Andreotti government (1989-1992) on its side: critics of that bloc contended that the growth of Berlusconi's empire was beneficial to the triumvirate formed by Craxi, Andreotti, and Forlani. In particular, the powerful CAF was interested in the birth of a new venue for information, the news on the commercial channels. In the summer of 1989 those critics found their suspicions confirmed when the managing director of Fininvest admitted that its news programs would become the only news in line with Craxi, Andreotti, and Forlani's own understanding of liberty and freedom.

The interests at stake in the new broadcasting law were obviously very high. The PSI was playing a double role, as it needed to maintain control over RAI and, at the same time, favor the consolidation of a monopoly in the private sector. The Socialist Party even proposed to reduce the number of RAI channels from three to one, a move that was perceived by many as just another favor to Berlusconi. Craxi's party also supported Fininvest's offering its own live news, forbidden until then, not only because that added immense value to the commercial channels, but also for *lottizzazione* purposes; indeed, the beginning of news broadcasting on Fininvest channels favored a massive hiring of Socialist and Republican (PRI) journalists.[37] The DC was consumed between internal dissent and factions, acutely aware of the slipping away of its power inside as well as outside RAI: its left wing supported the public broadcaster, while its right wing opposed regulations on the commercial competitor. The PCI was also caught in the midst of an identity crisis: a longtime supporter of public service broadcasting had by then become part of the *lottizzazione* system, a position that undermined its credibility.

The new law, which finally passed in August 1990, kept things as they were. Apart from the usual opening statements, which acknowledged that "pluralism, objectivity, and complete information, openness to diverse political, social, cultural and religious opinions . . . represent fundamental principles for the broadcasting system,"[38] the law legitimated the existing duopoly, or, as critics contended, the DC/PSI duopoly. As expected, the commercial monopolist was the real winner: Fininvest's ownership of three national channels was accepted, which also implied that Silvio Berlusconi would continue to control more than 61 percent of advertising revenues for the television market and share over 90 percent of the audience with RAI channels.[39] Other national television broadcasters, 1,400 local broadcasters, and 4,000 radio broadcasters were left with the crumbs. The Mammì Law had also other negative effects on the cinema industry and the print media. The cinema was compromised by the fact that television broadcasters were given permission to air a high number of movies every day. The print media, which in 1980 could count on 60 percent of the total advertising resources, by early 1990s had only 40 percent of those resources available.[40]

The Ideology of "Late" *Lottizzazione*

Soon after law no. 223 was passed on August 6, 1990, another series of controversial appointments, which had been put on hold until then, was decided. The *lottizzazione* of that summer was, according to many observers, one of the most pervasive ever:

> The parties had already figured out everything. First of all they had multiplied the positions inside each Tg in order to increase the number of potential seats. Then they proceeded to occupy those seats. This latest delicate alchemy of power, which everybody denies but of which everybody keeps track in their handwritten memos, was accomplished according to the strictest rules of *lottizzazione*. It was done through a careful operation consisting of sharing powerful positions among the parties on the basis of their political and electoral weight, and according to the equilibrium among all factions.[41]

A novelty of those appointments was that minor government parties, including the PRI (the Republican Party), the PLI (the Liberal Party), and the PSDI (the Social-Democratic Party), participated more aggressively in the partition. This was accomplished by multiplying the number of Tg vice-directors:

Manca [RAI president] decided to increase the number of vice-directors for each Tg from two to three. His intent was to reorganize news programs according to time bands. Indeed, this was a prelude to a sub-*lottizzazione* by "time band" [*lottizzazione a ore*], as it was defined. As a result, Tg1 ended up having a Liberal Party color at noon, when the vice-director on the shift was a member of the Italian Liberal Party. It then assumed a republican tone at night, when there was a PRI vice-director. A similar logic was followed by Tg2 and Tg3.[42]

Now more than ever, the crucial thing for a journalist was to have some kind of party affiliation; indeed, those who did not have a party acronym next to their name could not even hope to work.[43] It seemed as if *lottizzazione* had become a mechanism whose only scope was to perpetuate the inertia of the system. Press journalist Giorgio Bocca commented:

Not one, not two, but four vice-directors for each Tg. One for me, one for you, one for us, the government parties, one for the opposition. After all that has been said and written against *lottizzazione* by RAI top leadership as well as by politicians and by public opinion, everything remains the same. It seems as if there were a rubber wall, one that always reminds us of the discrepancies between the party system and society, one that underlines that there is no sense of democracy, and a general lack of respect for public opinion.[44]

But the intensification of party interference was also a symptom of the incipient crisis within the party system. As parties were losing touch with their electoral basis and civil society, their control over the broadcaster was intensifying; they relied on the power of television with an exaggerated trust in its ability to shape public opinion.

Lottizzazione in Crisis

The 1990s were years of dramatic changes in the Italian political landscape, years that had profound repercussions for the public service broadcaster. The Clean Hands bribery scandal of that period exposed corruption at the highest levels of politics, bringing to the surface the decades-old practices of illegal financing of parties. As Italians were growing increasingly disaffected with their parties, the ideological substratum that had made *lottizzazione* possible was changing. The dominant discourse began incorporating calls for more objectivity in reporting, and an end to political interference, together with a general outcry for more transparency in public administration, greater efficiency, and a new customer-oriented ethos in sectors that had previously enjoyed decades of monopoly status (like the postal services, the public school system, the national health care system, and RAI itself, which in 1996 instituted a center for customer satisfaction and in 1997 opened a call center, *Aperto al pubblico*, where citizens could call to voice their opinions).

At a time when the end of ideologies seemed sanctioned by history, *partitocrazia* was seen as a cancer, spreading from state apparati to the public administration. Political alliances became synonymous with corruption. Eugenio Scalfari, editor in chief of the daily *La Repubblica*, commented:

> State institutions have been infected by the parties, which, on their part, had been occupied by immobile apparati, sheltered from any electoral mechanisms. Indeed, such electoral mechanisms as the majoritarian system, considered to be responsible for the power that parties had acquired in Italian social and political life, were created to crystallize the status quo, to prevent any change from happening, to support and promote corruption.[45]

Meanwhile, inside RAI, journalistic values such as objectivity and balance were being cherished as the antidote to political contamination. Salvation appeared to lie in business concepts like efficiency and competition, embraced by the technocratic administrations soon to follow in RAI (1993-1996). It seemed as if the new language of market and efficiency might emancipate the public broadcaster from its previous relationship with political powers.

However, to this supposedly new freedom from political parties a desire to assume leadership in quality programming, experimentation, innovation, in other words, to enrich and expand the identity of the public service broadcaster did not correspond. And eventually, RAI's independence from the party system came to signify its subjection to the tyrannies of the market, and the demise, or at least, the confinement within circumscribed and secluded areas, of its public service ethos.

During the 1990s, RAI's programming became increasingly similar to that of Fininvest (Mediaset since 1996), as the attention to audience and the reliance on advertising money caused the public broadcaster to concern itself more with winning the ratings war than with fulfilling its public service mission.

The Success of RAI3 and the Anti-*Lottizzazione* Campaign

Intense corporate restructuring, which had already begun in the late 1980s, proceeded at a fast pace through the early 1990s. Commercial activities became centralized under the supervision of the vice-director of television programming, while much attention was devoted to adjusting RAI's scheduling to that of its competitor, and strengthening the identity of each channel. RAI1 maintained its character as a generalist channel geared toward popular entertainment, news, and public affairs; RAI2 became the fiction channel (with most of its fiction imported from the United States in an effort "to penetrate the market, cater to people's preferences, and keep costs low");[46] and RAI3 continued to provide news, public affairs programs, and reality TV.

The ratings for RAI3 improved considerably during the late 1980s and early 1990s, showing that it was possible to marry the search for audience with quality productions;[47] for many the success of this channel was an example of how good things could get once *lottizzazione* was perfected. But the times when parties could openly admit their influence over the broadcaster were gone, at least during the bribery scandal years, and the broadcaster was losing its longtime supporters, among them the PSI. Threatened by the Catholic-Communist alliance at the foundation of RAI3's success, the Socialist Party began to attack *lottizzazione*, an attack that, one might argue, was intended to legitimate its own next move, namely, tightening its grip on Tg2:

> The main problem in the public broadcaster is RAI3 and the journalists' union [Usigrai]. In the third channel, Communist cultural operators are first of all the emissaries of their political ideology. Only in the second instance are they journalists. There is no solution: either the other two channels [Channel 1 and 2] become increasingly partisan, or the entire public broadcaster will become an instrument in the Communists' hands.[48]

The Socialists' criticism against a "communist occupation of RAI" and against the party system that allowed it went hand in hand with populist sentiments calling for mindless entertainment, private pleasure, and a disengagement from political participation[49]—odd though it may seem to hear such sentiments expressed by a famous Socialist, Craxi's right hand in RAI, Ugo Intini:

> What we as Socialists really want is a public broadcaster more efficient, modern, a real corporation where there will be no more three Tgs and three channels; a public broadcaster that will be closer to those citizens who cannot identify themselves anymore with a political party, but rather as young or old, interested in entertainment or in-depth information, in popular topics or in more sophisticated ones.[50]

The fear of the Communists' success at leading Channel 3 was probably a good enough reason for the Socialists to champion their campaign against *lottizzazione*. If *lottizzazione* meant more space given to the Communists, then the PSI could probably do without it. Moreover, at a time when citizens were growing dissatisfied with the political system, it was convenient for the Socialists to ride the wave of anti-*lottizzazione* and anti-*partitocrazia*.

After the Mammì Law passed, the PSI proposed to reduce the number of Tgs and channels. This was interpreted by other political parties and especially by the main journalists' union, Usigrai, as an attempt to "eliminate the public broadcaster *tout court*, and as an attack on democracy of information."[51] Other parties, including the Italian Republican Party (PRI), rejected the proposal and supported the notion that "new mechanisms should be implemented in order to liberate RAI journalists from having their careers determined exclusively by the politicians."[52] Also, the DC, the PLI, and the PCI expressed their discomfort with the tripartition system in RAI, but none of them seemed able to propose alternatives to the notion that the end of the tripartition would also mean the end of pluralism in RAI. Or maybe none of them dared to make the first move and step back from the control of any of the three Tgs and channels. After all, *lottizzazione* and pluralism had been inseparable since the Reform Law of 1975: one secured the other, and the common wisdom was that when somebody tried to eliminate *lottizzazione*, pluralism would also suffer. It is also important to point out that the discourse on *lottizzazione* was often instrumental to the parties' own interests. The PCI, for instance, considered any attack against RAI as an attack on democracy of information. To reduce the number of Tgs was interpreted as an attempt to hegemonize information. The DC, as we know, was internally divided. On one hand, its left wing was still supporting the public broadcaster, and consequently, the logic of partition; on the other hand, the DC right wing condemned *lottizzazione*, but behind that position hid support for the monopoly in the commercial sector.

Criticism of *partitocrazia*, and of RAI as a bastion of the "government of parties," was strongly embraced by the right, and became a key element of Berlusconi's electoral campaign of 1994. However, the absence of a tradition of objective and independent journalism, which alone could legitimate any sound criticism of *lottizzazione*, made such criticism seem purely instrumental, ideological, and self-interested. Having shallow roots within Italian intellectual and journalistic tradition, accusations against *lottizzazione* bore no fruit; without a solid political will to separate television from the parties, the inertia of the apparatus could not be modified.

The End of the Old RAI

During the years of the Clean Hands scandal, inside RAI tension was high, and one of the hottest spots was the Tg1 newsroom. In April 1992, Tg1's director, Bruno Vespa, released an interview to the daily *Corriere della Sera* in which he admitted that "the editor in chief of Tg1 [was] the DC, particularly the right wing of the DC."[53] In effect, he told the truth, and the harsh reactions on the part of RAI's journalists and top management to his interview were emblematic of the double-sided quality of public discourse surrounding *lottizzazione*. It was a phenomenon that everybody knew about and many practiced, and it was acceptable as long as it remained secret, within the private context of informal meetings, talks, and phone calls. But officially and in public, it was rebuked, rejected in shame, especially after the April 1992 elections, when "the internal geography of RAI, designed in the image of the party system, was suddenly erased."[54] The confusion of referents in the political/party system was well expressed when, during a popular talk show on RAI, TG1 director Bruno Vespa and the secretary-general of the PRI, Giorgio La Malfa, engaged live in a heated discussion about the public broadcaster and the party system. On April 6, 1992, once the results of the national elections had sanctioned the end of the DC, in front of millions of viewers, La Malfa accused Vespa of being *lottizzato* and declared that the ways in which parties had misused public television showed that RAI was indeed the "first problem that need[ed] to be addressed [by the new government]."[55]

In September 1992, Vespa received a no-confidence vote from the Tg1 newsroom assembly, which led, in early February 1993, to his resignation. According to most of the newsroom's representatives, the main reason for Vespa's ouster was his bias toward the Forlani DC faction. At a time when political scandals were exploding and making headlines daily, he was accused by the national press and by most of his own reporters at Tg1 of downplaying any charges of Christian Democrats' involvement in corruption and Mafia-related crimes. Vespa's ouster reflected not only the crisis within RAI, but also the DC's own crisis. Indeed, neither Fanfani nor anybody else from the right wing of the party, so powerful only a few months earlier, stepped forward in Vespa's favor. Some argued that his fall as news director marked the end of an era:

> Bruno Vespa fell because he thought that neither his party nor the corporation would ever abandon him. Instead, they did. Forlani, who put Vespa there, did not move one finger to help him. Director-general Pasquarelli, who never really wanted him there, acted as if nothing had ever happened.[56]

Giovanni Valentini enthusiastically commented on *La Repubblica*:

> The stepping down of Vespa represents the victorious outcome of a revolution coming from below, from journalists against *partitocrazia*. We can now finally say that the old era is over in RAI, even though a new one has not yet begun. What happened in RAI, is a reflection of the earthquake that is shaking Italian political life. . . . What is happening is the loyal mirror of the regime's crisis.[57]

However, Valentini's hopes for a real change inside RAI were naïve. Vespa did not disappear. After staying away from the TV screen for some time, he came back with *Porta a porta* (Door to Door), a talk show on RAI1 which was given great resonance and high visibility.

Vespa was replaced with Albino Longhi, right-wing DC, a protégé of then RAI director-general Gianni Pasquarelli, a man known for his ability to negotiate among different factions, and defined by some as the "man in gray." His Tg continued to protect what was left of the DC by giving scarce relevance to the daily updates on the Clean Hands scandal; on the opposite side, Tg5, directed by former Tg2 journalist Enrico Mentana, regularly opened its editions with information on the latest events related to the political scandals. Italians appreciated the novelty, and indeed, the audience share of Tg5 surpassed that of Tg1 on various occasions during the spring and the summer of 1993. Viewers preferred, at least at some point, what the Fininvest channels could offer: a different kind of information, less focused on the *Palazzo* (as Italians call the political establishment), more interested to the every day chronicle, and therefore, so it seemed, free from the parties' influence.

A Law to Eliminate *Lottizzazione*

With a corporation whose 1993 annual budget had a debt of 80 billion lira, and a work force in the region of thirteen to fourteen thousand employees, of whom twelve hundred were journalists, plus thirteen thousand external collaborators, a new law was necessary to guarantee some kind of direction at a time when direction and references were lost.[58] A first attempt was made with law no. 206, passed on June 23, 1993, whose intent was to end *lottizzazione* and lay the foundations for a more efficient corporation. The new law substantially modified the 1975 Reform Law and, most importantly, modified law no. 10 (1985), the so-called Berlusconi decree. Because the parliament's control over the public broadcaster had been used as a Trojan horse by the parties, the new law reduced the seats on the board of directors from sixteen to five (to prevent the parties from allocating seats in the customary way), and gave the power of appointment to the presidents of the two houses (Senate and the Deputies' Chamber), rather than the Parliamentary Committee. The law also established that the board should consist of people "chosen for their professional prestige and their independence."[59] The board, a sort of collective managing director, acquired other tasks in addition to its usual administrative duties, including elaborating and approving editorial plans, allocating financial resources to different areas of corporate activities, approving annual budget proposals, elaborating investments and restructuring plans, and personnel policies. The board was also granted the authority to approve and revise the corporation's annual broadcasting and production plans, and to appoint vice general directors, other high-ranking officials, and the president.

The law drastically reduced the power in the hands of the director-general, especially for what concerned the director's role in hiring and programming. It did so by placing much of that power in the hands of the board of directors and by giving them a decisive, unprecedented role in the nomination of the director-general. The Reform Law of 1975 had already made provisions to limit the power of the director-general and dilute that power among the members of the board of directors and the Parliamentary Committee. That included hiring and promoting journalists, news directors, and other top-level executives, and the power to define the corporation's annual programming plans. By contrast, the Berlusconi decree of 1984 had repealed those limitations, establishing that the director-general would propose the appointments of vice general directors and other executives to the board of directors, that he would be responsible for assuring pluralism of programming, ensuring the efficient use of resources and personnel, and supervising the overall activities of the corporation. Obviously, the DC was not pleased with the limitations imposed by the new law because it wanted to have a powerful director-general; instead this provision was supported by the opposition, including the Democratic Party of the Left, which preferred a director with reduced power over RAI editorial policy. The law also established that the mandatory license fee would be adjusted to inflation and that RAI's concession fee for the use of the airways would be "lowered to the price paid by commercial radio and television broadcasters" (art. 4)—a conspicuous reduction from 160 billion lira to 1 billion.

The so-called council of five sages was appointed in July 1993 to lead the broadcaster. The new board consisted of Paolo Murialdi, Claudio Demattè, Elvira Sellerio, Tullio Gregory, and Feliciano Benvenuti. All of them were politically independent, that is, they did not hold party cards. This new phase, which lasted until July 1994, was known as *la televisione dei professori*, the professors' television.

The professors urged efficiency and competition. Improving RAI's financial health was seen as the key to emancipating the broadcaster from party interference. Giovanni Valentini expressed well this move:

> A genetic mutation is happening in the public service broadcaster thanks to the new editorial program presented by the new administration. We are moving away from the parties' RAI toward the citizens' RAI. Maybe the new RAI is not born yet, but certainly, the old one is dead. Maybe it is not the end of *lottizzazione*, but certainly it is the beginning of de-*lottizzazione*. The three channels will be redefined. Their common goal will be to reach the maximum possible number of viewers. [I]n other words, it is now a matter of how to orchestrate an exact marketing strategy, by directing each product toward a given target.[60]

RAI News and Its Viewership

Between 1993 and 1994, the offerings of children's programs, light entertainment, and talk shows on all RAI channels grew considerably, while in-house production—including coproduction—diminished on RAI (from 73.8 percent to 65.2 percent of total production), and grew on Fininvest channels (from 23.1 to 47.7 percent) between 1988 and 1994, with the highest amount of imported fiction and films for television on RAI2.[61] By 1994, there were more hours dedicated to "light entertainment" on RAI channels than on Fininvest channels—light entertainment represented 59.5 percent of total output on RAI versus 40.5 percent on Fininvest. Sports and films diminished. This might be part of the reason why RAI maintained its supremacy: in 1995, its average audience share was 47.93 percent, versus 42.75 percent of Fininvest and 9.32 percent of other TV stations.[62]

Competition between RAI and Fininvest had extended to news and current affairs since 1992, when, as a result of law no. 223 (1990), commercial broadcasters were allowed to have their own news programs with live reporting. Fininvest's flagship channel, Canale5, aired its first news program, Tg5, in January 1992. International competition through satellite broadcasting had also started one year earlier on the occasion of the first Gulf War, when RAI competed with the Cable News Network (CNN). RAI's exclusive rights to sports events also ended in the early 1990s, adding considerable pressure on the public corporation in an intensifying competition for revenues and audience.

News and public affairs programs maintained an acceptable audience share on the public channels: from 32 percent in 1987-1989, the total share had increased to 38 percent in 1990, and to more than 40 percent in 1991. The offer of news and current affairs programs in prime time also increased during those years. However, when the competition with the commercial broadcaster began, news on RAI resented the effect. From 1992 to 1993, the audience share of Tg1 at 8 p.m. went from 31.7 to 30.1 percent. In the same period of time, the Tg5 audience share went up from 21.3 percent to 23.5 percent. Between 1992 and 1993, only the regional news (TGR) saw an increase in its audience share.[63] Things improved in the next years: between 1994 and 1995, the audience of Tg1 at 8 p.m. increased 2.43 percentage points—from 31 to 33.43—while the share of its direct competitor, Tg5 at 8 p.m., continued to grow from 24.5 percent in 1994 to 25.47 percent in 1995.[64] Overall, Tg1 at 8:00 p.m. maintained its first place during most of the 1990s. In 1995, for instance, its average daily audience was over 7,000,000 people (a 33.43 percent share), whereas its direct competitor, Tg5, counted 5,500,000 viewers (equal to a 25.47 percent share). In 1997, Tg1 had an audience share of 32.8, while Tg5 had 24 percent; as a whole, RAI channels had a total audience share of 66 percent, 33.3 percent for Mediaset channels.[65]

Overall, throughout the 1990s and early 2000s, news programs on RAI, especially on Tg1, remained competitive on average, showing that RAI still represented an authoritative source of news for most Italians. At times of crisis, or national emergencies, this became even more visible.

For instance, immediately after the September 11, 2001, terrorist attack on New York City and Washington, D.C., RAI news and current affairs programs drew an unusually high number of viewers. The day after the attack, the total audience share for RAI news programs was 52.83 percent in prime time, compared to 36.85 percent for Mediaset. On September 12, 2001, RAI's press office reported that more than 8 million people watched *Porta a porta*, on RAI1. And when the president of the republic gave his speech on the same day, people watched it on RAI1, even though the same speech was being broadcast live on all the national networks. According to television analyst Francesco Siliato, such behavior seemed to indicate that in times of crisis, the majority of Italians still tended to "identify RAI [and particularly RAI1] with the institution[66] of broadcasting. Notwithstanding the crises of the political system and *lottizzazione*, Italians continued to consider RAI as an authoritative source of information.

Excellent public affairs programs were aired in the 1992-1993 and 1993-1994 seasons. During the winter of *tangentopoli* (the Clean Hands bribery scandal of 1992-1993) about 22 million viewers (almost half the population of Italy), from Monday to Sunday, had the opportunity to watch politicians and other exponents of the first republic being questioned by journalists, jailed or put on trial. Among the most watched public affairs programs and talk shows were *Milano, Italia*, hosted by Gad Lerner (who would in 2000 become Tg1 director); *Mixer*, a well-established moderate talk show created and hosted by Giovanni Minoli; *Il rosso e il nero* (The Black and the Red), a leftist public affairs program hosted by Michele Santoro; and *Tocca a noi* (It Is Our Turn), hosted by journalist guru Enzo Biagi. Such high profile public affairs programs contrasted with the trend at Tg1 and Tg2, which often failed to highlight the unfolding events.

The Professors, the Journalists, and *Lottizzazione*

Although Italians continued to maintain some kind of trust in RAI as an institution, choosing it as their number one source of information, the leadership of the corporation, especially at the time of the "professors," showed signs of intense disaffection with the news programs, which soon became the main target of their anti-*lottizzazione* campaign. Indeed, by the end of October 1993, all the old news directors had been removed and each Tg had a new head. Tg1 director Albino Longhi, too easily identifiable with the old DC, had already been replaced in July by Demetrio Volcic; Paolo Garimberti became Tg2 director; Andrea Giubilo, left DC, was appointed director of Tg3; Michele Santoro became vice-director of RAI3, under director Angelo Guglielmi; Nadio Delai (a Catholic former director of the Institute of Social Research CENSIS) became director of RAI1; Giovanni Minoli, Socialist, became director of RAI2; and Franco Iseppi, DC left wing, was appointed director of scheduling. As always, notwithstanding the supposedly independent procedures of such nominations, criticism against the appointments came from various directions:

> Too many DC people, this was the critique from PDS, Reconstructed Communism (RC), and the PRI. The so-much-celebrated *delottizzazione* seemed to represent rather a step backward from the notion of pluralism. Most of the neo-directors came from the DC left wing. The PDS confirmed: "There is an increasing presence of left wing DC people . . . whereas the presence of any leftist party is decreasing."[67]

The Republican Party argued that the appointments were sending out a "clear political sign." Even the journalists' union Usigrai criticized them: "We did not notice elements of difference in comparison to the past *lottizzazione* schemes."[68] Others joined in protest. Former RAI president Enrico Manca said that "from *lottizzazione* we are now back to *latifundium*. In particular to a left DC *latifundium*."[69] As a matter of fact, not only were the news programs in the hands of one faction, the left DC, but also important structures like the production of fiction and scheduling were in the hands of the Catholic faction. For Achille Occhetto, secretary-general of the PCI from 1988-1990 and of the PDS from 1991 to 1994, the professors' choices expressed a "postmodern centrism,"[70] too similar to the previous centrism of the DC era.

Giornalismo all'Inglese? No, Grazie!

The Anglo-American model of objective journalism was championed by the new RAI leaders, who were especially critical of Tg3's openly partisan editorial line; objectivity and neutrality became key words in remarks by RAI's president. But those aseptic Anglo-Saxon models were strongly questioned by many observers:

Objectivity, neutrality, journalistic truth. The question is: "Do these things really exist?" RAI's president has no doubts. He proclaimed, "Journalistic truth exists, there are no doubts about this." He would like to see all conditional tenses disappear from news reporting, in the illusion that only certainty and facts would remain.[71]

Once more, the question whether objectivity in journalism was attainable or even desirable stirred up interesting debates among intellectuals and journalists. One of them commented:

> Those who advocate "truth" do not understand one thing about journalism, and that is that journalism is politics, partisanship. In this respect, the real shortcoming of Italian journalism is that newspapers and news programs are becoming one and the same.[72]

According to this last commentator, the problem was the homogenization of the three newscasts, the perceived lack of diverse viewpoints expressed by them, rather than the lack of objectivity. But the board of directors had a different perspective and believed that in RAI "we only need one Tg, because news is news and therefore we don't need to present it three times."[73] Therefore, proposals were made to reduce the number of newscasts from three to two by eliminating Tg3. According to this hypothesis, Tg1 would remain the generalist news bulletin, Tg2 would target younger audiences, and Tg3's national edition would disappear and the entire Channel 3 would be transformed into a regional channel. This option, however, was soon discarded by Paolo Murialdi, a board member in charge of restructuring the news. The reason: a unified Tg would become easy prey of the government of the day.[74]

The debate about the nature, and the number, of Tgs, had vast echo. Some proposed to keep the three news programs, but to differentiate them on the basis of their editorial projects, rather than party affiliation. Lilly Gruber, a prominent journalist at Tg1, proposed one Tg for news stories, one for in-depth analysis, and the third for sports and local information. Demetrio Volcic, director of Tg1, suggested a similar idea: keep the three Tgs, give each one its own editorial mission, and get rid of ideological affiliations.[75] In the end, the tripartition remained, even though ideological affiliations were slightly reduced: Tg1 continued to be the pro-Catholic news; Tg2, whose password was *decraxizzare*, with the mission to marginalize, and possibly eliminate, journalists too close to Craxi, focused on its lay tradition; and Tg3 continued to be the left-wing news program. The sports desk was unified in one autonomous department, and the three radio news programs were consolidated under one director.

The Professors' Challenges

The reactions to the changes imposed by the professors varied. Usigrai, the powerful journalists' union, fiercely criticized the new leadership. Behind the neutrality of notions such as objectivity, market strategies, and efficiency, other interests seemed to lurk, according to Usigrai secretary-general Roberto Natale, who believed that the professors were, albeit unwillingly, playing cards that would weaken the public broadcaster to the full benefit of its commercial competitor:

> We did not have any problem with the professors' intent to end *lottizzazione*. In fact, we had been trying to do that already for some time. We had our problems with the image that the professors were publicizing of the public broadcaster [corruption; inflated expenses; inflated salaries and unclear compensations to external collaborators]. That image was so clearly negative that it neutralized any commitment to renovation and reformation that they said they had. In other words, I think the professors were supporting (perhaps unwillingly) the positions of the enemies of RAI, those who claimed that the broadcaster should have been not only reformed, but indeed split into various branches and finally sold.[76]

Major tensions between the leadership of the public broadcaster and Usigrai arose when President Dematté proposed that RAI and Fininvest sell one channel each as a means to reinvigorate the broadcasting market. The journalists' union never liked this idea, nor did it ever agree with the professors' plan to privatize or sell parts of the corporation:

> [W]e got very mad when the director-general said, "The public broadcaster should be sold," on the basis that RAI was too big a corporation. We were suspicious, and rightly so, of a board of directors that was trying to get rid of parts of its corporation. From the managing director of FIAT you would not expect something like this, would you? You would expect to see a director who works to consolidate his assets. You wouldn't expect a managing director to say, "Here, get a piece of my corporation!"[77]

Others, however, suspected that Usigrai wanted merely to defend corporatist interests and the status quo. Francesco Siliato suggested that the "changes imposed by the board of directors upset the top, the icebergs of corruption in RAI, those lobbies whose main objective was to defend their own obsolete values and their own interests."[78] Still some RAI journalists, including Roberto Mastroianni, had positive comments to make, especially regarding the management of human resources:

> [During] the period of the so-called CAF . . . managers at all levels had been appointed without any need. We had managers and top officials in RAI who could not be fired but were completely useless, or worse, they were negative. The professors commissioned a very well organized research effort, done by a research firm. They checked curricula, they called managers and interrogated them for hours. . . . The results of the research showed that the middle and top management had indeed been inflated. . . . Many people in RAI were frightened.[79]

However, Mastroianni also argued, the reformist potential collapsed because of the professors' lack of knowledge of RAI and the excessive vigor of their actions. Their campaign failed because of "tactical mistakes":

> Their first mistake was that as soon as they arrived they attacked the journalists. They began by questioning the expenses of foreign correspondents and other expenses. They failed to recognize that the internal power groups and the journalists were going to destroy you in only a couple of days if you did something like this. . . . The management, furthermore, came from a journalistic background, so all of them had connections with each other. So, once you attack the management, you will have the journalists against you as well, and vice-versa. . . . Another tactical mistake was to publicize the worst possible things about the corporation. During the professors' administration the lid was slightly lifted on a big mess. But that was not the way to do it. From that small lifting, however, a terrible smell came out.[80]

Some critics questioned the effectiveness of the actions taken by the board to resolve RAI's problems. They argued that appointing new directors alone, without simultaneously implementing structural changes, was not sufficient to actually improve things inside the corporation. Enzo Forcella was among those critics. He defined the whole experience of the professors in RAI as *gattopardesca*, using an adjective taken from a famous novel by Tommaso Di Lampedusa, *Il gattopardo*, which indicates one's ability to pretend that one is changing whereas in reality all remains the same.[81] Others, including Alessandro Curzi, a Tg3 director removed by Demattè because of his partisan leadership, accused the professors of doing their own *lottizzazione*: "The novelties that they brought along were indeed old and gray."[82] At the same time, the public broadcaster was also being criticized by the political parties, especially the DC right wing. One party representative lamented:

> The proof of the DC's complete failure in the political and social life of the country is exemplified by current events in the public broadcaster. RAI has betrayed the Christian Democratic Party. The fief where the DC used to decide the good and the bad for decades is not responding anymore. No more long interviews with DC politicians, no more invitations to talk shows and to the Tg. Where has the traditional regard gone?[83]

Given all this criticism, the professors' attempts to innovate were clearly doomed to end, their efforts nullified by RAI internal powers, but also by political parties such as the PDS and the DC. Meanwhile, dark clouds were taking shape on the horizon of the Italian political panorama. At the end of 1993, for the first time in ten years, Publitalia, the advertising collecting agency for Fininvest, showed a negative balance, while the Fininvest holding had accumulated a debt of 4,000 billion lira. It was then that Silvio Berlusconi decided to enter politics with his new party, *Forza Italia*, in a calculated attempt to solve the financial difficulties of his media empire.

The Old Joins the New

The progressive coalition, consisting of the PDS and some of the small parties emerging from the ruins of the former DC, confronted the conservative coalition *Polo delle Libertà*, consisting of *Forza Italia, Alleanza Nazionale*, and *Lega Nord*. The political confrontation resulted in a confrontation between the two national broadcasters, RAI and Fininvest. Allegedly, the center-left was supported by the public broadcaster, whereas the center-right was supported by the Fininvest channels. At the end, thanks to his powerful media empire, Silvio Berlusconi won the elections and became prime minister. On the grounds that the state's television service could not possibly oppose the government (as Berlusconi argued it was doing) and that the previous administration had failed to carry to completion its de-*lottizzazione* mandate, the professors were removed in July 1994. The presidents of the Senate and the Chamber of Deputies appointed a new board of directors, with Letizia Moratti president and Gianni Billia director-general.

Efficiency, productivity, entrepreneurial spirit, and journalistic objectivity continued to be the watchwords of the new leadership. Whereas only a few years earlier the emphasis had been on offering multiple perspectives and different points of view based on the parties' perspectives, in 1994 the stress shifted to "objective reporting." Speaking to this purpose, RAI's annual report of 1994-1995 stated that the broadcaster "must provide news that is absolutely and without any possible doubt complete and objective."[84] Internal competition among the three public channels, which was one of the traits of *lottizzazione*, was definitely abandoned. "Channel politics," indicating ideological distinctions among the three channels, was replaced by an editorial politics in line with the new corporate style within the overall project of redefining the broadcaster's public service mission. RAI1 continued to be a generalist, popular channel; RAI2's mission was to offer more news and in-depth news analysis; RAI3's task was local and regional programming. Even though the board of directors continued to emphasize that RAI must "dedicate enough and appropriate spaces for the development of the core public services,"[85] various observers and commentators cried out against what they saw as a U.S.-style design to relegate the public service broadcaster to a niche, ancillary (as Letizia Moratti defined it) to the lead role that commercial channels would take.

The State of the Industry

After the new appointments in the fall of 1994, RAI had 805 top managers: there were 31 directors (during the Demattè era they were 28), 5 codirectors (2 more than at the time of the professors), and 8 vice directors (there had been 54 at the time of Demattè). The number of newsroom heads went down probably because many of them were promoted to higher positions.

Meanwhile, the offer of fiction had increased considerably from 24 percent of total programming in 1984 to 31 percent in 1994. Light entertainment had also grown compared to previous years: in 1994 it represented 11.8 percent of total output on RAI1, 7.1 percent on RAI2, and 9.8 percent on RAI3. Interestingly, RAI1 and RAI2 were broadcasting more light entertainment than their commercial rivals: on Italia1 light entertainment represented 4.5 percent of total offering, and only 3.5 percent on Rete4. The number of imported shows continued to grow. Those from the United States went from 1,532 hours in 1994 to 2,264 hours in 1995. The most significant increase was on RAI2, from 647 hours of U.S. imports in prime time in 1994 to 1,264 hours in 1995.[86]

In the meantime, television had become the most important mass medium in Italy. In 1984, it shared 47.2 percent of the total advertising revenues (13.5 percent to RAI, 26.3 percent to Fininvest, 4.1 percent to other private national televisions, and 3.3 percent to private local TV stations). The print media controlled 43.1 percent of the resources; cinema, 0.2 percent; public service radio, 1.7 percent; and private radio stations, 2.2 percent.[87] By 1994, television—public and private—controlled 54.6 percent of the advertising market (RAI's share was 16.8 percent, Fininvest 32.7 percent, other private televisions 5.1 percent); public radio controlled 1.3 percent of advertisement money; private radio 2.5 percent; the print media 38.2 percent; and cinema 0.3.[88]

By the end of 1995, RAI had approximately 11,000 employees: 1,665 journalists, 410 directors, 1,013 managers, and 7,953 technicians. There were 16 million subscribers, 51 percent of them from the north, 20 percent from the center, 20 percent from the south, and 9.4 percent from the island.[89]

Lottizzazione Continues

In January 1994 a commentator for the daily *Corriere della Sera* made the following remarks with regard to the public broadcaster and its ability to develop into something different from what it had been:

> State television blew up because of the same explosion that destroyed the old political system. But it keeps standing up and walking, like an empty dress. . . . It is dangerous that after the explosion the empty dress is still up on its feet. Because the body of a political system identical to the old one could be tempted to slip back into it . . . it is not out of the question that, after having been produced by a certain political system, RAI could even reproduce it."[90]

This commentator was right: indeed not much was changing inside the public broadcaster. Contrary to the right-wing coalition's promise to end *partitocrazia* and *lottizzazione,* many accused the Moratti administration of restoring the old regime:

> We are back to the old practices. *Lottizzazione* has started again. Before, it was the CAF (the trio Craxi, Andreotti, Fanfani) doing all the hiring in RAI; now we have Berlusconi and Fini [secretary-general of *Alleanza Nazionale*] taking care of things.[91]

The moderate *Corriere della Sera* confirmed that in line with the old tradition, the three Tgs were being shared among the winning parties: Tg1 went to *Forza Italia,* Tg2 to *Alleanza Nazionale,* and Tg3 remained with the opposition. The appointments of directors and vice directors of news faced fierce internal opposition. A senior journalist recalls these struggles:

> Carlo Rossella was appointed Tg1 director in place of Volcic? An absurdity. Who was Rossella? They told me he had even worked for me at one point but I could not even remember him. And then they put Mimun as director of Tg2! They've got to be kidding! They got him from Fininvest where he was their news vice-director, and Mentana [a Socialist former journalist for RAI] was the news director. I could not believe it! We gave Mentana (our former Tg2 vice-director) to Fininvest, and by now RAI had stooped so low to the point of accepting Mentana's vice, Mimun, as our new director! How humiliating! In the newsroom, we fought against him furiously. There was my faction (the Mattioli faction) against his faction. But he never decided to resign. Mimun was a former Socialist (of some faction, I can't remember which one). And then he migrated to the *Polo* [*della Libertà,* the center-right coalition], as many Socialists did. That's why he was appointed Tg2 director.[92]

A phenomenon knows as *mediasettizzazione* of RAI began and various people from the Fininvest entourage went to work for the public broadcaster. Meanwhile, old journalists, famous at the time of Craxi, were quite miraculously resurrected. One commentator noticed: "The old nucleus of Craxi's *lottizzazione* came back to reign. But the worst kind of the old nucleus: the fourth row, the ones nobody ever wanted to promote."[93] Another observed:

> Everything that could be recuperated from the Craxi era, plus a powerful group of people from Fininvest, the ones who were CAF's prefer-

ence and the ones who worked for Berlusconi, represent the new public broadcaster of the new era. Carlo Rossella and Clemente Mimun come from Fininvest; Piero Vigorelli [director of Channel 3] is the ancient herald of Socialism; and finally, to complete the happy memories of the old CAF, Claudio Angelini [director of Channel 1] is ready to come back to life.[94]

Many regretted the good old days, including Enzo Biagi, who wrote: "This new *lottizzazione* is softer, because its technique is softer. It works on details, such as emptying the corporation, sending away people who count, while at the same time respecting the old power groups."[95] Others shared this negative judgment:

> RAI now is crowded with former Christian Democrats, crypto-fascists, former Socialists, and people from *Lega Nord*. This is becoming truly amazing. Halfway between the grotesque and the horror genre, this tragicomedy in RAI represents, with a certain theatrical effect, the deep nature, the wild instinct, the "animal spirits" of the current government coalition. The government coalition told us at first: "Let us work, and then you'll see what we will be able to accomplish." I am afraid, however, that there will be not much left to be seen, as the public broadcaster is being completely destroyed.[96]

The return of the ghosts of the CAF era spotlighted the old-style government of the new coalition, and the fact that the so-called second republic was not so different from the first one, especially since the ruling coalition happened to be headed by a media mogul who owed his fortune to *partitocrazia*. Commenting on the conservatives' failure to provide a truly innovative leadership, Sergio Romano expressed his discouragement:

> I had hoped that Letizia Moratti and Ennio Presutti [president and director-general of RAI], entrepreneurs from Milan, would have brought with them to Viale Mazzini [RAI's headquarters in Rome], their Milanese 'philosophy'. I had hoped that they would have kept faith with their principles and training. Instead, they have agreed to negotiate the appointments with the parties, taking up to 40 days to do what the top management of any corporation would have done in only a few hours. They should now go home and stop covering up with their Milanese aura a typical Roman mess.[97]

Not only was the administration incapable of true innovations, but also the broadcaster itself was incapable of supporting any novelty:

> RAI headquarters in Saxa Rubra give the impression of contravening the laws of time. Everything seems immobile, frozen, and hibernated. Tg2, full of talented journalists, is at its historic low point. The journalists accuse Mimun, their director, of being unable to carry on a correct working relationship with them, of having a certain inclination toward *lottizzazione* logic, and of expressing open favoritism toward those who are politically protected by the *Polo*. Above them all, above Tg2, the ghost of Bettino Craxi is still floating around. Here, the first republic meets the second.[98]

This was the impression that I got myself, walking through the halls of the various news production departments on different occasions between the fall of 1996 and the summer of 2002. Journalists, especially at Tg2, still used to refer to their colleagues as "Communists," "Socialists," or "Christian Democrats." The old parties had ceased to exist, but there were still those who identified themselves with one or the other group. One of my respondents, Roberto Mastroianni, expressed well this feeling of anachronism: "There are people in RAI who are like the last loyalists to the Japanese Emperor: they keep fighting to be loyal to their emperor against the dirty American, without realizing that the war is over."[99] He was right. Clearly, the "old" way of doing things inside the public broadcaster had not disappeared with the end of the old parties. RAI journalists knew well that the system of party reference, the direct line from the newsroom to the new party's secretariat, was still the preferred way to get a career advancement or support a friend's hiring.

The new appointments to directorates and vice-directorates of news and channels were opposed not only by the progressive press (like *La Repubblica*, always harsh against Berlusconi) and the moderate press (like *La Stampa* and *Corriere della Sera*, this latter traditionally more conservative); opposition came also from inside the winning coalition itself. Umberto Bossi, leader of the Northern League, accused his ally Silvio Berlusconi of fully controlling six national channels, a "confirmation," Bossi declared, "that in Italy there is not just *lottizzazione*, but rather an absolute monarchy over information."[100] But the spirit of this declaration is to be questioned. The partition of seats along party lines had become so much a part of the politicians' conception of power and politics, of their most intimate psychology, that the ones who, like Bossi, did not get their men in the positions they wanted accused the others of *lottizzazione*. Paradoxically, the only solution to *lottizzazione* seemed to be an even more complete, an ideally perfect *lottizzazione*. In this regard, a commentator wrote, "Condemnation of *lottizzazione* will continue in the name of a more perfect *lottizzazione*, and everybody will continue to do it, while, at the same time, hating it."[101]

Meanwhile, Berlusconi's conflict of interest between his media empire and his new position as prime minister became increasingly more problematic: it became the "lead on the wings" of his first government, as *Corriere della Sera* wrote in June 1994.[102] Berlusconi divested some of his financial share of Fininvest, but retained majority ownership, and the three TV networks remained Fininvest property. The lead was heavy enough to bring Berlusconi down only a few months after his investiture, in the fall of 1994.

More Victory for Berlusconi: The 1995 Referendum

The menace to democratic practice represented by a situation in which Silvio Berlusconi could potentially control three public channels and three private channels called for a revision of the 1990 broadcasting law. In 1994, the PDS proposed that no single operator should own more than one national broadcasting channel. The intent was to limit the duopoly over advertising revenues, avoid the consolidation of dominant positions, and deny any privilege to the public broadcaster. This plan, similar to one presented by the Popular Party, the heirs to the DC, and one by the *Lega Nord*, proposed that RAI would have only one national broadcasting channel, paid for by advertising revenues, and one regional channel, without advertising and supported only by the license fee. However, this plan was never implemented.

On June 11, 1995, referenda were held to decide twelve different controversial issues in Italian politics, four of which pertained to broadcasting policy. Before the referenda, Berlusconi used his television channels to conduct publicity campaigns hoping to prevent the position of the Democratic Party of the Left (PDS) from winning. He was successful, and his positions were supported on all four counts. Italians voted "no" to limit individuals to the ownership of one television channel; "no" to do away with advertising breaks during televised films; "no" to limit the activities of advertising companies (such as Publitalia, a Fininvest company) to two national channels; and "yes" to allow RAI to be privatized. The results undermined Constitutional Court sentence no. 420 of 1994, which had declared that the concentration of three national channels in the hands of one operator—legitimated by article 15 of the Mammì Law—was unconstitutional.

La RAI dell'Ulivo

The Moratti administration, appointed by the first Berlusconi government, led the public broadcaster for almost two years. In April 1996, the heterogeneous center-left alliance *L'Ulivo* (Olive Tree), dominated by the Democratic Party of the Left (PDS), and comprising the influential Popular Party (PPI, formed from the Christian Democrat left, numerous ex-Socialists, and the Greens) and Reconstructed Communism won the national elections.

In RAI, a new board of directors was appointed by the presidents of the Senate and the Chamber of Deputies. An intellectual close to the PDS, Enzo Siciliano, became president, and Franco Iseppi, close to the DC left wing, was appointed director-general.

The appointments were applauded by some, but, as usual, criticized by many. Among those favorable, the business daily *Il Sole 24 Ore* recognized the high cultural level of the new board and expressed satisfaction with the significant representation of women, which included Liliana Cavani, film director, Fiorenza Mursia, publisher, and Federica Olivares, manager. It was the first time in the history of RAI that women were the majority on the board. But the financial paper was mostly concerned with the ability of the directors to ensure the broadcaster's central role in the multimedia sector: echoing a concern expressed by others, *Il Sole 24 Ore* wondered how a board whose members knew very little about television (and whose president proudly claimed to never watch it) could face the challenges of an increasingly competitive media market.

As usual, criticism came from all directions. Some journalists argued that little had changed in RAI after the 1996 elections and that *lottizzazione* procedures were still in place:

> Even today any change, i.e., moving one journalist from one position to another, promotions, etc., must follow political criteria. There are various people of the PDS who are getting upset because, even if their loyalty to the party is well known, they have not received the advancement that they had expected from their party. They consider their party's intercession as a given. But the parties want people who can be manipu-

lated—The one who makes it is the one who is going to speak and perform as the parties want.[103]

Party affiliation continued to represent a powerful variable in hiring and career advancement, according to Rodolfo Brancoli, a well-known journalist who, for a brief period in 1996, was director of Tg1. He recalls having seen "a secretary at the director-general's office looking at a list of candidates for some positions. Next to each of those names there was the usual acronym of the party to which that person was affiliated, within parentheses."[104] Also, the partition of *telegiornali* across party lines remained almost intact after the center-left coalition won the elections. Tg1 retained its historic role as the government's news program; Tg2 went to the National Alliance, and generally, to the opposition *Polo delle Libertà*; while Tg3 remained in the hands of the PDS as the main party within the government coalition. In October 1996, data from the Media Observatory of the University of Pavia, in charge of monitoring airtime devoted to political leaders and coalitions on all national broadcasters, confirmed Tg2 and Tg3's affiliation: Tg2 gave almost 29 percent of its time to *Polo delle Libertà* and Tg3 devoted more than 30 percent to the government coalition. Tg1 gave 42 percent of its broadcasting time to the government.

Journalist guru Indro Montanelli also joined in to express his disappointment with the methods used by the presidents of the Senate and the Chamber of Deputies to elect the new board of RAI: according to him, the usual intense negotiations between coalitions, and among factions within each coalition, were a sign that the traditional methods were being implemented once more. In particular, Montanelli criticized the center-left government for having refused the proposal that a high commissioner be appointed to lead the broadcaster. This proposal, made by a member of the group *Comunisti Italiani*, envisioned a single quasi-CEO, head of the corporation, who would report directly to the president of the republic, and would thus be freed from any sort of relationship with the government of the day. But the proposal never went anywhere, because, as Montanelli suspected, the government needed more than one seat in order to place people on the RAI board.[105]

Not surprisingly, also according to *Forza Italia* and *Alleanza Nazionale*, the appointment of the board members, all of whom came from a center-left background, demonstrated the continuation of old practices. A journalist commented:

The weight of the parties must always be taken into consideration. Indeed, the parties haven't ceased to be parties just because they have changed their names. Certainly, *lottizzazione* is now less blatant than before; but how could anybody negate the importance of parties inside RAI and neglect their reactions?[106]

Once again, commentators on national dailies lamented that the "political system that brought Italy to the disaster should have been dead by now. Instead, one needs only to switch on the TV set to see that its ghost is still moving, giving orders, and judging."[107] Any genuine will to separate television from the influence of the political system was absent. The inability to approve legislation able to govern the market, rather than simply describe the situation as it was, had traditionally been the weakness of the Italian system. Solutions, as always, were sought in the appointment of new people, but there was little desire to implement structural changes. Lietta Tornabuoni wrote in the columns of the daily *La Stampa*:

> [I]t is not sufficient to put new people inside the corporation to change the rules of the game. Neither a director, nor a vice-director, nor a president, can really do much to improve the course and the programs on RAI. A person's good will is not enough: a real change needs structural interventions and profound mutations.[108]

She was right: the continuous reciprocal accusations among parties as well as the recurrent dances around the new appointments masked the weakness of the political system, its inability and unwillingness to produce concrete changes, and the substantial lack of any intention to separate the broadcaster from political power.

Programming

The second half of the 1990s marked a further homogenization of programs and genres between the public and the private broadcaster. RAI showed little ambition with regard to its public service role, and its offerings distinguished themselves from those on Mediaset channels only on rare occasions and extremely rarely during prime time. Critics contended that even the news programs had become increasingly similar to the ones on the commercial channels.[109] Also the number of public affairs programs was reduced, and some of them, like the famous *TV7*, were relegated to late night. Another example was Michele Santoro's public affairs production unit, *Tempo reale* (Real Time), inaugurated in 1994 and dismantled in 1996 when the popular journalist, the author of much of the fortune of RAI3, left the public broadcaster and went to work for Mediaset.

The public broadcaster also lacked any significant offering of domestic and European programming. Law 122 of 1998 required both national broadcasters, RAI and Mediaset, to devote a higher percentage of their revenues toward domestic and European production of audiovisuals. However, even though in 1999 23 percent of the annual fee was used to produce Italian and European audiovisual products, the Italian public service broadcaster was still producing less domestic fiction than other European broadcasters. After plummeting to a minimum of 220 hours per year in 1996, RAI's 1998 domestic production had reached only 357 hours versus 621 hours for France, 851 for Spain, and 1,321 hours for the United Kingdom. The domestic production of fiction and documentaries also decreased: formats imported from overseas and entertainment abounded on all national channels. Lietta Tornabuoni was right when she noted in RAI a "real passion for appointments, and a total indifference to programs."[110]

The State of the Industry in the Late 1990s

By the end of 1996, full-time RAI employees numbered almost 11,000, excluding more than 1,000 part-timers. Of those full-time employees, 1,659 were journalists, 979 of whom worked in RAI regional news. Of the 10,955 employees, 1,018 were top managers and 382 were high-level executives. This high number of managerial and executive positions contradicted the corporation's claims that it was cutting administrative positions in favor of the news department given that the production of news programs was not increasing.

RAI maintained its audience leadership on the "average day" and in prime time, but the gap between the public and the commercial channels was steadily decreasing (from a difference of 18 percentage points in 1990-1991 to a difference of 2 percentage points in 2000-2001).[111]

Restructuring

RAI's internal organization was subjected to major changes throughout the 1990s. From a corporation controlled by IRI until 2000, the public broadcaster was transformed into a holding. After the restructuring of 1996, the corporation added a few new vice-directorates directly under the director-general: the vice general directorate for service and support (finances, control, business development), and another vice-directorate for production. Customer satisfaction, technical quality, and the RAI school (instituted in 1995 to train journalists and technicians) reported directly to the director-general. Financial conditions improved in the second half of the 1990s: from being heavily in debt in 1995 (700 billion lira) to an active balance of an estimated 100 billion lira in 2001.[112] The separation between the editorial and industrial divisions (1999) paved the way for the privatization of various services. In 1999, RAI established three digital thematic channels free-to-air (RAI Sport Satellite, RAI News 24, and RAI Educational) and its multimedia services (RAI Net) in an effort to direct interactive and multimedia services and strengthen RAI's role as content provider in the new media market. In 2001 RAI began offering additional services, such as the website RAI.it and RAI Med (RAI Mediterranean: a satellite channel broadcasting to Europe and the northern coast of Africa), and new pay services, such as RAI SAT Fiction. RAI Trade became the commercial branch with the task of overseeing the distribution of RAI programs and copyrights in the international market.

A Change of Leadership

Critiques against Siciliano's leadership intensified in the winter of 1997-1998, when RAI's president was rebuked for not knowing enough about television and for having an elitist conception of the role of public service media. His administration was accused by the right of a supposedly center-left bias, but was accused by left parties, like Reconstructed Communism, of being too moderate. Siciliano finally resigned in January 1998, and his resignation anticipated the government crisis to follow. Indeed, accused of not being able to deliver on its promises of institutional reforms and economic improvements, the Prodi government lost the support of some of its constituents and fell in the autumn of 1998.

In the absence of new legislation, the presidents of the Senate and the Chamber of Deputies appointed the five members of the new board: the new president, Roberto Zaccaria, left DC, was a university professor of law, and had been a member of RAI's board of directors for many years; Stefano Balassone was very close to Alessandro Guglielmi, the former director of RAI3; Vittorio Emiliani, former director of the daily *Il Messaggero*, was close to the Green Party; Giampiero Gamaleri, university professor, was connected to *Alleanza Nazionale*; and Alberto Contri, was associated with *Forza Italia*. Pier Luigi Celli, from the PDS area, became the new director-general. The separation of the news along party lines continued: according to the Observatory of the University of Pavia, in May 1998, Tg1 gave 68 percent of total airtime to the *Ulivo* coalition; Tg2 gave 38 percent to the opposition and 62 percent to the government coalition; and Tg3 allocated 24 percent of its news time to the opposition and 76 percent to the government coalition.

Among public affairs programs, it is important to mention the pro-*Polo* talk show hosted by journalist Bruno Vespa, *Porta a porta* (Door to Door), aired on prime time on RAI1 five nights a week. Michele Santoro came back to RAI after his 1996 exodus to Mediaset with new talk shows, including *Sciuscià*, which started in 2000, a kind of investigative journalism where much attention was given to sensationalistic and dramatic elements to capture the audience. Another talk show, *Il raggio verde* (The Green Ray, 2001), was fiercely attacked by the center-right government because of its allegedly anti-Berlusconi stance during the election campaign of spring 2001.

La RAI della Destra

After Berlusconi won the May 2001 elections, he did not push for a change of RAI's board of directors right away, even though RAI's leadership lamented pressures from his government. President Zaccaria complained that "the independence of the corporation [was] under attack," and that RAI could not offer pluralist and balanced information because of the "continuous government scrutiny."[113] Others, instead, did not notice any significant difference between the center-left and the center-right governments and their respective influence over the public broadcaster. The director of RAI2, Carlo Freccero, regretted that the old *lottizzazione* was over, because at least there had been different voices. Nowadays, he lamented, "Television has to wear a condom, and the differences that once characterized our system have by now disappeared and been replaced by a tempered middle way, a climate of generalized consensus that is shared by the left as well as by the right."[114] Others agreed: one reason why Berlusconi did not immediately change the board and news directors was that he did not need to do so, as RAI had become bipartisan, producing programs that were rarely controversial and trying to please the left as well as the right, in a world where "diversities were increasingly looked at as a real threat."[115] In reality, some programs had clearly upset the prime minister, especially during the preelection months in the spring of 2001. When in January 2002 the mandate of the old board of directors was finally expiring, Berlusconi declared that "public television had been taken hostage by the partisan left and used against [himself]."[116]

In February 2002, a new board of directors was appointed with former Judge of the Constitutional Court Antonio Baldassarre as president. The appointments were decided after the usual lengthy negotiations among all the parties inside the government majority and between this and the opposition. Berlusconi wanted Carlo Rossella, the director of *Panorama*, one of the prime minister's magazines, to become president of RAI. In the end, Rossella was perceived as too close to Mediaset and therefore put aside. RAI veteran Agostino Saccà, previously director of personnel, was appointed director-general.

If the professors' RAI and the RAI of Moratti's administration had both tried to break with the past, at least in words, the RAI of the center-left and the post-2001 center-right RAI—also referred to as a "monstrous synthesis of RAI and Fininvest," or "Rainvest"—were more blatant about their political and party affiliation. As a commentator wrote in the daily *La Stampa*, there were "many RAI but one unchangeable reality: their dependence on the parties."[117] And if during the era of the professors and Moratti it was not politically correct to talk about journalists' party cards and their political identity was loosely defined in terms of "areas" and "backgrounds," the RAI of the center-right did not seem to have problems with clearly identifying the parties it wanted represented inside the broadcaster. In winter 2002, Maurizio Gasparri, the minister of communications, stated that the moment had come to "stop flying and come back on earth. Let's forget the *super partes* [above parts] journalists," he declared, "we prefer the ones who are loyal."[118] And loyal people they got—like Fabrizio Del Noce, the new director of RAI1, who had been elected senator in 1994 on the ticket of *Forza Italia*, Berlusconi's party; or like Antonio Marano, director of RAI2, who "is the *Lega Nord*, as *Lega Nord* reflects itself in Antonio Marano";[119] or like Tg2's director, Mauro Mazza, through whom the second public Tg was secured in the hands of the *Alleanza Nazionale*. The impact of the new course on programming was soon felt, as journalists disliked by the right were put aside. For instance, soon after Berlusconi, during an official visit in Bulgaria in the spring of 2003, accused both Enzo Biagi, author and host of a famous public affairs program on RAI1, and Michele Santoro, author and host of other popular programs on RAI3 and RAI2, of "doing a criminal use of television," the two journalists were clamorously denied renewal of their contracts for television season 2002-2003.[120] Talking about this case, the president of the RAI Parliamentary Committee, Claudio Petruccioli, lamented that: "each voice that RAI loses is a loss for pluralism."[121] On one hand, Biagi and Santoro's case was soon taken as an example of the "old" RAI, of the tradition of quality and partisan journalism that Italians respected; on the other hand, their marginalization was a sign of what was going to happen to the public broadcaster in the Berlusconi era. Many argued that the decisions to remove those popular and acclaimed journalists were the result of a precise plan to diminish the role of RAI, particularly of its information services, to the advantage of Mediaset channels. Moreover, the continuous interference of the government in programming—in the fall of 2002, RAI's director refused to show episodes of a satire program poking fun at the prime minister—resulted in problems within the board of directors itself. By the end of 2002, three members of the board had already quit to protest policies that they said made public broadcasting less competitive against the rival network. Things only got worse during the first months of 2003: after RAI clamorously failed to provide live reporting of Hans Blix's testimony on the search for forbidden weapons in Iraq in front of the United Nations Security Council in February 2003 and of the antiwar rallies in various Italian cities in the same month, the remaining two members of the board, supporters of Silvio Berlusconi, resigned under intense pressure from public opinion, political opposition, and even from the governing parties. The public broadcaster was left without leadership and in complete shambles.

The sense that the Berlusconi government was purposefully running public television into the ground for the benefit of the prime minister's private interests in the television business was reinforced by an analysis of the conditions of RAI in its first two years of center-right administration. In a market in which the overall television audience grew (in 2002-2003 the average number of viewers during prime time was 27,300,000, 800,000 more than the previous season), RAI's share suffered. Even though RAI1 maintained its primacy on the average day, Canale5 won the competition in the most lucrative time slot (24.9 percent share for Canale5, 23.2 percent for RAI1). All three public channels lost ground in prime time: during the first months of 2003, their total share went down to 43.9 percent, from 46 percent in the 2001-2002 season, and 47.1 percent in 2000-2001.[122] The decision to eliminate Biagi and Santoro from the schedule certainly had an impact on the audience share. During the 2002-2003 season, the program that replaced Enzo Biagi's *Il fatto* in its prime-time slot lost the competition with the popular *Striscia la notizia* (Strip News) on Canale5, which gained 5 percentage points. RAI2 suffered the most without Santoro, losing 10 percent of its share on the average day and 12 percent of its audience in prime time.

RAI's finances also suffered: from a surplus of 95 million euros in 2000, the public broadcaster accumulated a deficit of 190 million euros in 2003. Advertising revenues also declined during the first months of 2003: 7 percentage points were lost in February while 15 percentage points were lost in March.[123]

In March 2003, RAI's leadership was completely renewed, and attempts were made to ensure the independence of the new board. Lucia Annunziata, former press journalist, ex-director of Tg3, and close to the area of the *Democratici di Sinistra*, was nominated president. The four members of the board were chosen among intellectuals and academicians gravitating around the center-right coalition. The director-general's seat, traditionally a fief of the government party, was assigned to Flavio Cattaneo, close to the *Alleanza Nazionale*, but also appreciated by the *Lega Nord* and a personal friend of the Berlusconi family, in particular of Paolo, Silvio's brother. Many rejoiced at the appointment of Annunziata, considered by far one of the best possible choices—a female journalist with vast experience as a press and television reporter. But many saw the trap of a strategy that was designed to quench the opposition's critiques against Berlusconi's iron fist in the information sector without, however, making substantial changes. In this regard, prominent intellectual Paolo Flores d'Arcais defined the composition of the new board—a left-wing president surrounded by four center and right-wing board members—as an "authoritarian Bulgarian-like solution, one that will ultimately ensure complete control over the television system."[124]

Since the appointments of winter 2002, only RAI3 remained under the auspices of the center-left, and was repeatedly accused by the head of the government of being partisan and opinionated. A worrisome example of the quasi-censorship climate reigning in RAI was when, after an edition of Tg3 in May 2003 paused on the image of a protester shouting anti-Berlusconi slogans outside the Milan tribunal where the prime minister was on trial for bribery charges, RAI's director-general sent officials of the internal auditing division to the Tg3 newsroom to control tapes of the newscast, interrogate journalists and reporters, and question Tg3's director about his editorial decision.

The opposition, as usual, cried out against the "complete occupation of RAI on the part of Berlusconi." But it is undeniable that the center-left coalition bears a large part of the responsibility for not having been able, during the four years in power from 1996 to 2001, to pass a law that would have regulated the broadcasting and telecommunications system and the conflict of interests between public office and media ownership.

Notes

1. Elaboration on data from Francesco Siliato, *L'Antenna dei padroni* (Milan: Gabriele Mazzotta Editore, 1977), 101; and from table 49 *Sviluppo delle televisioni private. 1972-1977*, in the "Mezzi di comunicazione" section of the Data Bank Compact Disc included with *Guida all'Italia contemporanea*, ed. Massimo Firpo, Nicola Tranfaglia, and Pier Giorgio Zunino (Milan: Garzanti, 1998).

2. Data gathered from RAI, Radiotelevione Italiana, *Annuari RAI, 1988-1989*, 16.

3. Data from Francesco Pinto, *Il modello televisivo. Professionalità e politica da Bernabei alla terza rete* (Milan: Feltrinelli, 1980), 189.

4. As a comparison, in 1970 circulation numbers of daily papers in the United Kingdom was 45 per 100 inhabitants, and 43 in 1979; in France it was 24 copies, down to 20 copies in 1979; and in Germany, 32 copies in 1970, 41 in 1979. Data from Enzo Cheli, quoted by Edoardo Novelli, *Dalla TV di partito, al partito della TV televisione e politica in Italia 1960-1995* (Florence: La Nuova Italia, 1995), 201.

5. Data from table 42 *Tiratura dei quotidiani (dato per 100 abitanti). Alcuni paesi europei. 1970-1990*, in the "Scuola e istruzione" section of the Data Bank Compact Disc included with *Guida all'Italia contemporanea*, 1998.

6. Divisione Affari Generali Documentazione e Studi, RAI, Radio Televisione Italiana, "Televisione 1975-1986. Programmi a diffusione nazionale," in *Annuario RAI, 1988-1989*, xxix-xxx.

7. Alberto Severi, interview with author, tape recording, RAI headquarters, Saxa Rubra, Rome, March 11, 1998.

8. Piero De Chiara, interview with author, tape recording, Olivetti Foundation, Rome, April 3, 1998.

9. De Chiara, interview cit.
10. De Chiara, interview cit.
11. De Chiara, interview cit.
12. The decree was named the Berlusconi decree to indicate that it was promulgated to accommodate Fininvest's interests.
13. See Marco Gambaro and Francesco Silva, *Economia della televisione* (Bologna: Il Mulino, 1992), 159.
14. De Chiara, interview cit.
15. De Chiara, interview cit.
16. Italo Moretti, interview with author, tape recording, RAI headquarters, Rome, March 1998.
17. In the 1980s, the *aziendalisti* were those who reflected the tradition of the 1950s *aziendalisti*, characterized by loyalty to the corporation and a commitment to the public service.
18. Roberto Mastroianni, interview with author, tape recording, RAI headquarters, Via Mazzini, Rome, January 1998.
19. Paolo Murialdi, "Per una ricerca sulla lottizzazione" (Notes toward a Research on *lottizzazione*), *Problemi dell'informazione*, 22, no. 1 (March 1997), no page number available.
20. Enzo Forcella in Laura Delli Colli, "Ottanta nomine in arrivo alla RAI," in *La Repubblica* (Rome), February 29, 1987.
21. Forcella in Delli Colli, "Ottanta nomine in arrivo alla RAI."
22. De Chiara, interview cit.
23. De Chiara, interview cit.
24. Enzo Forcella, "E adesso i comunisti hanno il Tg1," in *La Repubblica* (Rome), March 6, 1987.
25. Anonymous, "È stato il PRI a candidarmi per dimostrare che non vuole lottizzare," in *La Repubblica* (Rome), August 10, 1990.
26. Anonymous, "Dal clamore su Brenneke al caso Orfei: che strana coincidenza," in *La Repubblica* (Rome), August 10, 1990.
27. Anonymous, "Tutti i candidati a quelle poltrone," in *La Repubblica* (Rome), February 17, 1987.
28. Miriam Mafai, "Il miracolo della RAI-TV," in *La Repubblica* (Rome), August 11, 1990.
29. Forcella, "E adesso i comunisti hanno il Tg1."
30. De Chiara, interview cit.
31. De Chiara, interview cit.
32. De Chiara, interview cit.
33. Amused, De Chiara recalled that, together with Roberto Natale, the representative of Usigrai, they "spent one entire night composing the political affiliations of the finalists." When not sure about the party affiliation of a given candidate, they would guess or make it up to ensure a smooth hiring: "If one finalist was ever seen going to church, that would be an easy case as we would consider it a good enough evidence to put him into the DC quota. We had lots of fun!" De Chiara, interview cit.

34. Rodolfo Brancoli, director of Tg1 in 1996, director of the magazine *Liberal* at time of interview, interview with author, tape recording, *Liberal*'s headquarters, Rome, March 1998.

35. Data gathered from Walter Veltroni, *Io e Berlusconi (e la RAI)* (Rome: Editori Riuniti, 1990), 150.

36. Reality TV focused on real life events (court hearings, in particular), without the sensationalist element that characterized the later development of the genre across Europe and the United States.

37. Many Socialist journalists went from RAI to Fininvest. One of the most famous was Enrico Mentana, from Tg2, who in 1992 became director of Tg5, the news on Canale5.

38. Law no. 223, August 6, 1990, *Disciplina del sistema radiotelevisivo pubblico e privato* (Discipline of the Public and Private Broadcasting Sector), Title 1, Art. 1 (General Principles).

39. The almost one thousand private television stations ended up being the losers. The *Federazione Radio Televisioni* (a national federation of radio and television stations) condemned the 1990 law warning that, for effect of market concentration, 60 percent of television stations would close down their operations. "Così si dichiara la chiusura di seicento emittenti italiane," in *La Repubblica* (Rome), August 10, 1990.

40. For more details, see Roberto Zaccaria, ed., "Radiotelevisione," vol. 2, *Trattato di diritto amministrativo* (Padua: Cedam, 1996), 8-9.

41. Loredana Bartoletti, "RAI, la carica dei vice. Radio e telegiornali, c'è posto per tutti," in *La Repubblica* (Rome), September 19, 1990.

42. Maurizio Ricci, "Alla RAI nasce la lottizzazione a ore," in *La Repubblica* (Rome), August 10, 1990.

43. Mario Pastore, "Chi comanda alla RAI-TV," in *La Repubblica* (Rome), October 10, 1990.

44. Giorgio Bocca, "I lottizzati della RAI," in *La Repubblica* (Rome), October 20, 1990.

45. Eugenio Scalfari, "Lo sgomento del paese," in *La Repubblica* (Rome), May 8, 1991.

46. *Annuario RAI 1990-1991*, 34.

47. Giovanni Cesareo discusses this phenomenon in his essay, "Televisione," in *La cultura italiana del Novecento*, ed. Corrado Stajano (Bari: Laterza, 1997), 766.

48. Ugo Intini, quoted in Sandra Bonsanti, "Alla RAI voltiamo pagina. Il PSI butta sul tavolo della verifica il tema-Tv," in *La Repubblica* (Rome), January 30, 1991.

49. Populism, endorsed by "yuppie" Socialists during the 1980s, was at the foundation of the so-called Ideologia Milanese. Indeed, the Milanese ideology, which represented the cultural context in the north favorable to both Craxi's and Berlusconi's success in the 1980s, was characterized by "a mix of hatred of political life; mistrust of the state; contempt for abstract rules (and again for the state which inevitably produces lots of abstract rules); and the preference for

concrete pragmatism always aiming to find solutions outside the sphere of principles and regulations." Ernesto Galli Della Loggia, quoted in Eugenio Scalfari, "La vittoria del partito azienda," in *La Repubblica* (Rome), August 4, 1994.

50. Ugo Intini, quoted in Sandra Bonsanti, "Alla RAI voltiamo pagina," *La Repubblica* (Rome), January 30, 1991.

51. Vincenzo Vita (former head of the PCI mass media division) quoted in Bonsanti, "Alla RAI voltiamo pagina," in *La Repubblica* (Rome), January 30, 1991.

52. Bogi, vice secretary of the PRI, and Sandro Fontana, DC, director of the newspaper *Il Popolo*, quoted in Sandra Bonsanti, "Alla RAI voltiamo pagina," in *La Repubblica* (Rome), January 30, 1991.

53. Bruno Vespa, quoted in Corrado Ruggeri, "Vespa: il mio editore si chiama DC," in *Corriere della Sera* (Milan), April 9, 1992.

54. Paolo Conti and Fernando Proietti, "La scossa elettorale fa tremare il villaggio RAI," in *Corriere della Sera* (Milan), April 15, 1992.

55. Giorgio La Malfa, quoted by Conti and Proietti, "La scossa elettorale fa tremare il villaggio RAI," in *Corriere della Sera* (Milan), April 15, 1992. The live broadcast was on April 6, 1992.

56. Concita De Gregorio, "Primo della classe col vizio di Forlani," in *La Repubblica* (Rome), February 4, 1993.

57. Giovanni Valentini, "Addio al Tg di regime," in *La Repubblica* (Rome), February 4, 1993.

58. By comparison, in 1995 Fininvest counted 12,400 employees, including the Mondadori group. Fininvest channels alone counted 3,300 employees, of whom 300 were journalists. Data from Maria Grazia Bruzzone, *L'Avventurosa storia del TG in Italia dall'avvento della televisione a oggi* (Milan: RCS Libri S.p.A., 2002), 370.

59. Law no. 206, June, 25, 1993: *Disposizioni sulla società concessionaria del servizio pubblico radiotelevisivo* (Dispositions regarding the public service broadcaster), art. 2, "The Board of Directors."

60. Giovanni Valentini, "La RAI dei cittadini," in *La Repubblica* (Rome), October 1, 1993.

61. Data from *Annuario RAI, 1995-1996* (Rome: ERI, 1996), 110.

62. Data from *Annuario RAI, 1995-1996*, 24.

63. Data from *Annuario RAI, 1994* (Turin: Nuova ERI edizioni RAI Radi Televisione Italiana, 1995), 59.

64. Data from *Annuario RAI, 1995-1996*, 203.

65. Telemontecarlo had an audience share of 0.7 percent. These data are from *Annuario RAI 1997-1998*, 44.

66. Francesco Siliato, telephone interview with author, October 3, 2001.

67. Loredana Bartoletti, "Ecco la nuova squadra di Demattè: I miei direttori saranno i capicantiere della ricostruzione," in *La Repubblica* (Rome), October 23, 1993.

68. Usigrai representative, quoted in Bartoletti, "Ecco la nuova squadra di Demattè."

69. Enrico Manca, quoted in "Accuse e polemiche sulle nominee RAI; C'è chi rimpiange le lottizzazioni," in *La Stampa* (Turin), October 24, 1993.
70. Achille Occhetto quoted in "Accuse e polemiche sulle nomine RAI."
71. Anonymous, "Giornalismo all'inglese? No grazie siamo italiani," in *La Repubblica* (Rome), August 18, 1993.
72. Giorgio Bocca, quoted in Anonymous, "Giornalismo all'inglese?"
73. Tullio Gregory, quoted in Anonymous, "Giornalismo all'inglese?"
74. See Paolo Murialdi, *Maledetti "Professori"* (Milan: Rizzoli, 1994), 32.
75. Demetrio Volcic, quoted in Enrico Singer, "Ecco le mie notizie senza etichette politiche," in *La Stampa* (Turin), September 16, 1993.
76. Roberto Natale, interview with author, tape recording, Usigrai headquarters, Saxa Rubra, Rome, March 1998.
77. Natale, interview cit.
78. Francesco Siliato, media expert, interview with author, tape recording, Milan, January 31, 1998.
79. Roberto Mastroianni, interview with author, tape recording, RAI headquarters, Via Mazzini, Rome, January 1998.
80. Mastroianni, interview cit.
81. Enzo Forcella, telephone interview with author, December 6, 1996.
82. Alessandro Curzi, quoted by Anonymous, "Giubilo sotto choc 'È stato un colpo chissà se di fortuna'," in *La Repubblica* (Rome), October 23, 1993.
83. Ombretta Fumagalli Carulli (DC politician) accused RAI of being in the hands of the PDS: "It has become clear by now that the public broadcaster has become the PDS megaphone as that party got most of the seats in the last round of appointments." Fumagalli Carulli, quoted in "La DC si sente tradita 'Viale Mazzini ai rossi'," in *La Repubblica* (Rome), December 16, 1993.
84. *Annuario RAI, 1994-1995*, 6.
85. *Annuario RAI, 1994-1995*, 6.
86. *Annuario RAI, 1997*, 98-99.
87. Unidentified other competitors shared 5.4 percent of total advertising resources in 1994 (data from *Annuario RAI 1995-1996*, 138).
88. In the same year in the United States 37.5 percent of advertising revenues went to television, 11 percent to radio, and 37.1 percent to newspapers; in Japan, 41.8 percent to TV, 5.4 to radio, and 28.9 to newspapers. Data from *Annuario RAI 1995-1996*, 138-139 and 143.
89. Data on RAI's personnel and subscriptions from *Annuario RAI 1995-1996*, 210-211.
90. Saverio Vertone, "Repubblica nuova, vecchia TV," in *Corriere della Sera* (Milan), January 26, 1994.
91. Corrado Ruggieri, "L'ira di Saxa Rubra finisce in sciopero," in *Corriere della Sera* (Milan), September 20, 1994.
92. Mattioli, interview cit.
93. Beppe Giulietti, quoted in "E Del Noce scavalca in critiche anche Giulietti," *Corriere della Sera* (Milan), January 16, 1996.

94. Anonymous, "Metà Caf, metà Biscione ecco la RAI 'rinnovata'," in *La Repubblica* (Rome), August 31, 1994.

95. Enzo Biagi, RAI journalist, quoted by Fabrizio Ravelli in "Lottizzano peggio di prima," in *La Repubblica* (Rome), November 2, 1994.

96. Giovanni Valentini, "Macerie televisive," in *La Repubblica* (Rome), November 2, 1994.

97. Sergio Romano, "I Manager e l'aria romana," in *La Stampa* (Turin), November 2, 1994.

98. Nello Ajello, "Il tempo si è fermato sull'ora di Bettino," in *La Repubblica* (Rome), February 28, 1995.

99. Mastroianni, interview cit.

100. Official communiqué from the Northern League, quoted in Gianluigi Rold, "Bossi: rifare tutto. Scoppia il caso Del Noce," in *Corriere della Sera* (Milan), September 20, 1994.

101. Saverio Vertone, "Il senatur e la rosa sfiorita," in *Corriere della Sera* (Milan), September 19, 1994.

102. Guido Gentili, "La vera anomalia," in *Corriere della Sera* (Milan), June 8, 1994.

103. Sandro Petrone, interview with author, tape recording, Tg2 newsroom, Saxa Rubra, Rome, January 8, 1998.

104. Brancoli, interview with author, tape recording, *Liberal*'s headquarters, Rome, March 1998.

105. Indro Montanelli, "Che delusione," in *Corriere della Sera* (Milan), July 9, 1996. Rodolfo Brancoli also supported the notion to create a high commissioner in charge of RAI. See Brancoli, "No, non è la Banca d'Italia," in *Corriere della Sera* (Milan), July 2, 1996.

106. Stefano Tomassini, interview with author, tape recording, RAI headquarters, Saxa Rubra, Rome, January 1998.

107. Saverio Vertone, "Repubblica nuova, vecchia TV," in *Corriere della Sera* (Milan), January 26, 1994.

108. Lietta Tornabuoni, "Quel triste balletto della Tivù," in *La Stampa* (Turin), August 8, 1996.

109. See Bruzzone, *L'avventurosa storia del TG*, 437-514.

110. Tornabuoni, "Quel triste balletto."

111. Elaborations from "Stagioni televisive individui Giorno Medio Share," Studio Frasi, Milan.

112. RAI (2001), *Il Bilancio 2000. La situazione economica e finanziaria* (The financial and economic situation 2000). Available on the RAI website (under "Azienda") at www.ufficiostampa.rai.it/.

113. Roberto Zaccaria, quoted in Roberto Ippolito, "Troppi condizionamenti soffocano le news RAI," in *La Stampa* (Turin), October 20, 2001.

114. Carlo Freccero, quoted in Fulvia Caprara, "Il conduttore torna su RAI2 con 'Sciuscià' edizione straordinaria," in *La Stampa* (Turin), November 13, 2001.

115. Freccero, "Il conduttore torna su RAI2."

116. No author, "TV & politica-RAI in mano alla sinistra? Scontro premier Zaccaria," in *Il Sole 24 Ore* (Milan), January 31, 2002.

117. Pierluigi Battista, "Dalla prima repubblica ai professori, dal super-ulivismo di Zaccaria al centro-destra. A caccia del nuovo che non esiste," in *La Stampa* (Turin), April 17, 2002.

118. Maurizio Gasparri, quoted in Augusto Minzolini, "La 'svolta' nelle trattative," in *La Stampa* (Turin), February 13, 2002.

119. Battista, "Dalla prima repubblica."

120. In the spring of 2003, RAI offered Santoro the opportunity to work again, but only on the condition that his public affairs program would be broadcast either at 2 in the afternoon, or at 1 o'clock in the morning, instead of its regular prime-time slot. Clearly, Santoro did not accept the offer.

121. Petruccioli, quoted in Maria Grazia Bruzzone, "Ogni giorno che passa un calo di prestigio," in *La Stampa* (Turin), June 6, 2003.

122. Data from Francesco Siliato, "I risultati delle reti-Conclusa la stagione 2002-2003: RAI1 leader nell'intera giornata, Canale5 nel prime time; Il pubblico televisivo cresce ancora," in *Il Sole 24 Ore* (Milan), June 3, 2003.

123. Data from Bruzzone, "Coro di consensi per la nomina, Mentana si distingue: 'Scelta tutta interna al centrodestra'," in *La Stampa* (Turin), March 15, 2003.

124. Flores d'Arcais, quoted in F. Mar., "Cofferati gelido: La sinistra farebbe meglio ad occuparsi di pace e non di lottizzazioni," in *La Stampa* (Turin), March 8, 2003.

Chapter 4

Lottizzazione: A Normal Practice for Public Service Journalists

> *I began my career more than half a century ago, when il duce was in power. Everyday, the ministry [of popular culture] sent us a memo telling us what was appropriate and what was inappropriate for publishing. Today, there are those who "interpret" without the need to be given orders, and there is a diffused tendency not to bother anybody.*[1]

The institution of public service broadcasting and the political culture in which it evolved (the "blocked democracy"[2] and the party system) created a terrain conducive to *lottizzazione*, which was then legitimated, explained, and rationalized theoretically. But for *lottizzazione* to become an "organic ideology" it must also touch everyday common sense. As Antonio Gramsci wrote, "The coherence and organic historical effectiveness of such an ideology can only be found when and where philosophical currents enter into, modify and transform the practical, everyday consciousness."[3] This chapter highlights how *lottizzazione* has become common sense, modified and transformed, normalized, as it were, to the point that it has become impalpable, taken for granted, almost an unconscious presence within the professional ideology of public service journalists. In particular, this chapter investigates journalists' experience: How has *lottizzazione* been experienced and perceived by people inside the system? What, according to them, is the nature of the problem (if it is a problem)? How has *lottizzazione* affected their jobs? As I expected, the Spada versus Murialdi debate represents the range of possible positions inside and outside the broadcaster on the issue of *lottizzazione*. There are journalists who do not even see it, there are those who see it and do not think it is a problem at all, and there are those who see it and think that it is a problem for the broadcaster and for Italian democracy.

This chapter begins by giving special attention to the access to the profession, as a way to ensure initial selection of journalists who are "suitable for the job" (people who have a social, cultural, and political background in line with the accepted values required for the job). Through the interviews with practicing journalists, it delineates the consequences of *lottizzazione* for the profession and for the public broadcaster, its positive and negative sides. Finally, it considers whether or not *lottizzazione* has corrupted any ideal role for public service journalism within Italian democracy.

Access to the Profession

The First Decades

During the first decades of television broadcasting, journalists' entry into RAI was determined by political and social homogeneity with the government party. In some cases the broadcaster itself trained its journalists, who were chosen from among young intellectuals, often in line with the dominant ideology of the time. Candidates were selected upon the recommendations of political leaders and friends of the director-general and, only on rare occasions, they were selected from among the winners of national exams. Selection procedures, which consisted mostly of interviews, written and oral tests, and professional tests, were often fictitious, while determinant factors were personal and party connection and the "right" recommendation:

> Generously compensated, rigorously selected from the Christian Democratic press, . . . RAI journalists constituted a privileged group, extremely loyal to the corporation. Their homogeneity was controlled

from the beginning. First of all, national exams were rare. . . . More often the hiring was done ad personam, and because of it, the Christian Democratic Party was able to fill RAI with Christian Democratic journalists, and, during the phase of the center-left, with progressive Catholics. . . . Overall, more than professional abilities, a position in RAI required political loyalty.[4]

However, even though party connections and "political loyalty" were valuable currencies, the political area of journalists' affiliations was broadly defined. More than strict party affiliation the important requirement was the candidate's political and cultural affinity with the dominant ideology. In other words, being a moderate, progovernment fellow was good enough. For instance, during his tenure as RAI director-general, Ettore Bernabei made sure that the new hires were "good Christians,"[5] but that did not necessarily mean that all potential employees had to have a DC party card, nor that valuable, promising applicants from other political areas were left out. As former Tg2 foreign correspondent Francesco Mattioli recalls,

[W]hen I was hired in RAI in 1968, *lottizzazione* was already evident, and everybody knew that there were people who were going to get in, no matter how badly they might do at the exams [or interviews]. Indeed, Bernabei hired everybody who was proposed by the Christian Democratic party. But he was smart enough to reserve a small quota of spaces for journalists who were not Christian Democrats, or were only loosely associated with the party.[6]

Mattioli demonstrates a widespread sense of respect for the former head of RAI when he notices that "Bernabei continuously showed disdain toward those journalists who were mere servants of the regime and was able to surround himself with valid professionals."[7] Others share similar memories: it is true that Bernabei inflated the structures of the broadcaster to create jobs and appease the various currents of the DC, but he also had an eye for creative, intelligent people. The power he had and the freedom he enjoyed to function independently from strict party logic allowed the director-general to gradually open the broadcaster to the Socialists. As Bernabei himself puts it, he used to hire "Christian Democrats, Social Democrats, Liberals, Socialists, and Communists. All of them with only one condition: that they were good!"[8]

The 1970s and 1980s

As the relationship between the Socialist Party (PSI) and the Communist Party (PCI) worsened in the late 1970s and early 1980s, and competition with private TV channels intensified, the partition of RAI on the basis of political party affiliation became stricter, more carefully detailed, and closely scrutinized. Rather than just a loosely defined affinity with the dominant ideology, an unyielding adherence to party politics became an absolute prerequisite. As a respondent put it, at times "they even wanted to see your party identification card."[9] In the 1980s, when the two news programs (Tg1 and Tg2) became respectively more identifiable with the Christian Democrats' and the Socialists' news, the party secretariats became particularly concerned about hiring journalists of proven loyalty as competition between the two Tgs intensified.

Journalism Schools

But if ideological affinity first, and strict party affiliation later, were necessary requirements for any credible candidate, formal education was not. In the mid-1970s, for instance, only 30 percent of RAI's journalists had a master's degree. In the absence of professional schools (the first school for journalists was instituted in Milan in the late 1970s, but the first school for broadcast journalism was established only in 1992), the main training field for future broadcast journalists was the press, especially the party press. Up until the end of the 1980s the majority of RAI journalists were former press journalists and many of them came from upper-middle-class backgrounds.

Since the early 1990s, new schools have been created. Through the years, they have provided formal training to aspiring journalists and also contributed to changing the demographics of the workforce.[10] By 2003, ten schools had been approved by the National Order of Journalists. Most of them were located in the north and center north (Milan and Bologna), and in the center (Rome, Urbino, and Perugia—this latter founded by RAI and the University of Perugia to educate future broadcasting and multimedia journalists and for the in-job training of RAI personnel). One school was in the south (Scuola di Giornalismo "Suor Orsola Benincasa" in Naples), and one in Sicily (Scuola di Giornalismo e Ufficio Stampa at the University of Palermo).[11] Schools only offer a limited number of openings each year, therefore there is a strict selection process to get in.

Prerequisites are a master's degree and excellent knowledge of the English language. Additional credits are granted for previous journalistic experience.

What Employment Opportunities Are There for Journalism School Graduates?

In an attempt to depoliticize the recruitment process, the main union of RAI journalists, Usigrai, has strongly supported the hiring of graduates from journalism schools. However, the job shortage has created an overabundance of professional journalists on the market; indeed, the union's promise that by the year 2000 the first two years' graduates from the Perugia school would be hired by RAI was not fulfilled.[12] In fact, according to data from the *Istituto Nazionale Previdenza Giornalisti Italiani* (the National Retirement Fund for Journalists) and other data from the Perugia journalism school, only 10 percent of the Perugia graduates landed a job in RAI.

Nevertheless, the efforts to introduce objective criteria, including university degrees, certainly had an impact on the overall characteristics of RAI's workforce (even though, of course, those criteria do not necessarily rule out the relevance of party affiliation and nepotism in determining who is going to be hired). As a whole, Italian journalists are better educated than they were before. For instance, in 1995 between 70 and 80 percent of them either had a university degree or were university students.[13] This trend is also reflected in the composition of the RAI workforce. During the 1990s, the educational background of RAI employees, across qualifications, improved considerably, and with it, also came more gender diversification. Out of a total of 11,809 employees[14] working for RAI in 1994, 14.4 percent were university graduates; of these, 14.5 percent were female. In 1996, 15.3 percent of a total of 10,995 employees were university graduates, while 16.1 percent of them were female.[15] Whereas in the early 1970s, female journalists represented only 4.2 percent of the total number of RAI journalists and were usually relegated to lower positions, through the years that percentage grew considerably. Out of a total of 1,634 journalists in 1998, 395, or 24.2 percent, were women; in 1999, the number of females increased to 406 (or 25.1 percent); in the year 2000, 428, or 25.8 percent of the 1,660 journalists, were female.[16] Whereas the number of journalists from 1998 to 2000 increased only 1.6 percent, the number of female journalists increased 8.4 percent. During the second half of the 1990s efforts were also made to have more women in the public broadcaster holding executive positions, including news directors and board members.[17]

Salaries

Salaries of RAI journalists have traditionally been privileged, not only compared to press journalists, but also to other professionals working for the public broadcaster. According to the 1972 national contract of the National Federation of the Italian Press (F.N.S.I.), the minimum annual salary for a RAI managing editor[18] was 536,500 lira, approximately 134,000 lira more than a journalist with the same qualifications working for the print media, 142,000 lira more than the maximum salary for an RAI television director (50 percent of whom at that time had a master's degree), and double the salary of an experienced cameraman.[19] Salaries continued to be higher than those paid to journalists working for the press and sometimes even higher than the salaries of those working for the commercial television broadcaster. In 1995, the average annual salary of an Italian journalist was approximately 45,000 euros; in the same year, a journalist working for RAI was making approximately 62,000 euros.[20] According to research done in 1997 by *Il Mondo*, weekly supplement of the daily *Corriere della Sera*, between 1995 and 1996 salaries of top journalists and managers of the public broadcaster were often higher than the salaries of Mediaset journalists of comparable rank.[21] In addition to higher salaries, until the mid-1990s a permanent job contract with RAI had that particular prized Italian status of a public service employee, with virtually guaranteed employment. Other privileges were the *indennità video* (a sort of extra fee granted for each appearance on camera, a fee that Mediaset journalists did not obtain until 2001), the fact that until recently certain positions could be passed over to one's child as inheritance, and the opportunity for journalists to access private pension funds earlier compared to other public sector workers.

Lottizzazione and Hiring Procedures

The Negative Sides

Besides "official" recruitment procedures, through the years the architects of party logics and the bureaucrats of *lottizzazione* carefully designed "parallel" highways defining hiring procedures and career advancement in RAI. How has that mechanism of access to the profession based on *lottizzazione* influenced the quality of RAI's workforce? Understandably, there is a general tendency to think that political restrictions on access have been detrimental. According to Piero De Chiara, responsible for the PCI mass media division during the 1980s, the mechanism based on party affiliation did not usually "guarantee that the best journalists were recruited in the long range."[22] In fact, he says, the mechanism of access and promotion based on purely political criteria have impoverished the corporation in the medium to long run, as layers over layers of journalists have accumulated through the years:

> When there is an opening that is reserved for a certain party, the corporation first calls the leader of that party. It invariably ends up that a certain journalist, formerly employed by the party paper, gets the job. The guy could be good, but he could also be not good. Party officials also get hired as RAI journalists. But it's the same thing: Sometimes, they end up being good journalists, sometimes, they don't.[23]

Sandro Petrone, journalist at Tg2, shares a similar negative judgment:

> What happened in RAI as a consequence of *lottizzazione* was that the journalists we had were not really the ones that the corporation needed. The only thing the corporation wanted was to hire somebody from the PSI; this was their primary goal; being a journalist or not was often a secondary concern. They hired people from the party press offices, from the party secretariats, they hired their own friends, children of the bankers with whom they had debts, etc. People were hired who came from all sorts of previous jobs. The real prerequisite was that once they were in they would represent the interests of the given party that had put them there.[24]

Not only the parties were determinant in establishing who would be hired, but they also had a say on career advancement. Indeed, a major problem was the proliferation of positions of responsibility that continued to be created through the early 1990s without having any real function rather than to please certain currents and political parties. Sandro Petrone shares a widespread frustration when he comments about the political maneuvering associated with career advancement:

> [I]n RAI, you also got promoted on the basis of political merit. Therefore, very often those who were promoted were not those who were

able to do television, but rather those who could show more loyalty to their own party. Loyalty to the party meant, specifically, that one had to distort the message, namely disregard any correct journalistic criteria. When such journalists, who had no idea of how to do television in the first place, became powerful, they destroyed, absolutely destroyed, any kind of technical and professional organization inside the corporation. They came from the press or, even worse, from nowhere, and had no idea of how to create a piece for television broadcasting. What they did was to stand in front of the camera and talk; the result was nothing other than some kind of televised political announcement.[25]

The number of directors and vice-directors increased with every change of government administrations and/or at every change of balance within any major party. On those occasions, directors and vice-directors were replaced by the new leadership without, however, losing either their title or their salary. Moreover, since jobs were, at least until the mid-1990s (since then Usigrai and the corporation have changed their policies and temporary contracts have become the norm for new hires) secured for life, the irreparable and consistent damage was that, once hired and/or promoted, people could neither be fired nor demoted.

The Positive Sides

There were also times, however, when hiring procedures based on party logic benefited the corporation. Given the high level of ideological confrontation during the 1970s and 1980s, and the opportunity, granted by the Reform Law of 1975, to have journalists representing all major political areas inside the broadcaster, the parties' secretariats, as well as the corporation, had a vast pool of aspiring journalists to choose from and were motivated to search for the best professionals available. At times, the quota system offered the possibility to recruit a variety of professional journalists coming from diverse backgrounds who brought into the broadcaster a wealth of alternative ideas and perspectives. There are cases when procedures based on *lottizzazione* encouraged the hiring of journalists such as Michele Santoro, who, from an anonymous small party paper in the south, was hired by RAI in the PCI quota and became, in a brief period, an innovator of talks shows and public affairs programs, obtaining critical recognition as well as high audience shares. Other famous names are usually mentioned as an indication of the "relative" goodness of *lottizzazione*. There are those who say that people such as

Arrigo Levi, Corrado Augias, Sergio Zavoli—the "big shots" of Italian journalism—would never have been hired without the *lottizzazione* system. Indeed, many agree that in earlier times *lottizzazione* had a selective function that was also based on quality. After the collapse of the party system in the early 1990s, though, things drastically changed, according to Paolo Giuntella, head of *Tg1 Speciale* (an in-depth supplement of Tg1):

> In the last few years, from the CAF [the Craxi-Andreotti-Forlani triumvirate, 1989-1992] on, promotions have been done based only on political reasons. In the earlier phases of lottizzazione, both the PCI and the DC were interested in having the best journalists around, and therefore they would call up top people from their respective newspapers to work here. From 1989 on, people have come to RAI not because they are good, but just because they are friends of this or that politician, they are the daughters of this or that, lovers of this or that, etc.[26]

External Collaborators and *Precari*

One way in which party logic often interferes in hiring procedures is through the lists of "external collaborators." Indeed, besides national examinations and the *ad personam* call, according to which a news director has the faculty, in special circumstances, to directly hire a certain journalist of his or her choice, RAI has a contractual obligation to hire journalists who have been working for a given number of years as "external collaborators" and are on a special list of temporary workers, called *precari*. Piero De Chiara explains how this happens:

> To be an "external collaborator" means that you have a pretty good chance to be hired. The mechanism works like this: a certain party newspaper (like *L'Unità, L'Avanti*) gets restructured and certain "chosen" people are laid off. The party starts moving in a given direction to create a "correct" way for these people to be hired by the public broadcaster. The way is this: the journalists laid off begin to work for RAI as "external collaborators," and, after a few years, get onto a preferred kind of list, the list of temporary, or *precari*, journalists. After two years on this list, they obtain the protection also of the union. By that point, their way in is assured.[27]

The privileged *precari* list is usually, although not always, the last step before one is finally hired. This list is also controlled by Usigrai, the journalists' union, whose support, as De Chiara suggests, is crucial to ensure that things go as planned.

National Exams

Representatives of Usigrai agree by implication that *lottizzazione* is detrimental but express more confidence in their own efforts to end it. Since the late 1980s, the union has been particularly active in introducing national examinations and scholarships (internship programs) for hiring new journalists. The union believes that national examinations can represent a neutral, party-free procedure, and takes pride in the increasing number and the high professionalism of journalists who have been hired through the 1990s and early 2000s thanks to these selection procedures. For instance, in order to participate in the selection process for the 2001 national examination, candidates were required to have a master's degree and be fluent in a foreign language. They also needed to be trained in broadcast journalism.

Roberto Natale, Usigrai secretary-general, points out the union's main areas of intervention, namely, hiring procedures and promotion processes:

> Until the early 1990s it was rare to be hired in RAI through a normal selection process. The only selections were held in 1968, then in 1978, and then we had internship programs in 1980 and 1981. More national selections were done in 1989, in 1992 [and another one in 2001]. Thanks to these national examinations, more than one hundred journalists were hired without any connection to parties, namely, in a clean, transparent way, so that nobody had to thank any political patron for getting the job. . . . So, right now, hiring through political patronage represents only 10 percent of the total.[28]

However, Natale admits that national examinations do not take care of the problem of the *precari* and external collaborators, an "area where there is still a certain degree of shadow,"[29] and claims that Usigrai is considering a system to avoid political and party interferences with the mechanism that regulates external collaborations. "The point," he said during our interview, "is that we know well that the ones who get onto the *precari* list have good political connections. Indeed, when one says, 'I have a contract with RAI,' people laugh and say, 'Ah, ah, we certainly know how you got that contract!' The union wants to change that, and we are changing that."[30]

What Usigrai has been thinking about is to extend selection procedures also to first-time external contractors, so that a more rigorous selection is required not only to get permanent appointments, but also to obtain the first collaboration. Still, many among *precari* and the external contractors feel marginalized by Usigrai's strategy, which, they say, is mainly preoccupied with ensuring the well-being of those journalists who are already fully employed by the corporation, and seems to be hostile to those who have been working for years with temporary contracts. For instance, in its 1990 charter, the union promised that only 50 percent of available permanent positions would be reserved for the winners of national examinations (at any given time) and the remaining 50 percent would be allocated among other candidates, including the *precari*. However, on the occasion of the national examination of 2001, no posts were reserved for those who had been working for years as part-time, or temporary, contractors. Natale had also promised that by 1999 "all *precari* would be hired by the corporation,"[31] but that did not happen either. In fact, the number of collaborators who are still on temporary contracts remains very high: as an example, in 2001, one-third of the 120 journalists working for Tg1 were *precari*.

Are National Exams Lottizzazione *Free?*

Whether or not national examinations can represent a step toward a *lottizzazione*-free public broadcaster is controversial. Reflecting on ways to reduce political influence on hiring procedures, RAI journalist Stefano Tomassini, head of the foreign desk at Tg1 and member of Usigrai, points out that

> if *lottizzazione* can ever be considered a problem, one must admit that the union has done a lot in the last few years to ensure that journalists are hired through national exams so as to reduce party interference. Many things have changed since the early 1990s: look here in my newsroom, I have at least three people hired with the national exam of 1992; others come from the *precari* list; others come from our school in Perugia. The system has changed a lot.[32]

Giorgio Balzoni, former secretary-general of Usigrai and head of the Tg1 domestic affairs department, shares the same optimism:

> Thanks to the Usigrai things have changed and national exams have been introduced as a channel for hiring young journalists outside the quota system. The politics of quotas has been sidetracked a bit because of these exams and because of the party system's collapse. Politicians have had other things to worry about, instead of being busy filling in the boxes.[33]

Recruitment based on national exams has been especially important in the post-1992 scenario when ideological and political identities have increasingly been turned into mere commodities. Sandro Petrone explains:

> After the Clean Hands scandal, politicians went through a period of uncertainty, in the sense that nobody knew which logics were in place anymore. Things have changed slightly since the Usigrai has tried to introduce national exams, scholarships, and a list for unemployed journalists from which the corporation is supposed to hire people. This probably gives more chances to be hired to people who know how to do their job but lack the necessary connections.[34]

But Petrone also shares the skepticism of many others when he asserts that, even though things have "changed slightly," the underlying dominant logic has remained unaltered:

> Directors continue to be nominated on the basis of political affiliation. The editorial line of each Tg is still established by the parties. . . . Advancements and hiring are still determined on the basis of political criteria. . . . In RAI this is what happens: it is not the best one who survives; the survivor is the one who is able to tell the story as the politician wants it to be told.[35]

Petrone is right. The notion that national examinations provide a *lottizzazione*-free selection process is, at times, naïve. Technically, such exams are supposed to ensure equal opportunities for each candidate, be free from political interference and personal networking, and ensure that only the candidate's knowledge is scrutinized. But there are always ways to get around the formal rigor of these examinations, in RAI as well as in other public service sectors. For instance, it is a normal and well-accepted practice for aspiring public school teachers, post employees, and other candidates for jobs in the public administration to ask their political patron for help. Very often, having good connections with certain politicians, especially with local representatives of a given faction, party, or coalition, is almost a guarantee to get a job. It is reasonable to assume that political networking might be beneficial also to those candidates taking RAI national examinations.

As a matter of fact, Usigrai itself acknowledges the recrudescence of *lottizzazione* even when national examinations are used to select journalists. Indeed, the union notes that "unfortunately, in various cases, old *lottizzazione* practices have been implemented anyway, as the winners of national exams have still to look for political patronage."[36] For instance, a 1993 report from the union details the strict party logic implemented on the occasion of the 1989 national exams:

> Some of the candidates who were declared "suitable for the job" by the committee were "advised" to search for a political patron to be formally hired. On that occasion, the corporation continued to adopt the old norms of "*casella-casella*," the box-to-box *lottizzazione* principle. According to that principle, each selected candidate was forced to be counted in the quota of a specific party even if the candidate did not really have any sympathy for any party at all.[37]

Those candidates were finally hired only after Piero De Chiara and Roberto Natale made up their party affiliations. The PCI mass media division head and the Usigrai representative accepted to do a "fake *lottizzazione*" in order to answer the corporation's questions about the party affiliation of each candidate so that quotas could be satisfied, potential "impure" elements could be weaved out, and the winners could be hired.

Another reason why national examinations might not be completely immune from *lottizzazione* has to do with the composition of the examining committee: How could national exams be *lottizzazione*-free when the committee members administering them are often people who have themselves been engaged in *lottizzazione* activities (the committee usually consists of six members, three nominated by the broadcaster, and three by Usigrai)? For instance, at the 1992 national examination, the president of the committee in charge of the selection was Socialist Enrico Manca, former president of RAI in the 1980s, who was supposedly heavily involved with *lottizzazione* during his tenure. How can a committee presided by Enrico Manca guarantee the "purity" and "transparency" of the examination? It is also troublesome to notice that Usigrai does not address the issue of the composition of the committee, and does not ask for guarantees of impartiality of their members.

This notwithstanding, the union believes that requiring national examinations is the way to attack *lottizzazione*. This system based on national examinations, the union says, "should also serve the purpose of minimizing forms of *lottizzazione* through hiring pseudo-unemployed journalists [those from the party newspapers]." However, the Usigrai acknowledges that more needs to be done to change the promotion procedures, "otherwise, 'clean' hiring will afterwards be nullified by 'polluted' promotions."[38]

The Experience of *Lottizzazione*: Does It Exist or Not?

While conducting the interviews, it became clear that journalists have a very different understanding of what *lottizzazione* is, whether or not it still exists, and how it affects their performance. What do they think about it? First of all, do they even acknowledge that such a practice exists? How do they judge it and what is their experience with *lottizzazione*? Among my respondents there are those who can be defined as being anti-*lottizzazione* and those who are clearly pro-*lottizzazione*. The following are the leitmotifs that characterize the anti-*lottizzazione* people. They deny the existence of *lottizzazione* and tend to:

- Disregard the phenomenon of party interference with their work, thereby asserting that *lottizzazione* no longer exists and that it has been grossly exaggerated by external enemies, mostly in the press and in the commercial media, to destroy public service television.
- Believe that the main reason why *lottizzazione* does not exist nowadays is because there are national exams regulating the access to the profession. Those exams are believed to ensure an objective selection process for journalists.
- Assert that, if there were any residue of *lottizzazione*, it would only affect the mechanisms regulating the external collaborator/part-time system (*precari*), career advancement and promotions, and not regular hiring procedures.
- Recognize that *lottizzazione* does exists but it only affects hiring and promotions, not practice and the content of programs—for proof, they say, "See the data coming out of the various watchdog organizations that monitor the air time we dedicate to politicians, parties representatives, and representatives of the government."[39]
- Concede that *lottizzazione* exists, but only "in the other Tgs, not in mine."[40]
- Concede that *lottizzazione* does exist but "I was an exception":

- I was hired by exam.
- I don't schmooze for promotions.
- I don't hire that way, I've only heard gossip about others doing so.

On the pro-*lottizzazione* side, the leitmotifs are:

- Everybody does it: Italian commercial TV, other Italian state agencies, and other European public broadcasters.
- *Lottizzazione* is a two-way street; the journalists are just as active as the politicians.
- Political control is somehow better than commercial/market control.
- It was a fairly good system, but deteriorated during the 1990s as political affiliation became more of a commodity rather than a sign of ideological commitment.
- The close relationship between political parties and journalists beats the current system, which is based on personal connections.
- It broadens pluralism beyond a tiny oligarchy.
- It underlines the fact that journalists, especially good journalists, have values and political ideas.
- It affects programming more now than it used to in the classic days when it was done right.
- It beats the spoils system.

Apparent points of agreement between the pro- and anti-*lottizzazione* people are:

- *Lottizzazione* is closely connected with privilege, high salaries, and sinecures.
- Nowadays it affects promotion more than hiring.
- Usigrai, the journalists' main union, is to some extent involved.
- *Lottizzazione* does not have a direct influence on the journalists' work and programming.

Those who dismiss or deny the existence of *lottizzazione* tend to be recent hires, junior journalists. To many of them *lottizzazione* appears to be an obsolete practice, something that belongs to the past history of the corporation, to the earlier phase of the first republic, something with which they have nothing in common. Politically these journalists tend to be right wing, sometimes former Socialists, and followers of Berlusconi's coalitions. They declare that they are doing fair objective journalism and deny any democratizing function of partisan journalism.

Senior journalists, on the other hand, are more likely to acknowledge the existence of *lottizzazione*. They usually underline the different historical phases of *lottizzazione* and delineate the consequences of each phase. Often I found that the most recent phases of *lottizzazione* are considered to have had undesirable consequences for the quality of public service journalism. To the current phase, my senior respondents counterpose the earlier phases of *lottizzazione* (up to 1989), when, they say, excellent partisan journalism was valued, encouraged, and appreciated. Many of these journalists participated in the making of the Reform Law of 1975. They tend to emphasize the positive, prodemocratic function of the earlier phases of *lottizzazione*; politically they tend to be leftist and/or Catholics (former DC).

Lottizzazione Does Not Exist

Let us begin our analysis of how journalists and top officials experience *lottizzazione* with Valerio Fiorespino, who was head of the journalists' division of the personnel office at the time of the interview. Fiorespino refused with strong determination to admit the existence of *lottizzazione* or of any form of political interference with his job:

> We follow the national journalists contract and always try to work together with the union when we hire journalists. We stick firmly to the rules. Nobody, not even a news director, can say, "I want this journalist working for me" and actually get that person unless there are well enough documented reasons, professional reasons that is, for hiring that particular journalist. It is clear that any corporation as old as RAI might bring along with itself some kind of dead weight. But that is absolutely normal.[41]

To my questions about whether or not he thought that some of that "dead weight" could have been determined by *lottizzazione* practices influencing hiring and career advancement, he replied:

> Yes, of course! That's what people think about us. But, see, the reason for so much publicity about us is because this is RAI, and anything about RAI, and in particular, negative things about it, make big head-

lines. However, the reality is another one. We have precise rules, and I can assure you that such rules are respected.[42]

Fiorespino did not really address my question; instead he complained about negative publicity for RAI. However, the fact that he followed the norms does not necessary rule out *lottizzazione*. In fact, *lottizzazione* itself consisted of a precise set of rules. He continued his complaints about the perceived public opposition against RAI:

> Positive things happening in RAI are of no interest to anybody. They are not considered newsworthy. On the contrary, any possible negative event happening here becomes newsworthy. Anyway, the reality is what I am telling you there is no *lottizzazione* here.[43]

It can be very frustrating to talk to a high-ranking RAI official about *lottizzazione* and be repeatedly told that it does not exist. It is disorienting: it is like being told, during a gray, rainy day, that the sun is shining outside. I continued to point out to Fiorespino that *lottizzazione* had seemingly been a common practice and, for many, many years, a crucial variable for the selection, the hiring, and the career advancement of journalists in the public broadcaster. But in his replies he firmly emphasized his lack of knowledge of *lottizzazione*:

> I really don't know much about this *lottizzazione* thing. I don't know about it directly, at least. I know about it as you do, because I read about it in the newspapers. But, sincerely, I have never been an active part of it. *Lottizzazione* means sharing seats according to party affiliation. I never did such a thing. Neither did I see anybody doing it. Maybe, sometimes on some occasions I might have deduced that that was what happened, but I can't describe things to you as if I were an active part of it, because I was not. Neither I would be able to tell you who is *lottizzato* and who is not. I read the newspapers; that's how I get to know things. The reality, however, is that my only job is to merely observe changes, who is appointed, how career advancements are implemented, etcetera.[44]

As head of the journalist division of RAI's personnel office, Fiorespino did not simply "observe" changes: he was a determinant actor in the hiring and career advancements of journalists. He consulted directly with the director-general, and his reports on any given proposed appointment were crucial. Nevertheless, he insisted: "Likewise, I observe changes of leadership at any given channel. Those changes, each one of them, as far as I know and as far as I am concerned, are exclusively dictated by professional reasons and internal equilibriums."[45]

One might well wonder what Fiorespino means here by "internal equilibriums." Very often such "internal equilibriums" merely indicated detailed quotas for the various parties and the various currents—in short, the mechanism by which *lottizzazione* works. At any rate, he said that whether or not "such a thing" (*lottizzazione*) existed, was not something he needed to be concerned about:

> I have no idea if one journalist or another is affiliated with this or that party. And even if I were aware of people's party affiliations, I am not sure that such information has anything to do with the changes and the appointments that we make. Anyhow, whether or not such changes and such appointments are determined by *lottizzazione*, it's none of my business.[46]

When pressed, he grudgingly recognized that maybe, yes, *lottizzazione* had existed, at least with respect to career advancements, but only—or mainly—in the past, and that, yes, perhaps it might have had some negative consequences:

> Certainly, career advancements and promotions to higher positions created some problems in the past. . . . [T]he newspapers have all the rights to say that the corporation pays high salaries to directors and vice-directors who don't work. But we also need to objectively recognize that the corporation has made incredible steps forward during the [1990s]. We have been accused of multiplying directorships and vice-directorships and paying lots of money to people who keep their positions without actually performing their roles. But this phenomenon has now been minimized. It happened in the past, and a very few cases are perhaps still happening today. . . . If then this is the result of *lottizzazione*, such a thing is an external element. I am a man of the corporation and, inside the corporation, such things do not count. And, to be honest with you, I don't know how much they really count.[47]

As to defend himself, Fiorespino went on to emphasize the technical aspects of career advancement and the process of hiring journalists, as if technical aspects were neutral, *lottizzazione*-free. The questions I had straightforwardly posed to him about *lottizzazione* had visibly irritated him.

Other respondents showed a similar reluctance to talk about *lottizzazione*. Some, like Francesca Nocerino, Tg2 reporter, do not even know for sure whether or not *lottizzazione* exists, or what it is:

> What does *lottizzazione* mean? Political influence? I am not really scandalized by it. . . . [D]id *lottizzazione* ever happen? Yes, of course. But that happens everywhere, not only here in RAI. People usually have such a negative vision of what political influence might mean for us in RAI. If politicians are able to fulfill their mandate and do what they are supposed to do, then I don't see why political influence is such a terrible thing. And then, what political influence is here in RAI after all? When there is corruption, scandals, we have never attempted to cover them up or minimize them; we have always tried to uncover them. That is what we have always done, I believe. Besides this, politics is not a bad word. It is not, in itself, evil.[48]

Nocerino must have a short memory since she did not recall that, for instance, when the scandal over illicit financing of parties first began in 1992 with the imprisonment of a low-rank Socialist Party official in Milan, Tg2 gave little emphasis to the unfolding events. In fact, the news on RAI2 always showed some special consideration toward its longtime godfather, Bettino Craxi, especially when charges of corruption began to pour in against the former prime minister. As a result, the news that concerned him, and other PSI officials, were usually downplayed.[49] Furthermore, by redefining *lottizzazione* as simply "political influence," Nocerino is enabled to argue that it is not necessarily bad—and at the same time that, even if it is bad, "everybody does it." To my question about the ongoing practices of *lottizzazione*, she answered with an ironic smile:

> Who says that *lottizzazione* is not practiced anymore? And on what basis do they say so? In one sense it is true. National examinations and *precari* lists for professional journalists who are out of jobs have done a lot to improve the situation. Compared to earlier times, the mechanism of hiring has become more transparent. But see, then you need to check what happens when people are inside the newsroom. Political affiliations . . . who knows how much those count inside the newsroom for determining career advancements? Those are independent from any hiring procedures. But, after all, what can I say? The ones who are going to acquiesce will always exist everywhere, not only here.[50]

Nocerino became very defensive. I had to reassure her that I was not trying to accuse her of corruption and that I wanted to approach the issue of *lottizzazione* from an open-minded perspective without prejudgments.

One element that emerges from Nocerino's interview, as well as from the previous interview with Fiorespino, is the corporatist spirit ("I am a man of the corporation," Fiorespino underlined). This spirit emphasizes the in-house rules ("We firmly stick to the rules regarding hiring," the head of the journalists' division at the personnel office said), the journalistic ethos of pursuing truth ("When there is corruption we try to uncover it,"[51] the Tg2 reporter affirmed). Most importantly, both respondents emphasized how important it is to stand together, in unity and solidarity against external attacks, especially those coming from what seems to be RAI's main rivals, newspapers and Mediaset.

It's a Bad Word!

Many respondents got very irritated just hearing the term *lottizzazione*, which clearly had very strong, negative connotations for them. During a telephone interview with a top RAI official, I discovered that the use of the term alone was enough to actually irritate people:

Q: I am interested in the relationship between the party system and the corporation, and one of your colleagues told me to talk to you.

A: I would not know what to tell you. My experience is really limited on such a subject whereas, as I understand it, you want to go 180 degrees. Moreover, in order to be interviewed by you I should ask the corporation for authorization. . . . [S]o, I really don't know how and why you might find it useful to interview me.

Q: Well, I would be really interested to talk to you about *lottizzazione*.

A: Oh, here we are! This is an even more delicate issue. Imagine if the corporation knew, if the office of the director-general as well as the president's office knew . . . if I would present them a request like this . . . oh no, they could never possibly accept it, and I would fully understand why.

Q: I have interviewed many people already in RAI; nobody told me anything about this need for authorization.

A: Well, OK. I admit it, I am an *aziendalista*.[52] And anyhow, I'm telling you, I wouldn't know what to tell you regarding *lottizzazione*. I would have to base myself on gossip, on things heard, word of mouth. . . . [B]ut really, I couldn't imagine how you might be interested in such things.

Q: I would be.

A: Well, listen, I am telling you, you would not benefit from an interview with me whatsoever. Goodbye.[53]

With that, he abruptly hung up. In this interview, the unofficial nature of *lottizzazione* was being used as an excuse for refusing to acknowledge its existence. In fact, it is properly through word of mouth and decisions made behind the scenes during informal meetings that *lottizzazione* has worked through the years. That was exactly what I was looking for. Paradoxically, in a kind of negative circular logic, the specific way in which *lottizzazione* worked was proposed as the evidence of its nonexistence. At the same time, however, by admitting that the only way to know anything about *lottizzazione* is through gossip, one implicitly admits its existence.

Not only some RAI officials but also some politicians refrained from talking to me as soon as they heard the word *lottizzazione*. One of them was Bettino Craxi, former prime minister (1984-1987) and ex-secretary-general of the extinct PSI. Needless to say, Craxi was a man who had enormous power and influence over broadcasting legislation and RAI, besides being a personal friend of Silvio Berlusconi. I began an interview via fax with Craxi at the spring of 1998. At that time, he was in exile in Hammamet, Tunisia, to escape the jail sentence that was pending on various charges of corruption linked to the illicit financing of his party. When I introduced myself to the former premier, I stated that I was interested in the interrelations between the party system and the public broadcaster. Craxi replied warmly and enthusiastically: "I like your project," he said, "and I think it is a very important one. Please, fax me the questions and I will promptly reply."[54] In my next correspondence I specified the object of my research and said that I was interested in the PSI political culture in relation to the public broadcaster during the 1980s. It was then that I used the word *"lottizzazione."* Craxi replied with a short, abrupt message, stating that whatever he had to say about such a topic he had done so in one of his books. He told me to read it and wished me good luck.⁵⁵ I tried to reach him repeatedly thereafter: unfortunately, he never replied.

I had another similar experience with Daniele Ronzoni, who was the head of the domestic political affairs department at Tg2. He too asserted the nonquantifiable nature of *lottizzazione* and negated any professional implications with the system of political parties. Similar to the logic of the previous RAI official, the nature itself of the phenomenon (its nonquantifiable, impalpable nature) becomes, also for Ronzoni, proof of its nonexistence. Asked about his perspective on the relationship between the political sphere and public service journalism, he replied very defensively that he "had no point of view to share" and that, as far as he was concerned, he had "no impressions and no opinions."⁵⁶ That he had no experience, neither opinions nor perspectives with regard to *lottizzazione* was obviously hard to believe given that any political affairs department had traditionally been a place where parties' influence was prevalent, and that was even more the case at Tg2.

When I explained to Ronzoni that I wanted to know his impressions of, and his experience with, *lottizzazione*, he too seemed extraordinarily surprised and offended:

> You misled me. You told me that you were interested in the relationship between political sphere and journalists. But now you are telling me the truth, namely that you want to talk about *lottizzazione* . . . but these two things are not the same thing. If we want to talk about *lottizzazione*, that is the history of the corporation. But, if that is the case, then you should talk to other people and not to me. I was not here when it happened; those were other times. As far as I know, *lottizzazione* is ancient history. And plus, I can't talk for others. Talk with my colleague, the one who mentioned my name to you. He should know better than I do. Anyhow, if you want an interview, I am available.⁵⁷

But, when I reiterated that, yes, I did want an interview with him, he insisted that he had nothing to share. However, pressed to reply to my questions, Ronzoni responded:

> What you are asking me is a very serious thing. The only thing I have to say is that we only have a journalistic relationship with the political sphere. I am part of a team, and at Tg2 the only thing we do is news, we just do news. As such, political events are treated as plain news. Whatever happens, we treat it across many editions of our Tg throughout the day, and we present a large range of perspectives and points of view.⁵⁸

Toward the end of our conversation, however, he finally said: "See, asking me about *lottizzazione* is like asking the host how his wine is." Was this Ronzoni's way to say: *Lottizzazione* does exist, but how could I say that (1) it exists; (2) it is a negative characteristic? As for Ronzoni's analogy, nobody can realistically expect the host to say that his wine is bad. But if the host himself is saying, "You can't ask me how my wine is," one might rightly wonder about both the quality of his wine and the sincerity of his words.

Overall, the tone of these last three interviews—surprise, indignation, uneasiness, aggressiveness—makes it particularly difficult to believe what the respondents explicitly or implicitly argued, that is, that they had nothing to do with *lottizzazione*.

Conspiracy Theory

During our interview, Valerio Fiorespino argued more than once for a sort of conspiracy theory according to which any attack from outsiders (in particular, from newspapers) against the corporation (especially accusations of *lottizzazione*) was meant to weaken the public broadcaster. In an attempt to defend the corporation, he explained:

> We are actually lowering the salaries we pay to Tg directors, vice-directors, and so on. . . . But still, the supposed high salaries in RAI make the headlines, whereas the salaries of ENEL [the former publicly owned Electric Company], which are much higher than ours, are of no interest to public opinion. Anyhow, I challenge anybody to say that today, right now, there is a systematic *lottizzazione* that is causing more damage compared to all the good things that we have done throughout the years.[59]

Certainly, Fiorespino is not alone in feeling under attack. There seems to be a widespread sense of external menace also in the words of Daniele Ronzoni, who opposed any allegation of *lottizzazione* and fought back: "What are all these accusations of *lottizzazione*? Why does nobody accuse our colleagues working for Mediaset of such a thing?"[60]

Following the scandals that brought down the political party system in the early 1990s, it is understandable that RAI journalists and its officials are especially sensitive to allegations of political corruption. In part true and in part instrumental, attacks against the public broadcaster are perceived as blows against public broadcasting per se, orchestrated by those who want to destroy the public service to the benefit of the private sector. Stefano Tomassini, from Tg1, exemplifies these general feelings when he says, "I don't want to seem cynical or too pessimistic, nor too relativistic, but I objectively think that the problem lies in the fact that RAI is now considered the last bastion against commercialization to be conquered."[61] It is understandable how accusations against RAI might be perceived, especially at times when a dislike for public services is prevalent, as attempts to diminish the broadcaster's image in the eyes of the Italian people and to promote, willingly or not, the image of its competitor, Mediaset. If RAI, the last bulwark against Berlusconi, is destroyed, a public jewel will be lost and Mediaset will triumph: this is a recurrent theme. As Tomassini put it, "There is a body of public opinion out there that is constantly and consistently adverse and malevolent toward our specific category of public service broadcast journalists, and toward the corporation in general."[62] Although the fear that political maneuverings are being carried out in order to marginalize the role of RAI is understandable, that should not preclude one from practicing self-criticism, when appropriate. The risk is that a strenuous defense of the public service might tend to avoid any criticism, even when justified.

Like Fiorespino and Ronzoni, Francesca Nocerino also defended herself against accusations of *lottizzazione*, arguing that external attacks always try to denigrate the corporation. She added a new element to the analysis when she mentioned that such attacks also come from RAI's leadership: "The problem is that everybody likes to bash RAI, even people inside the corporation and its own top management."[63] Here Nocerino is referring to the professors' television era of 1993-1994,[64] when the board of directors accused many journalists of being *lottizzati* and encouraged many of them to leave. The Tg2 journalist is voicing a complaint shared by many of her colleagues:

> To be attacked from the outside and then even by your own leadership inside the corporation was extremely sad, very painful. Those who should have defended this corporation instead denigrated it. I don't think it was fair at all. In RAI there are very competent people who work really well and very hard. But such positive things are never spread around. . . . Everybody only talks about the negative sides of RAI.[65]

Can *Lottizzazione* Be Quantified?

During our conversation, Daniele Ronzoni pointed out that in 1995 a watchdog was instituted with the University of Pavia to control quantity of airtime that each Tg (on public and commercial broadcasters) devotes to political parties' representatives, members of parliament, and representatives of the government and the opposition. Ronzoni recommended that I talk with those who work in those institutions. "They check us out," he ensured me, "they analyze Tg2 and then judge it. They'll tell you if we are *lottizzati* or not."[66] Of course, the work done by Pavia and other similar institutions, like *Centro di Ascolto Radiotelevisivo* in Rome, provides a wealth of valuable quantitative information. But that information is not sufficient to understand the phenomenon of *lottizzazione*. Even though the data of the observers do at times show some fairness in the allotment of airtime, and demonstrate a heightened awareness of the need to be quantitatively accountable (which is also a requirement of the 1999 *par conditio* law that establishes norms to guarantee fair and balanced representation of all parties during preelection times), these data are not sufficient. More qualitative information is needed to assess the impact of party influence on information and to determine whether or not a certain news program is biased toward any given party. Voicing the reservations of many others, Stefano Picchi, foreign correspondent for Tg2, argues that "measuring" the news is not a way to get rid of *lottizzazione* because on television giving equal airtime to opposite views does not necessarily mean equal, or balanced, presentation of those views. But certainly, even he recognizes that the formula adopted by Tg2 has shielded it against accusations of partiality by appealing to objectivity, facts, and thereby transforming the old political commentary into plain, quantifiable information.

Lottizzazione versus the Spoils System

When I asked Daniele Ronzoni of Tg2 what all the talk about *lottizzazione* was in his newsroom, he replied outraged:

> Hey, here you are! You are a little behind in time, aren't you? *Lottizzazione* is obsolete nowadays. Those things used to happen during the first republic. Now the public broadcaster goes to whoever wins the elections and *lottizzazione* has become an obsolete term. We implement the spoils system just like the Americans do. Not even newspapers talk about *lottizzazione* nowadays, nor do they use such a term anymore.[67]

That newspapers do not talk about *lottizzazione* anymore is absolutely not true. In fact, I literally went through hundreds and hundreds of pages of newspaper articles reporting on *lottizzazione* in RAI in recent years. It is true, however, that the practice of political influence over the public broadcaster is resembling more and more the spoils system in use in democracies such as the United States: indeed, since 1994, RAI basically goes to whoever wins the elections. Because of the change in the electoral system (from the proportional system to the majoritarian system) and the legislation introduced in 1993 according to which the two speakers of the houses (who are government nominees) appoint the members of the board of directors and the president of RAI, the power of each government administration inside the broadcaster has considerably increased. But whereas for some, including Ronzoni, such a spoils system is a positive, encouraging development, according to the journalists' union and people like former RAI journalist Gianni Minà, this evolution creates a condition of total occupation on the part of the government of the day over the public broadcaster.[68] Others have similar concerns: former RAI director-general Ettore Bernabei argues that because of the new spoils system the leadership of the public broadcaster does not respond anymore to the will of the voters as represented by the parliament, and, therefore, it is no longer legitimated by the people.[69]

In addition to the practices connected to the spoils system, according to which top-level bureaucrats are called by the executive power to lead certain state agencies, in Italy the government interferes also within internal administrative affairs of the broadcaster and with programming. In 1994, during his first term as prime minister, the media mogul Silvio Berlusconi was clear about his vision of public service broadcasting when he said that in no other democracy was a public broadcaster and its programming against the government as RAI was in Italy. Once again, Berlusconi voiced his ideas on public service broadcasting soon after the victory of the right-wing coalition at the May 2001 general elections, when he expressed disappointment for the work done by journalists Michele Santoro and Enzo Biagi, and comedian Daniele Luttazzi. According to the prime minister, they were guilty of openly expressing their antipathy toward his political coalition, *Casa delle Libertà* (the house of freedoms), during the previous election campaign. Consistent with the prime minister's desires, once the new RAI board of directors was appointed in February 2002, both Biagi and Santoro's programs were eliminated. Daniele Luttazzi's political satire, *Satirycon*, was also axed. All of them were accused, by government representatives and the conservative press, of exercising "political killing" against the ruling coalition.

Overall, it is perhaps true that the system in use is getting closer to the spoils system. But this, especially in Italy, is extremely problematic. In a country where the owner of the public broadcaster's main competitor has political influence over RAI, there is always going to be, as Roberto Morrione, director of RAI NEWS 24, noted, a "generalized worry and an overall intent not to create problems for the Mediaset channels."[70] One wonders, therefore, if such a spoils systems does not reinforce a sort of tyranny over the media rather than representing a sign of an advanced democracy, and a source of pride, as Ronzoni seems to believe.

It Exists, But Only in Other Tgs

At times the interviews shift dizzyingly from protestations that the journalists really had no idea what *lottizzazione* meant to displays of detailed knowledge about it. Daniela Vergara, anchorwoman of the prime-time evening edition of Tg2, was hired without any exam or formal selection (another way to say that she was hired according to political quota) and began working for the radio news on RAI channel 3, GR3, in the 1980s. Then she went to Tg3, and in 1996 she finally landed a job at Tg2. During our interview, she denied any direct experience with political parties' interference in her work, indicating that, since she arrived at Tg2 late, she could not possibly have any recollection of *lottizzazione*. Perhaps, she was implying that by the time she joined the newsroom of the second channel—Tg2 became very close to *Alleanza Nazionale*, a right-wing party, after Berlusconi won the 1994 elections—*lottizzazione* had ended. I provoked her by saying that it was common knowledge that Tg2, especially during the 1980s, was Craxi's news program. I would expect Vergara to definitely know something about *lottizzazione*, also because, even if she was not at Tg2 during the 1980s, she was hired in RAI during those years, the apex of *partitocrazia*. "How was it to be in RAI during those times? How did it work?" I asked her. She replied: "As is easily understood, I have no idea about *lottizzazione*. Being in radio first, I was physically removed [RAI radio headquarters is in a different location than television production centers] from the television headquarters in Saxa Rubra. Therefore, I cannot help you in any respect."[71]

If it might be true that radio was, and still is, of secondary importance to the political elites, it simply cannot be true that Vergara's appointment at Tg2 was *lottizzazione*-free. When Vergara joined the newsroom at the second national channel, many in the press suggested that she got the job thanks to her mentors, Clemente Mimun (Tg2 director at the time) and Gianfranco Fini (secretary-general of *Alleanza Nazionale*). As journalist Carlo Gallucci wrote in the weekly magazine *L'Espresso*, at that time the "entire Tg2 was given to *Alleanza Nazionale*."[72] But Vergara defended herself:

> Honestly, I don't want to say either that I am *lottizzata* or that I am not. Or that other people were. My personal experience is atypical. ... I came into a radio news program that was of the Social Democrats, then I went to Tg3, and that was the PCI's news. Then, I went to Tg2, which, it needs to be acknowledged, is the most objective of all Tgs. My experience is very different from other people's experience. I worked a lot; that is how I went on with my career; I worked through different political and cultural realities. *Lottizzazione* has been my companion, but has never harassed me.[73]

But when I asked her whether or not *lottizzazione* had disappeared from RAI, she finally got a chance to talk about some of her colleagues at the competing news program RAI1, and that was when she showed off all her inside information. Perhaps her desire to talk about *lottizzazione* at Tg1 was motivated by a traditional rivalry between her newsroom and the flagship's news, a rivalry reinforced by the fact that Tg1 during the center-left coalition government of 1996-2001 was in the hands of the main party of the governing coalition, therefore opposite to her party affiliation:

> It is absolutely untrue that *lottizzazione* ceased to exist with the 1996 administrations and the new political climate. *Lottizzazione* is still practiced. I would even say that the reality now is more complicated than before. Before, the divisions reflected a clear scheme of reference. Since the mid-1990s, everything has become more intertwined. No, I don't think that the end of *lottizzazione* is a reality here in RAI.[74]

Vergara strongly criticized the news on the first channel for its presumed left-wing inclination. To the partisan approach of Tg1, Vergara opposed the objectivity and professionalism of the news program where she was working. She too, encouraged me to check with the Pavia watchdog: "Tg2's objectivity should be apparent to all. We are proof that it is possible to do excellent journalism and still be objective."[75]

Lottizzazione: *A Normal Practice*

If one supposes that Vergara is telling half the truth, and that she is at Tg2 in the quota for *Alleanza Nazionale*, her negative critiques of Tg1 become understandable. Given the aura of objectivity that Tg2 was creating around itself, one can also understand her position and the journalist's emphasis on news and information as the proof that "her" Tg2 was indeed *lottizzazione*-free.

I Was an Exception

In order to better understand the phenomenon of *lottizzazione* as it has defined hiring procedures through the years, it is important to explore how journalists rationalize their being hired by RAI. Even after admitting that *lottizzazione* is pervasive, many of them refuse to acknowledge that they benefited from it.

Indeed, even when the existence of *lottizzazione* is admitted, as is the case with Sandro Petrone at Tg2, when it comes to how a journalist got a job in a specific news program, the interviewee often presents himself or herself as a hero who, alone in the middle of corruption, made it without getting compromised. Even though Petrone recognizes that when he was hired at Tg2, "the real owner of the newsroom was Bettino Craxi's PSI, rather than the Italian people," he separates himself from the Socialist Party of those years:

> I worked a lot as an external collaborator. In 1977 RAI called me for an interview, but then, to be hired I had to wait and wait until 1993. . . . What I missed in 1977, as many people who don't have a lifelong contract with RAI still miss today, was not the ability to do the job, the right attitude for the job, or not being as good as others, it was exclusively . . . the lack of support of the political patron, of the political group to which one belongs.[76]

Petrone believes in the notion that journalists should always dig into the depth of any given event, always bearing in mind that their references, their publishers, so to say, are the viewers. His ideal journalist is one who can "put himself into the common people's shoes, and not in those of the politicians." But, if that is his ideal notion, how did he manage to work at Tg2 at a time when nothing happened in that newsroom without Craxi's implicit approval? Petrone explains:

> I came to Tg2 because it was closest to the political group to which I belonged. I have always been, since I was really young, on the Left. . . . But in 1979, when I began to do journalism, I left my political ideas behind me. From that time on, nobody has ever found out my political beliefs. This is just to tell you that I'm not into politics any more. Since I first began to work as a journalist, I have not cared anymore about political issues. I ended up not being interested in politics because I found it boring and uninformative.[77]

Lottizzazione certainly exists; yet it does not seem to directly concern Sandro Petrone. He does not care about politics; yet by implication he puts himself in "politicians' shoes," and he came to Tg2 because of his politics. The main problem preventing him from being hired sooner was that he, like many others, did not have the right political support; yet he was first interviewed in 1977 (a crucial time for the Socialists' expansion in RAI), knew people inside the broadcaster, and became an external collaborator. It is reasonable to assume that he must have had some good connections to even get to the interview stage and then become an external contractor.

It Does Exist: The Positive Aspects of *Lottizzazione*

Contrarily to those who refuse to admit any direct involvement with *lottizzazione*, and tend to consider it as a very negative aspect of RAI's history, there are also journalists, as well as observers and RAI top officials, who regard *lottizzazione* as an essential and often positive element. They are ready to admit its existence and, rather than being apologetic, they are proud of *lottizzazione*, which for them is a sign of pluralism and democracy, just as political/advocacy journalism was considered a symptom of the regained political freedoms in the postwar period.

One such top official is Celestino Spada, director of the RAI research department at the time of this interview, who believes that a corporation like RAI provokes, and looks for, the relationship with the political sphere. "Here in RAI," he says, "political power is not considered an interference; rather it is something that we look for."[78] This, according to Spada, is neither unusual nor bad. As a matter of fact, he recognizes that the political and media systems in Italy have traditionally evolved in a sort of dialectic relationship, a kind of fatal attraction. The fatal attraction does not only involve the public broadcaster, but also the commercial broadcaster. Indeed, during the 1980s, Berlusconi's channels flourished thanks to their alliance with the party system. What is structural, Spada affirms, is the economic and financial weakness of both corporations (RAI and Mediaset), rather than their relationship with the political system.

Spada also argues that *lottizzazione* is strong among journalists, and if there are any problems with it, they are the journalists' problems: "They are the ones who have gotten used to certain privileges. Like when in 1992 the *lottizzazione* system experienced a period of crisis, the journalists were those who suffered the most and experienced an identity crisis."[79] Francesco Mattioli, a former journalist himself, confirms: "Journalists have not overcome their habit to conform. Here in RAI there has been a true sedimentation of *lottizzazione* through the years, layer after layer, *lottizzati* of the first hour, *lottizzati* of the second, *lottizzati* of the third hour. And so, now we have a conspicuous cemetery of the elephants."[80] However, according to Spada *lottizzazione* is a marginal phenomenon. More than an analysis of its positive side, he points out its relatively small impact. Television is an industry. Its product is programming. "Only if the political sphere interferes with the production," Spada says, "then we would have a problem."[81] In an effort to defend the corporation, Spada forgets that, unfortunately, political interference with programming does happen, especially from the time Berlusconi became a politician.

Others express their relatively benign judgment about *lottizzazione*. RAI journalist Giorgio Balzoni, for instance, has a very Machiavellian, pragmatic view of it. According to him,

> *Lottizzazione* would not have reason to exist if this were a pure, perfect system. In such a case, it should be banned. But we do not have a perfect system. [Therefore] *lottizzazione*, done in a certain way, has its reasons to exist, because it means that inside a public system all voices are heard and acknowledged. This is much better than a public service in which only the voices of the most powerful groups are presented.[82]

Francesco Siliato, media expert in Milan, doesn't see *lottizzazione* "as such a dramatic element" either. He justifies it as the lesser evil: "political control is a guarantee against another type of control, namely, industrial control, to which some kind of political control is preferable."[83] Siliato expands on Spada's notion of the broadcaster's financial and economic weakness, a structural condition that has also been a characteristic of the print media. As such, Siliato argues, Italian journalism "lacks the resources for surviving without some sort of industrial control. This is true also in other countries, but especially true in Italy, where the main newspapers have always been owned by big industry."[84] In the context of the close connections that have always existed among the state, the private capital, and the media, "*lottizzazione* marked an attempt to release such oppressive industrial control, and overcome the alliance between state and industry." The relative positive characteristics of *lottizzazione*, according to Siliato, imply a fundamental truth, which is true everywhere, but perhaps even more so in Italy:

> The reality is that it is impossible to do any kind of communication media enterprise that is free from one kind of control or another. In order to have a newspaper, or a TV channel, one needs lots of money. Freedom of the press and freedom of speech are concepts that are a little bit up in the air, without actual foundation. If everybody had lots of money, then, yes, this kind of freedom would be possible. But since this is impossible, then such freedoms are only empty words.[85]

In Siliato's view, political control can and should even supersede economic control, and can be exercised as a separate power, without being conditioned by economic pressures. More importantly, at times the protection of the political system over RAI defended the broadcaster from the powerful alliance between the state and capital, and from the tyranny of market imperatives. Indeed, political control has become the defining element of public, noncommercial broadcasting. A niche protected from market imperatives is the only guarantee that the public broadcaster can produce quality programming. Contrary to the argument according to which the broadcaster's connivance with the party system might disqualify RAI as a true public service broadcaster, Siliato suggests that it is precisely RAI's connections with the political sphere that made survival possible through the years.

Contrary to their junior colleagues, most senior journalists are not afraid to acknowledge the existence of *lottizzazione* and its influence on their careers. Giorgio Balzoni, for instance, admits that,

> I too was hired on the basis of political quotas and have no problem acknowledging it. A colleague had just left the second radio channel. He was notoriously a Christian Democrat. I had begun my career as a journalist with *Il Popolo*, the DC newspaper, and then I was for a while newsroom head of the DC weekly magazine. When this opening in RAI was created, I was called to fill it. My situation was similar to 90 percent of other journalists here. I was finally hired in 1982, and that's

what used to happen at that time. Today it still happens, but in much less proportion than before.[86]

Balzoni, a left DC and former Usigrai secretary-general, provides a very interesting analysis, which should also help clarify the relationship of the journalists' union with the party system:

> What we, as the journalists' union, have always contested and opposed has been *lottizzazione* at its minimum, i.e., at its worst. After all, political life in Italy since the late 1980s has been at its worst, and RAI, which was linked to the political system, experienced *lottizzazione* at its worst. For instance, during Bernabei's leadership it is true that people were chosen on the basis of party quotas. However, Bernabei chose the best people on the market. Since the early 1990s, instead, politicians have not imposed on RAI the best, but rather the more loyal people, who are not necessarily the best journalists. As it is an aspect of pluralism, *lottizzazione* is a positive phenomenon. I understand that pluralism is a difficult thing to achieve, but a good democratic system always reveals itself through the realization of difficult things.[87]

The new element emerging in this interview is the distinction between negative and positive *lottizzazione*. Such a distinction is not based on historical reasons, which would suggest that *lottizzazione* was a positive, structural response against the "blocked democracy" at a particular point in history. The argument is not even based inversely on the degree, the intensity, of *lottizzazione*, on the assumption that in some cases and under certain conditions, *lottizzazione* might even be a good idea. Instead, the interview embraces the "essence" of *lottizzazione* in such a way that its intrinsic goodness cannot be disputed. "*Lottizzazione* . . . means that inside a public system all voices are heard and acknowledged. This is much better than a public service in which only the most powerful groups' voices are acknowledged": nobody could possibly argue against such a statement. If "*lottizzazione* at its minimum is *lottizzazione* at its worst," then it follows that *lottizzazione* should be maximized in order to offer its best, that is, as it was when party affiliation was a crucial factor determining hiring and career advancement, and political parties were motivated to get the best journalists in the market.

The Post-1992 Scenario

However, even among the hard-core supporters of partisan journalism and *lottizzazione*, there is a widespread feeling that post-1992 *lottiz-*

zazione has been detrimental. It continued to be administered by political figures, but instead of politics and quality, the basis for the selection of journalists increasingly became politics and personal acquaintance. As former Tg2 foreign correspondent Francesco Mattioli put it, political influence "continued in its most negative connotation, negative because politicians have been making their decisions regarding whom to hire without really caring about what they are doing."[88]

However, contrary to what one might imagine, the politicians are not the only ones to bear the responsibilities for the situation. To express the confusion that followed the bribesville scandal of the early 1990s and the collapse of the postwar system of political references, Mattioli comments on the journalists' role:

> Many former Christian Democratic journalists jumped from one party to another, and nobody knew exactly who they were anymore. . . . The Democratic Party of the Left [PDS], after winning the elections in 1996, gathered all these recycled people, who were professionally very cheap, but who, however, were by now expecting to become powerful because they had the PDS stamp on them. There was lots of arrogance among the neo-PDS journalists, who became PDS from one day to the next.[89]

Left-wing journalist Roberto Mastroianni shares similar stories. He is very critical of the way in which party affiliation has become almost a "shopping" activity for many of his colleagues:

> I have seen journalists changing their political affiliation from one day to the next. You should have seen the line of colleagues in front of my office door the day after the 1996 victory of the leftist coalition. There were people coming from the most diverse backgrounds, from the former *Movimento Sociale* [the extinct neo-Fascist party], *Alleanza Nazionale*, and also people whom I had never seen before. Everybody seemed to suddenly have been converted to the Left. Everybody was ready to swear their political faith and loyalty to the PDS. "Do you remember me?" people would ask, "We met at that convention. . . . " Really sad, dangerously shameful.[90]

As the earlier system of reference collapsed, party affiliation became less reliable and more flexible than before, less based on ideological principles and more determined by convenience. Once party affiliation lost any resonance with political ideas, *lottizzazione* also lost its soul. As such, it became empty and purely instrumental.

Political Influence and the Journalists' Experience

Indistinctively, most of my respondents shared that they do not perceive political influences, or unwanted pressures, on their job. Whereas that might be expected from those who refuse to acknowledge the existence of *lottizzazione*, it was somehow surprising to realize that also the pro-*lottizzazione* people do not seem to experience much pressure or influence. Why is that? And what does it mean? The answers lay, I believe, in the cultural, social, and political context of Italian journalism, and in the connotations that terms like "independence" and "objectivity" have acquired in it. Given our legacy of partisan journalism, the historical significance of the party press, and the systematic financial weakness of the media industry, notions such as journalists' objectivity and independence are for the most part vague and abstract terms.[91] For Stefano Tomassini, for instance, there is no political interference in RAI, but only a "close relationship":

> More than interference coming from political parties, I have experienced the strict, close relationship between the political sphere and television. But this is not necessarily an interference. Let's talk about my experience. I started more than twenty years ago at *La Voce repubblicana*, the newspaper of the Republican Party. Many people had similar experiences coming to RAI from *Il Popolo*, *L'Avanti*, and other party papers. Indeed, for many years one of the main nurseries for public service journalism in Italy was the party newspaper, which was also the training ground for most of the postwar Italian press. Many of the current editors in chief and editorialists of the main national newspapers come from *La Voce repubblicana*. Many, most of us, come from the party press. Is this good, is this evil?[92]

How this "close relationship can go together with any attempt to do objective reporting, which one might argue should be the purpose of a public broadcaster, is difficult to tell," Tomassini concedes, even though he has never had any "major difficulty with being objective." But then, what does objectivity mean to him? He shares the understanding of many of his colleagues, especially those in the pro-*lottizzazione* group, when he explains that "objectivity should not preclude the assessment of certain values." In fact, Tomassini argues, it is the duty of public service journalists to stand for some "basic principles":

> Once, I was in a meeting with a bunch of other colleagues. Somebody said, and I fully supported what he said, that there are certain values that a journalist should stand up for, even at the cost of not being objective. The example that this guy gave us was the anti-death penalty campaign. We as journalists of a public broadcaster should stand up for what we believe in, and being anti-death penalty is one of those things. What this means is that the objectivity of public service journalists cannot just mean that our work entails only a gloomy and depressing telling of facts. It is necessary to stand up for some fundamental values. ... Even if, as a remote hypothesis, public opinion in this country were pro-death penalty, public service journalists should still stand up against it. It's a question of values.[93]

It is clear that Tomassini's notion of objective journalism is very different from a North American journalist's understanding of it (not that he minds at all: "in the United States," he says scornfully, "they have little experience, nor do they have any tradition for thinking about something public in the information sector").

A few questions arise: What relationship can be articulated between *lottizzazione* and objectivity? Can they go together? Tomassini seems to truly believe that *lottizzazione* could exist in hiring without interfering in the journalists' subsequent work. Furthermore, for him objectivity is a relative value since even the "objective" public service journalist is supposed to have ideas of his or her own. (However, Tomassini does not specify the boundaries of what this means, and how, for instance, the values that journalists should stand for might become similar, too similar, perhaps, to those promoted by the politician who gave them the job).

Subjects to the Power Holders or Partisan Journalists?

The issue of autonomy and objectivity leads to another consideration. What, if any, is the distinction between political party influence on the journalists' work and partisan journalism in Italy? In stark contrast to the last interviews, Sandro Petrone, at Tg2, is adamant about his conviction in the value of objectivity in journalism. As such, he believes that the only hope for the future of public service journalism in Italy is if media professionals are liberated from the influence of political parties:

> I am one hundred percent positive that if we free many young, and even less young, journalists from the frustrating, marginalizing logic of po-

litical control, if we can save these people, we are going to have excellent, extraordinary journalists, who are now very few because the entire profession has become normalized, leveled down. We are going to have excellent news, a balanced journalism, technically valid, but most importantly, a product that will actually reach people, give them information that they need. . . . If we succeeded in liberating journalism from political control, then we would see an entire team of excellent professionals, who, rather than in the boring British way of doing news, might tell the truth about what happens in the lively Italian style.[94]

Contrary to those colleagues who value *lottizzazione* (or at least certain phases of it), express an appreciation for partisan journalism, and even go so far as to conceive political interference as just a "close relationship," Sandro Petrone harbors no doubts:

I don't think that the Italian tradition of political/advocacy journalism means that we are doomed to continue working in a condition of dependency on the political sphere. I don't think that the positive characteristics of Italian journalism would disappear if we tried to change the logic of political control. I believe, instead, that there is a perverse criterion in Italian journalism that praises and rewards those who do political and partisan journalism, who then become famous among the politicians and advance in their careers.[95]

The Tg2 journalist is not willing to acknowledge the unique value of partisan and political journalism. For him, journalism has only to do with facts. Facts are facts, and his job is to tell them. Perhaps only one with such a clear-cut, perhaps innocent, perception of things could consider *lottizzazione* to be a total corruption and fail to see a distinction between party influence and partisan journalism.

Roberto Morrione, on the other side, is ready to draw a line between the brutal reality of party influence from the noble tradition of partisan journalism. This is how the head of RAI NEWS 24 sees the role of a news person:

When something happens, the first question that a news director should ask to him or herself is: how can I provide this information in a way that people will critically think about it, and in such a way that all forces at play will feel like they were enabled to present their positions?[96]

What comes to the foreground is the tradition of pluralism, and that is where partisan journalism finds its dignified role. Morrione continues: "A completely different situation is when the director asks himself: is this piece of information going to bother my political reference and how is this going to bother him?"[97] In this case, we clearly have an unacceptable situation of subordination.

For those who, with a scarce sense of criticism, believe in the ideals of objectivity and impartiality, *lottizzazione* represents a corrupt practice of which political journalism is a part. For those who are more interested in the history and tradition of Italian journalism, and appreciate the complexities of social and political phenomena, objectivity and impartiality reveal fallacies. For them *lottizzazione* can be a sign of pluralism, enrich the democratic process, and represent an opportunity for "all forces at play" to express their positions.

Self-Censorship

I imagine that, for any journalist, the line between feeling the influence (and the pressure) of his political party and being aware of his own political ideas (and their impact on his work), at times can be a very fine one. How does one know where her own ideas and convictions end and the dictates of her party begin? Various respondents, including Stefano Tomassini, noticed that self-censorship has a stronger impact on the journalists' work than any external, political interference. The implication is that self-censorship might be more perverse than external influences. As Roberto Morrione argues, political powers might have an influence on news and the journalists, but that influence is never overt. What there is, instead, is a "gray zone of self censorship, where a series of relationships based on mental correspondences are created."[98]

But even though many agree that self-censorship is a force even greater than outside interferences, there are some important differences among the respondents with regard to the nature of self-censorship. On one side, there are those who consider self-censorship as a private matter, a personal question. One of them is Tomassini, who thinks that self-censorship is an innocent, benign phenomenon ("self-censorship cannot be considered guilty: you can't consider guilty a journalist who performs self-censorship," he says).[99] On the other side, some people, including Roberto Morrione, suggest that self-censorship is not simply a private issue, but is a problem that has social origins. According to this analysis, it is the backgrounds of RAI journalists that make self-censorship particularly predictable and natural. As I noted earlier, the process of hiring journalists is (or at least was until recently) "selective" from the beginning, in the sense that "impure" elements, not in line with the culture of the corporation, tend to be weaved out. Indeed, even though journalism schools have played an important democratizing role, there is still a powerful class osmosis between journalists and politicians that contributes to the normalization of self-censorship. Piero De Chiara speaks to this point when he says:

> There is a spasmodic interest in television on the part of the politicians. They know lots of people inside RAI, and journalists know lots of politicians. In no other corporation is there such a contiguous relationship. Furthermore, politicians and journalists are all in Rome, therefore their children all go to the same schools, have the same social life, do similar recreational activities, and so on. There is, in other words, a terrible osmosis of class.[100]

This proximity between journalists and politicians is certainly not a recent phenomenon. In the 1950s, Enzo Forcella already described the community of journalists and politicians as a close-knit one. He wrote:

> The atmosphere [is] like that of a school or a family recital in which the actors have known themselves since they were little kids. They play off at each other, they speak an allusive language, and even when it looks like they detest each other, they are still best buddies. They play just for their pleasure, of course, because there is no other public.[101]

Journalists and Politicians

This class osmosis is reinforced by another phenomenon: careers in politics and those in journalism have become almost interchangeable. There are many journalists who enter politics and various former journalists-turned-politicians, who, at the end of their mandate as members of parliament or as ministers, return to their previous jobs. There are also many famous politicians, like former prime minister Massimo D'Alema, who still hold a press identification card. Classic examples of journalists-turned-politicians are Giovanni Spadolini, former director of *Corriere della Sera*, who served as prime minister in the early 1980s, and Alberto Ronchey, former director of *La Stampa*, editorialist for *Corriere della Sera* and *La Repubblica*, who became minister in the early 1990s. During the 1990s, various journalists left their profession to pursue their political aspirations, including press journalists Furio Colombo, Giulio Savelli, and Gennaro Malgieri, and RAI journalists Beppe Giulietti and Gustavo Selva.

Surprisingly, however, the consequences of this osmosis have not always turned out in favor of RAI, at least in the long run. Former director of PCI media department, Piero De Chiara, explains why:

> RAI's strong relationship with the political system creates imbalances that don't always turn out to be beneficial to the broadcaster. There is, indeed, a high risk of too much attention on the part of politicians toward RAI because of the closeness of politicians and journalists. This excessive interest gives RAI a higher perception of itself than it should have, and causes the public broadcaster to consider itself more of a central player than it actually is. RAI sees itself as a major player in the global media sector, when, in reality, it is a small corporation. What happens as a result is that in RAI they don't work enough toward the affirmation of the public service idea, but more on the perception they have of being the big Italian media corporation. They should be more humble because they are not a major corporation; while, at the same time, they should be more ambitious in reinforcing their public service mission.[102]

Journalists' Autonomy

How is it possible to maintain or create for oneself spaces of autonomy in a context where self-censorship is fueled by an almost incestuous relationship between journalists and politicians? How is "autonomy" at all possible given that self-censorship is mostly an unconscious function? Romano Tamberlich, head of *TV7*, a special weekly supplement of Tg1, thinks that it is possible to work autonomously and independently, if one so chooses:

> *Lottizzazione* has always existed, at least since the 1960s. But rather than talking about it, we should discuss autonomy and professionalism or lack of them. I can assure you that Tg1 is rather autonomous, careful, and objective in its reportage.[103]

But even though balanced information is an attainable goal, Tamberlich recognizes that too much attention to the *Palazzo* (the political establishment) usually means that less airtime is devoted to other information:

> It is perhaps true that we give too much attention to the president of the republic, but we do so because it is breaking news. Yes, probably it

would be more useful to pay more attention to problems that are closer to people's lives, such as health care, public schools, unemployment. This is not to say that such issues are not covered, but certainly, in the effort of keeping our attention on the political world, we get sidetracked and our attention to the country and its real problems becomes a secondary task.[104]

One hears and reads a lot about events regarding politicians, the government, and the head of state, much less about issues directly related to citizens' lives. Again, Enzo Forcella's account of what journalism, in particular, political journalism, looked like in the 1950s, fits well with what Tamberlich is saying:

Political journalist in Italy can count upon one thousand five hundred readers: all ministers and under-secretaries, some members of the parliament, all parties' leadership, union leaders, the high clergy, and some industrialists. The rest [of the people] does not count, even if the paper sells three hundred thousand copies.[105]

But whereas for Forcella the journalists' lack of freedom was, and still is, a structural condition determined by the economic reality of the Italian media industry and by the dictates of *partitocrazia*, for Tamberlich the possibility of redemption is a personal decision. Even if it is true that those in power need loyal journalists, he still believes that it is possible, for those who do not want to be the spokespersons for a given politician, to decide not to do so. The head of *TV7* gives an account of his own career to make the point:

I have been in RAI since after the Reform of 1975. Soon, I got interested in political affairs and became head of the Tg1 newsroom. In the end I gave up the political affairs department, because they needed journalists who were more careful, more aware of certain things. You want to define this *lottizzazione*? And probably you are right. However, even in the midst of political pressures, I have always put the quality of my work first. . . . For instance, I became close friends with Giorgio Almirante [secretary-general of the MSI, the extinct neo-Fascist party], but that never meant anything. Our friendship was a professional one.[106]

The solution to politicians' pressures is a matter of personal decision. Each journalist's sense of "autonomy" and goodwill are critical characteristics:

> At times journalists make autonomous efforts, individual efforts to emancipate themselves from political pressures. So, what I am saying is that there are spaces of autonomy. I always tell the young journalists here in the newsroom that whatever they put on the air is their responsibility, and theirs only. [No matter what your boss tells one to do,] if the piece on TV appears to be imbalanced, the main responsibility lies with the author of that piece. Therefore, even if there is this *lottizzazione*, and there are some pressures to conform, there are people who try to do their job with a modicum of honesty, and there are those who just don't want to do so. And then, of course, there are the ones who are autonomous from everything, the big shots of Italian journalism.[107]

Autonomy, for Tamberlich, seems to be a private matter, as self-censorship was for Stefano Tomassini. But where would one acquire and how would one implement such notions as quality and professionalism, balance and objectivity, if the structure, the institution's philosophy, does not support them? Should not such ideals be rooted in the tradition of the profession and in the tradition of the institution in order to become effective, since the final product, the televised message, is the result of collective endeavors and is embedded in a complex system (editorial line and the overall scheduling strategy)? And, more poignantly, are autonomy and independence even realistic expectations? Enzo Forcella does not think so:

> No journalist will ever say, "I am not independent." But in reality, a journalist cannot possibly be independent. . . . One might talk about spaces of freedom, but not independence. Yes, it's true, Giorgio Bocca [one of the "big shots" referred to by Tamberlich] can write whatever he pleases. Nevertheless, the editorial line of *La Repubblica* is not what Bocca writes. Furthermore, the young journalist cannot possibly do the same, he or she can't defend his or her liberty. Only somebody like Bocca can defend his spaces of freedom, even though what he writes can be easily neutralized by the editorial line of the newspaper, which is established with the headlines. There might be different degrees of spaces of freedom, but overall, independence and autonomy are extremely ambiguous concepts.[108]

Indeed. Ideals like autonomy and independence presuppose some kind of personal freedom of the intellectual that historically has shallow roots in Italy.

Censorship

Enzo Forcella puts his finger on the dynamic between structural tendencies and private freedoms when he defines the spaces of freedoms that each journalist, in various degrees, might be able to create for himself or herself. But when senior professionals such as Romano Tamberlich say that journalists can always choose a way out, that it is up to them to decide whether or not to follow the norm of doing what will please a certain politician or not, then *lottizzazione* is emptied of its structural responsibilities. Any effect it might have on journalists can be neutralized by one's personal autonomy and independence. *Lottizzazione* becomes an external formality, a rite of passage that controls journalists' hiring and career advancements, without seemingly having a major influence on professional practice and/or the broadcaster.

Certainly, there are different "degrees" of influence, or, vice versa, different degrees of independence, which clearly correlate to job security and seniority. However, overt censorship seems to be a very rare occurrence. Massimo Ghirelli, author and host of *Non solo nero* (Not Black Only), a well-known program on immigration and multiculturalism during the 1980s, shares his experience as an "external contractor":

> Censorship, direct censorship, is rare and very prudent. It happened two times to me. After they scold you once, then, for a while, they are going to follow the program more carefully, just to make sure. They ask you to let the text be seen by a supervisor. In extreme cases the director-general will call you up. But generally, journalists will avoid to do things that will get them in trouble. Anyhow, two instances of censorship over a period of six years is not much. It is clear, however, that such a small degree of censorship happens because there is already a strong self-censorship to begin with.[109]

But if it was very rare to experience "direct censorship," there were other ways by which pressure could be exercised:

> What you can find instead is plagiarism, some kind of soft coercion. While I was doing *Non solo nero*, I noticed more than once that there was some kind of disappointment on the part of Carlo Martelli [deputy prime minister in the 1989 Andreotti government and author of the 1990 immigration law] because we did not invite him nor any of his men to our program. The complaint was that we never called them not even on the phone. I had the clear sensation of what their expectations were; besides anything else, they wanted more space, more visibility.

But there was never an explicit request coming directly from the "high spheres."[110]

However, once the Socialist Party collapsed in 1992 and Berlusconi was elected prime minister in 1994, things changed. Ghirelli's program was cancelled; the reason, some argued, was because it was a Socialist program. Most likely, *Non solo nero* was axed because of a change in political culture rather than a purely political shift. Ghirelli is convinced: "The new guys did not like to talk about immigration,"[111] he said. The Moratti administration appointed by the center-right government in 1994 apparently did not even take into account the fact that *Non solo nero* had a high audience share and was cheap to make. Once they made up their mind that immigration was not going to be a topic of interest, the production was over:

> To have created a great program was not good enough. If for political reasons they decide that it's "no," then it's "no" and there is no audience, no share that is going to make a difference. In 1991 we reached a 31 percent of audience share and that was the highest share compared to other similar programs, and it was not really an expensive one to make. But the fact was that there was specific political opposition to it.[112]

Since Berlusconi entered politics, other allegations of censorship have surfaced. Besides the cases of journalists Enzo Biagi and Michele Santoro, whose programs were eliminated after Berlusconi made negative remarks about them, RAI's center-right leadership has been particularly alert about satirical shows. For instance, the show *Blob* was cancelled in early October 2002 after broadcasting a selection of Berlusconi's speeches delivered during his 2001 election campaign. In a communiqué, RAI's director-general Agostino Saccà justified his decision to pull the show off the air by accusing the producers of engaging in "partisan satire." Editorialist Curzio Maltese commented:

> In Berlusconi's RAI, we have become used to censorship of any critical, or even simply independent, voice. . . . [B]ut the idea that Berlusconi, via his faithful Saccà, might even censor himself, that is something new. It is curious that RAI's director-general might even consider "satirical" . . . the broadcast of the prime minister's most famous speeches. Indeed, the most "revolutionary" thing that *Blob* did was to air, without editing nor comments, Berlusconi's whole preelectoral "Contract with the Italians" speech.[113]

In November 2003, Sabina Guzzanti's show was cancelled after its first broadcast. In her satirical program, called *RaiOt* (pronounced "riot")–*Weapons of Mass Distraction*, the comedian attacked the entire political establishment, including, of course, the prime minister. She showed a graph of Mediaset winning easily in the advertising war with the other Italian media, suggesting that Berlusconi's influence as prime minister might have positive consequences on his media empire. Mediaset responded with a statement accusing Guzzanti of disseminating "lies and extremely serious insinuations" about the corporation. RAI's director-general justified the cancellation of the show as a precaution against possible legal consequences.

Internal and External Forces

Enzo Forcella and others have emphasized that the individual journalist, especially a new hire, doesn't stand much of a chance of resisting the pressure to conform. The implication is that a stronger union, or even stronger internal power groups, might be beneficial to the journalists' ability to negotiate degrees of autonomy from the powers that be. Understandably, this is a widespread conviction, shared by many senior journalists, including Francesco Mattioli, who believe that it is very important to stay united as a bloc against the politicians:

> The single individual cannot resist alone, isolated. I personally made it because I was one of the untouchables, therefore they could not easily get rid of me. But the young journalist can't do this. . . . The news director can easily tell him, "You either do what I want you to do, or it's over." The point is that politicians as well as news directors should feel that it's the entire RAI that is resisting, and not just the single young journalist.[114]

The notion that internal unity among journalists might represent a bulwark against political interference is certainly more realistic than the idealistic hope for professional autonomy conceived as a personal, or private, quality. An opposition between politicians and journalists is underlined. The subtle argument behind such opposition is that the end of *lottizzazione* can be achieved once more power is given to the latter, the journalists. The contradiction is evident: the journalists who believe that more power should be granted to them collectively to counter the power of the politicians tend to be senior journalists, who are also the ones who recognize *lottizzazione*'s positive sides. They argue that when RAI, and especially its newsrooms, will become financially, politically, and professionally stronger, then *lottizzazione*, or at least the negative sides of it, will be swept away. Celestino Spada holds a similar position when he argues that a financially more powerful broadcaster would better protect itself from political influence.

The alternatives of political (external) influence and internal groups are presented as antagonistic—as if a stronger internal cohesion would liberate the broadcaster from external *lottizzazione*. Eva Etzioni-Halevy talks similarly about the function of internal power groups in public broadcasting institutions as an element indicating resistance against political pressures. She reaches, however, an opposite conclusion. The questions that she asks are, "Is internal power preferable to political power? Is it preferable that internal groups decide the political culture of the institution, or is it not better that the parties and political powers set the guidelines?" She considers the second alternative preferable, if nothing else because the elites in power are democratically elected, whereas the top broadcasting officials are not.[115] For me the question is: Is the corporatist, sclerotic power of internal groups going to offer a viable solution to *lottizzazione*? According to some respondents, the "internal resistance" (the RAI Party, what is left of the *aziendalisti*, at times Usigrai) was supposedly born to defend RAI from political pressures. Such internal resistance, however, also became a fulcrum of corporatism, aimed at the conservation of the status quo and special privileges. Is this a valuable alternative to political interference?

Furthermore, even if it were true that internal power groups function as a site of resistance against external pressures, it is unclear whether the defense of the public broadcaster means the defense of the "old order," or if it expresses a genuine desire to counterpose something of value against commercial competition. This leads to another question: Is there anything left to be defended in Italian public service broadcasting, behind corporatist interests, special privileges, and the remembrance of old glories?

RAI's Power Groups

Certainly, through the decades, internal power groups have played a very important role in ensuring RAI's survival. What are those groups and what is their relationship with *lottizzazione*? Here I will introduce the most prominent among them: Usigrai, the journalists' union; the RAI Party; and the Journalists' Caste.

Usigrai

The journalists' comments regarding Usigrai and its relationship to *lottizzazione* vary considerably: there are those who hate what the union does, and those who love it. People like Massimo Ghirelli, and the many other external contractors and *precari* who are still waiting to be offered more secure positions, are not the only ones who are unhappy with the work done by the union so far, and question its true intent to get rid of political interferences in hiring. Indeed, the Usigrai has been criticized often for supporting corporatist interests and being involved in *lottizzazione*. For example, former member of the RAI board of directors Paolo Murialdi calls it the "mother of *lottizzazione*," and Marco Taradash, former head of the RAI Parliamentary Committee, defines Usigrai as the "great *lottizzatore*."[116]

On the other side, while acknowledging the union's constructive efforts to reduce the impact of political and party pressures on hiring, some observers believe that Usigrai, heavily politicized by a solid left DC and PCI leadership, is also characterized by a powerful "unionist" culture. Especially from 1990-1991 on, when the external political and social context became particularly chaotic and the traditional system of party reference crumbled, corporatist tendencies grew stronger:

> At that time, the union started to defend only internal journalists, its own members, against any outside pressure. A climate was created in which unionists would defend and protect each other. Among RAI journalists, Usigrai would protect the ones who were members of the union, and among these latter, the union would support more extensively those who were most active inside the union. Usigrai indeed represented, at that point, a new element of power inside RAI.[117]

Because of such corporatist tendencies, Usigrai is often accused of being a force aimed at defending the privileges of its journalists. But Roberto Natale, the union's secretary-general, rejects any allegations of being agents of conservatism or privilege. Taking a stance against Paolo Murialdi, he says:

> Let's stop talking about the union as an entity that only wants to conserve the status quo because that is not true. RAI journalists do not want to maintain things as they are. We do not like to live with this kind of RAI that has a bureaucracy that is still stuck at the time when RAI was a monopoly, whereas everything around us has changed.... [W]e are ready to talk about a reformation of RAI; we have no problems about it. We are available to discuss a new hypothesis for reformation, such as the proposal to transform RAI into a holding company [eventually RAI became a holding in 1999, and various sectors of its operations were privatized].... [W]e also agree on having private capital coming in. Indeed, without partial private capital RAI is going to be a dwarf in the international scenario.... [W]e are certainly ready for a change.[118]

Others agree with Roberto Natale. Not only is Usigrai not an agent of conservatism, but for many the union played a fundamental role opposing political powers, especially at times when it felt that the broadcaster was in danger. According to former Tg3 codirector Alberto Severi, for instance, the role of Usigrai was especially important in the early 1990s, when the union did, in a way, what the "magistrates working in the Clean Hands scandal did: on one side it put a certain system under attack; on the other side, it searched for more guarantees, more 'spaces,' to ensure free and professional information to the viewers."[119] In 1994, when the center-right leadership led by Letizia Moratti was supposedly dismantling the corporation to the benefits of Berlusconi's channels, the journalists' union provided much needed internal resistance and guidance, and fought one of its most vigorous battles, a "war of resistance," as Severi defines it. But, Severi concedes, that was not enough: that war ultimately weakened the journalists and the union. The reduced power of the director-general, a growing opposition between the journalists and RAI's leadership, the end of the postwar order of *partitocrazia*, and the increasing competition from terrestrial and satellite channels contributed to the creation of an unprecedented confusion within the broadcaster. According to Severi, the "lack of strong professional referents and appropriate guidance, the lack of quality directors, vice-directors, and channel directors, and the absence of strong internal guidance, palpably weakened the journalists, who became more precarious and more exposed."[120] Since then, other unions have developed alongside the Usigrai. The right-wing Singrai (*Sindacato Giornalisti* RAI) was born at the time of Berlusconi's 1994 victory to represent the journalists close to him; others, not in line with the center-left tradition of Usigrai, partially separated themselves from the union's main body in 1995 and gave birth to the so-called group of one hundred.

The RAI Party

Another powerful group inside the public broadcaster is the RAI Party, which, according to many observers, traverses traditional political party boundaries. In moments of danger for the corporation, the sense of affiliation to this party overcomes any distinction based on other political affiliations. For some, the RAI Party is a corporatist power that corrodes the broadcaster; for others, it is a necessary counterbalance to the power of the political sphere. Once again, former RAI board of directors' member Paolo Murialdi is among those who underline the negative characteristics of this party:

> This is a party formed by people inside and outside the corporation. It is a phantom party, something that you can't see. But it is there. It is a galaxy, a powerful nebula. The big portion of it is internal to the corporation. A smaller portion of it is external. Nevertheless, the external connection is absolutely vital; without it, the party wouldn't be as powerful as it is. It is a cross-party because it goes from the Left to the Right. You can see it appearing in moments of necessity. At that point the components of the party, namely, the internal and the external, the Left and the Right, all join together. Their getting together lasts only the time needed to achieve whatever goal they have on their agenda. Afterwards, everybody goes back to their own business, to their own political party affiliation.[121]

Murialdi declares that also the RAI Party is "an entity linked to *lottizzazione* and it is difficult to be identified, as it appears and disappears according to any given situation and interests."[122] Others agree: the party exists to "support the corporation, its own survival, and its own high salaries."[123] Many claim that Usigrai and the RAI Party go hand in hand when it is time for new broadcasting regulations to be passed, for the license fee to be renewed, or for the contract between the state and RAI to be drafted.

Yet others emphasize the positive aspects of the RAI Party, underlining that it was born as a counterpower to party influence; as such, *lottizzazione* and the RAI Party are opposite entities. According to Celestino Spada, this party, to which he declared that he himself belonged, was created to establish a strong internal resistance against political pressures:

It was created out of necessity at the time *lottizzazione* began. Such a party defined itself in contraposition to political interference. When others ignored us, we stood up and voiced our concerns, which would have remained silent otherwise. The RAI Party cannot be objectively defined in isolation. It was born as a defensive subject. The intent was to reinforce RAI as a consistent subject despite continuous political changes.[124]

Also for Sandro Petrone the RAI Party protects the interests of the corporation, and that is a legitimate endeavor: "It defends the interests of everybody working in RAI, as it happens also with the BBC. Also in the U.K. you have the Party of the BBC, right? But of course, everybody in this country has to talk negatively about RAI."[125]

Former Tg3 codirector Alberto Severi affirms the historical importance of the RAI Party, but is suspicious of its strenuous defense of corporatist interests:

In RAI we have people who, throughout the years, have tried to keep high the profile of the public broadcaster in an ambiguous context in which competition with Mediaset was at its peak. These people were aware that the struggle was about the values of public service information and that the alternative was to debase cultural standards and diminish the quality of programs. They tried to convey the principle that it was not true that more freedom could be found in the commercial broadcaster, but rather that there were strong interests at stake. This was the RAI Party. On the other side, it is also true that the RAI Party is getting old, old in its thinking; it is a party that is remaining inside its logics, its positions, its interests. It has become inevitably sclerotic, not blind, not ungenerous, but certainly sclerotic. It has become very conservative; it defends the memory, it defends one kind of presence of the public broadcaster that is now in contradiction with the needs of society.[126]

The Journalists' Caste

During the early 1990s another power group, a second "party," emerged in the shadows of the RAI Party. Whereas the RAI Party comprises aging members of top and middle management, this other group consists primarily of journalists. This group, or sect, as Roberto Mastroianni defines it, is able to "ride all different waves," as the strength derived from affiliation with it has been a guarantee of professional success even in periods of political turmoil. In the phase of "personalized *lottizzazione*," where political affiliation is determinant, friendships and personal connections are important, and caste affiliation is crucial:

> Life and politics in RAI are not simply a matter of political alliances anymore. To speak in general terms, the journalists' caste in Italy has always been a very enclosed and very sectarian one. The one in RAI is even more closed and sectarian. It mostly consists of journalists, but not every journalist can subscribe to it. It is a caste, as I said. They take your blood sample, they analyze your pedigree. They do a careful screening because once you are an insider, you are in, you are protected. It works as with the secret lodges. You will be supported in difficult situations; you will be helped in your career. The criteria to join are criteria of caste, lodges, personal friendships. This journalists' caste, like any caste or lodge, administers power; it is therefore able to provide contracts, hiring, and career advancements.[127]

Usigrai often contrasted the initiatives of the journalists' caste, especially when it was time to defend "indefensible journalists." "Often, but not always," underlines Mastroianni, whose professional career at RAI was at times negatively impacted by the lack of good connections with the "caste." He worked as an external contractor for fourteen years, even though he had an "enviable Vita" with plenty of experiences in new technologies and radio journalism. Finally he was given a lifelong contract as an administrator assistant; only after a few years, he moved up to become a journalist.

Somehow linked to the journalists' caste are the so-called video-clans, consisting of the entourage of popular anchors, talk show hosts, and public affairs stars. The "video-clans," which also gained much power and recognition during the 1990s and early 2000s, represent another important key to understanding power in the RAI of the new millennium:

> Groups, groups' migration—this is the key to interpret power inside the public broadcaster. . . . What counts today is the people, the stars, the talk show hosts, the anchors: Clemente Mimun [close to the *Polo delle Libertà* coalition, and director of Tg1 since 2002], Giovanni Minoli [author and host of the acclaimed public affairs program *Mixer* on RAI2], Michele Santoro. Those are the ones who have created around themselves a web of collaborators through the years. What counts more nowadays are the internal webs of power. Sponsors, authors, external and internal collaborators, all together they create a certain power group inside the corporation. And when the leader leaves, everybody

else leaves. In this sense, the relationship with Mediaset is also strange. Indeed, when people go from RAI to Mediaset they bring along with them their own entourage; therefore you see entire pieces of RAI being transferred over to Mediaset.[128]

This phenomenon has gone both ways: it is true that "pieces of RAI" have been transferred to Mediaset, but it is also true that pieces of Mediaset have been transplanted into RAI. This is what Gianni Minà defines as the *mediasettizzazione* of the public broadcaster: the process by which during the 1990s and early 2000s the "old" creative talents of RAI were encouraged to leave or given early retirement packages, while Mediaset managers, casting directors, producers, authors, and presenters moved into the public broadcaster.[129]

Journalists and Politicians: A Two-Way Flow

The board of directors used to contact each of the parties' secretariats. Indeed, each party secretariat had somebody responsible for the mass communication division. In reality, he was the guy in charge of negotiating appointments in RAI.[130]

Lottizzazione typically occurred during informal premeetings among a few members of the board of directors and party heads of the various mass communication divisions. That was the time when members of the board met with the parties' representatives to discuss and negotiate proposals about hiring and career advancements. The results of those negotiations were then reported to the formal meetings, where decisions were usually ratified.

However, the actual working out of *lottizzazione* was, and still is, more complex than this. From the interviews considered so far, it may appear as if RAI journalists were rather passive elements in the hands of politicians. *Lottizzazione*, indeed, has usually been conceived as a unidirectional flow of power, from the party secretariats to the public broadcaster and to the journalists. This interpretation, however, fails to acknowledge the importance of internal groups and the active role of journalists in ensuring and determining the flow of power. In this regard, Paolo Murialdi points out that

on one side there are the parties that put heavy pressure on RAI; on the other side there are RAI journalists and employees who seek out the parties to receive some kind of protection from them. There is this double link: the journalists on one side, and those who exploit the corporation on the other.[131]

According to this version, journalists actively engage in the search for political protection. But, if this is true, how does this active search work? Tg2 foreign correspondent Stefano Picchi describes the process:

> What happens is that journalists organize themselves in groups in the shadow of a given party so as to advance in their career, acquire positions of power, go to New York as foreign correspondents, and so forth. Politicians are, so to say, in demand. When there is a political change in the air, RAI journalists are busy looking for politicians' protection. They offer themselves to a given politician, saying, "I can be your guarantor. You better take me, otherwise, you know, the Communists might take over. You politician need to maintain your position inside the newsroom, and therefore you need me."

Picchi uses a very powerful metaphor to better define the relationship between politicians and journalists:

> The journalist is the prostitute, and the relationship between politics and journalism is like the one between the prostitute and her customer. She is in the street offering herself; the customer sees her and takes her. Same thing happens between us and the politicians. We offer ourselves, and politicians buy us. Most of my colleagues here are convinced that they are doing a good job, that what they are doing provides information.... I believe, instead, that the relationship between politicians and journalists is a criminal one, and that in such a relation each part deserves half of the life sentence; and we journalists are to be blamed because we keep quiet about these things.[132]

The Identity of Public Service Journalism

This notwithstanding, there still is, among most of the journalists I talked to, a sense of pride in working for the public broadcaster. It is not just the money. "It's about status," one of them told me, "not only among your colleagues, but mostly in the social context; you are highly regarded if you are a RAI journalist."[133] In fact, you would not be considered a "real" journalist unless you worked for RAI. At least, that was the case until the early 1990s, when the identification of public service journalists with the public broadcaster began to be challenged from inside as well as from outside the corporation. Those were the years when competition with live news programs on Fininvest channels began; those were also the years when the discourse about journalists' professional autonomy became more pervasive.

Since then, the emphasis on professional autonomy has provided a justification for a growing number of journalists (especially the most successful among them) to present themselves as public service journalists without being committed to any specific institution such as RAI, and claim their status even when they work for the commercial channels. Ownership of the channels is not an issue, they say, professionalism and integrity is what counts. They conceive of themselves as freely floating across airwaves, from public channels to commercial ones without constraints.

One of them is Michele Santoro. In 1996, after months of negotiations, he left the public broadcaster to join Berlusconi's channels. Santoro's decision, caused also by disagreements with the RAI center-left leadership at that time, stirred up lots of polemics. Santoro, an established star of Italian broadcast journalism and an icon of the partisan tradition, was accused by his colleagues, the union, and the progressive press of betraying the ideals of public service journalism.

Santoro justified his decision as an issue of professional autonomy: given his integrity and his commitment to the left and to public service, ownership of the broadcaster would not be a determinant factor in his work, and he would continue to be a politically active and progressive reporter no matter who the owner of the "means of production" was. Many of his colleagues in RAI (especially Usigrai members), who still considered public service journalism to signify first of all a commitment to RAI, labeled his defense a rationalization. Giorgio Balzoni, in his address to the Usigrai convention in 1996, commented on Santoro's decision to join the competition:

> It really bothered me to find out what Santoro has been saying about his passage from RAI to Mediaset. What he did was simply to choose in the marketplace the situation that seemed to better fit him. What can you do about this? Nothing. If one does not deeply believe in the role of public service broadcasting and one considers RAI just one piece like any other one on the market, then it is justifiable that some people might find it really difficult to continue such a front-line kind of commitment. However, the union was always contrary to what Santoro was

doing here in RAI and never supported [his] video-clans inside the public broadcaster.[134]

When Santoro went back to RAI in the spring of 1999, Usigrai expressed more disappointment with the way in which the corporation handled his return. A communiqué of the journalists' union stated that, even though Santoro and his collaborators would certainly reinforce the image of the public broadcaster, RAI should not have favored Santoro and his entourage by offering them lifelong guaranteed contracts, when instead there were still many *precari* waiting to obtain more secure positions.

Other journalists followed in Santoro's footsteps, including Maurizio Costanzo (talk show host) and Enrico Mentana (who became director of Tg5). They too embraced the notion that it is possible to do public service journalism even in Mediaset. In the winter of 1998, a particular event on commercial television was claimed by Costanzo to represent the new public service mission of commercial television. Antonio Di Bella, a medical doctor who was experimenting with a new cure for cancer, was the host of Costanzo's popular talk show on Canale5, *The Maurizio Costanzo Show*. Mediaset televised live the debate between Di Bella and Rosi Bindi, the minister of health at the time. RAI had refused to air such a debate because the issue was considered too politically sensitive and very controversial—Di Bella's therapy was widely followed but not officially accepted by the government and the medical establishment. The show, which was aired on prime time in direct competition with the news on RAI's flagship channel, got very high ratings. Mediaset claimed that they were performing a public service function by broadcasting such a controversial, cutting-edge, and widely popular debate. Rhetorically contrasting RAI, as standing on the government side, with Mediaset (on the common people's side), Canale5 argued that they offered an authentic public service in spite of the typical Roman bureaucratic impediments.

Enrico Mentana, director of Tg5, promoted the image of his news program as providing public service. In 1992, when the Clean Hands scandal first broke out, Tg5 was the first newscast to station a reporter at the Palazzo di Giustizia in Milan, the headquarters of the investigative pool of magistrates. When various bombs went off in Rome and Milan the night between July 27 and 28, 1993, Tg5 broadcast live from the scenes before any RAI TV crew was even able to reach the site.

These are certainly welcome achievements of commercial television and speak highly of the professional competence of its journalists and technicians, and the efficiency of its decision-making capabilities. However, they are not enough to define Mediaset as a public service broadcaster. Sharing the feelings of many of his colleagues, a senior RAI journalist argued that

> The commercial broadcaster cannot claim to represent public service just because they aired the Di Bella versus Bindi debate or because they beat Tg1 one night. Public service means something else. It means you are a public service broadcaster 24 hours a day, round-the-clock, on all three television channels, on all four radio channels, on TeleVideo, on RAI Corporation. This is fundamentally different than Mediaset just beating us for a few nights.[135]

This is true: no matter what people like Santoro, Costanzo, and others at Canale5 say, public service cannot be achieved just by a few, well-intentioned individuals. Instead, public service should indicate an overall strategy, an organic offering, a philosophy overriding the entire broadcaster, and not just a few episodes of quality programs, which is obviously not the main goal of Mediaset. Besides the daily news, *The Maurizio Costanzo Show* is only one of the few programs that is self-produced by Canale5: much of the rest of the network's daily offering consists of imported formats, soap operas, and daytime repeats of *The Maurizio Costanzo Show* of the day before.

However, it is also true that, because of the political instabilities of the 1990s, the frequent changes of leadership, and the perceived necessity to maximize the audience at all costs, the public broadcaster too has failed to elaborate an organic editorial plan and an editorial line for its channels (especially RAI1 and RAI2) that can offer a valuable alternative to commercial broadcasting. The point is: if public service broadcasting means, as the interviewee argues, an organic scheduling and programming, then not even RAI would pass the test.

In summary, the debate about what constitutes public service journalism and which kind of institutions might better support it is indicative of the journalists' search for a new identity. The controversy and the struggle over the meaning of public service also draws attention to the prestige that public service journalism still maintains, to the point that it is an object of contention between the two broadcasters.

How Journalists See Themselves

What role is professed nowadays for the public service journalist? To answer this question one must look not only at individuals but also at various publications, such as those by Usigrai (including the "Charter of Rights and Responsibilities of the Broadcast Journalist," 1990, and the report from their 1999 annual meeting—*Relazione al Congresso di Sorrento*), by the *Consiglio Nazionale Ordine Giornalisti* (the National Journalists Association, which published a "Charter of Journalists' Responsibilities," 1993), and by RAI-Radio Televisione Italiana (for instance, "Information and Programming for Viewers and Personnel of the Public Broadcaster," 1995).

These documents manifest the need felt among public service journalists to reflect on their own profession, its function in society, and its relationship with public opinion. Nevertheless, most of the statements in these documents appear almost ludicrous if one reads them in the context of *lottizzazione* and of the power struggle over RAI at the time when they were written (1990, the time of the CAF pressures on RAI; 1993, the struggles between the internal power groups and the professors' leadership; 1995, the era of Letizia Moratti, the center-right president appointed by Berlusconi's government; 1999, the struggle over privatization of the broadcaster).

Usigrai's Charter of 1990, for instance, states that "journalists are free from political interference, and are not interested in bringing their political ideas into their work."[136] Yet "in case of a change in the political-editorial line of each newsroom, the journalist can legitimately ask to go to another Tg."[137] Why should such a "free" and professionally apolitical journalist want to change his or her Tg if its political line changes? Could this indicate that, after all, political affiliation and the political line of a given newsroom are important to the journalist working there? Perhaps what this means is that the tradition of partisan journalism has not been abandoned. This tradition in itself, I believe, is not a target for satire. What is ludicrous and ideologically constructed is pretending that journalists are objective, free, independent, and "not interested in bringing their political ideas into their work."

In 1993, during the scandal of the party system and the collapse of the old establishment, the National Order of Journalists, stated that "trust is the basis of the relationship between [journalists] and citizens."[138] Such a statement can be justified only as wishful thinking. It is difficult to believe that at the apex of the Clean Hands investigation citizens trusted journalists.[139]

In 1995, during the Moratti presidency, RAI published its own charter stating that the "primary duty of the public broadcaster is to be impartial and correct . . . and that the differentiation among the three channels should be based on professional and editorial criteria and not on ideological criteria." Impartiality is considered fundamental, and the journalist should "commit himself to represent reality in all its aspects and in all its various interpretations." However, "when a topic is controversial, the journalist should present the interpretations that are more widely shared, and, therefore, more meaningful."[140] The echo here is interesting; less than one year earlier, at a July 1994 press conference, Silvio Berlusconi said that the public broadcaster should never go against the interests of the governing coalition (at that point his own coalition), which represented the majority of citizens.

In 1999, in response to various proposals that had been put forward to privatize the broadcaster and relegate its public service mission to the third channel, Usigrai supported the idea of a unified public service that would also include the "editorial areas in part fed by the market."[141] But the document failed to specify how areas financed by advertising and other market resources would be able to deliver a public service. The document portrays the image of RAI journalists as hostages of political power, as those who are just waiting for the broadcaster to become financially stronger to finally break free. The union fails to recognize that there are other obstacles on the path to a distinctive journalistic offering on RAI channels. In fact, "gossip," "light news," "sensationalism," and other "trivia" have taken over much of Tg1 and Tg2. As a consequence, those news programs look more and more similar to those offered by the commercial channels. The document falls short of acknowledging that this trend is dictated by the need to compete for advertising money and fails to detail how it might be reversed.

What these documents tell us is that Italian journalism desperately wants to identify itself with liberal values that in Italy have weak roots and almost no history. Why is that? And what do such formal statements of "good intentions" seek to accomplish? Do they try to cover further political maneuvers? Do they just want to mystify reality?

Conclusion

To study *lottizzazione* in RAI is like entering a labyrinth. One starts looking for notions and testimonies about the relationship between the party system and the public broadcaster. Soon one realizes that such a relationship is neither unidirectional nor simple, but multidimensional, with each one of its dimensions having ramifications, streams, and subdivisions.

Lottizzazione is, at least, a two-way phenomenon in which politicians and journalists are evenly involved. In this sense it is symbiotic; the former could probably not exist without the latter, and vice versa. And because it is not a one-way process, its functioning intertwines with other forms of power internal to the broadcaster. The result is something that appears, at times, almost senseless, even absurd. Roberto Mastroianni, one of my respondents, told me something that I will never forget: "Here, everything is much simpler than it looks from the outside." He said. "The metastrategies, the political tactics, come after. They come in at a second moment. What is determinant is, very often, contingencies, minor things."[142] He gave an example. Why, he asked, "is RAI so behind in the development of high technologies and related infrastructures, especially fiber optics?" This is not just the result of a political plan to keep RAI at the margins. Things like this happen, Mastroianni argued, because those who are in charge of new technologies and innovations are incompetent:

> They were given the job because they were somebody's lovers or somebody's ex-schoolmate. But they know nothing about new technologies and for them there is no difference between cable and fiber optics. So, they make decisions that turn the clock back on the broadcaster, but nobody cares.[143]

This triviality may partly justify the sense of unreality and incredulity that some journalists expressed when I asked them about *lottizzazione*. This may help explain why *lottizzazione* has easily hidden itself within the shadow of "common sense." It has become invisible perhaps not as of the result of carefully thought out hegemonic plans, but mostly because of its banality. One of my respondents, Piero De Chiara, an acute observer and a real connoisseur of *lottizzazione*, could not stop laughing while describing to me the various theories and corollaries. *Lottizzazione* is so banal, so simple, so ludicrous in a way, that it becomes easily normalized, has easily built into itself the mechanism to balance, and therefore please, all the various power groups. By doing so, *lottiz-*

zazione has been able to survive. And perhaps, by doing so, RAI has been able to survive. The "zebra" theory, for instance, is perfect, a masterpiece in a sense. So perfect that the existence of *lottizzazione* has even been considered as an enrichment of democracy and its possible end is feared, as it might also bring with it the end of pluralism. *Lottizzazione* perfectly suited the Italian political system, the tradition of our journalism. It suited the needs of a deeply divided society, where political involvement and political participation were emotionally, religiously practiced, and where objective journalism could not become a realistic aspiration. As Enzo Forcella reminded us, "It is generally easier for a journalist to be objective in a society as homogeneous as the American one; in a society as profoundly divided as the Italian one is, any journalist must take a stand!"[144]

This is not to say that *lottizzazione* does not have its hateful side. Throughout the years, as the practice of *lottizzazione* has become empty and meaningless, but rigorously followed nonetheless, it has become even more difficult to legitimate on the basis of its classic justification, as a tool to provide pluralism and wider political participation. The testimonies of junior journalists, who aggressively and ironically dismiss its very existence, express arrogance. It is the arrogance of those who have "made it," who are part of a privileged class and don't consider even slightly questioning how they got there and how they are going to live their professional careers in the future. *Lottizzazione* is not a business that one should take lightly just because it is banal. It is banal, but it is real; it determines appointments, hiring procedures, promotions, and a modus vivendi among journalists.

What is the role of public service journalists in Italy? How do the journalists see themselves and what they do? Well, of course, the answers to these questions are directly correlated with what one thinks about *lottizzazione*. From an Anglo-American perspective represented by observers such as Wolfgang Achtner, Italian journalism might be conceived as deeply and irredeemably corrupt. According to him:

> Italian journalists know really well that their only role is to be a docile and passive instrument in the hands of the politicians. Therefore, they are very happy to perform such a role. They make good money and live much better than other journalists worldwide and don't really work at all. . . . In America, facts are important. In Italy, facts do not count.[145]

Obviously, this is not what most RAI journalists (with a few exceptions) think about themselves. The ones who do not acknowledge the existence of *lottizzazione* perceive their way of doing journalism as objective and impartial, directed to reporting facts, not politics. As I noted, political connections, *lottizzazione*, and partisan journalism are considered obsolete practices. Now the trend is toward factual, objective reporting.

According to others, especially senior and left-wing journalists, *lottizzazione* is not a negative practice, and it does not destroy an ideal function of public service broadcasting, since such an ideal does not even exist, and even if it did exist, it would be ambiguous, ideologically constructed. "You can't be a journalist and be independent at the same time. It's an internal contradiction."[146] For many of the old guard and for the intellectuals among them, independence, objectivity, freedom, on one side, and the role of journalists, on the other, are concepts that mutually contradict each other.

Notes

1. Enzo Biagi, "Strettamente personale. Coscienze lottizzate e libertà di coscienza," in *Corriere della Sera* (Milan), November 26, 1998.

2. "Blocked democracy" refers to the lack of alternate government that has characterized the Italian political system from 1947 to 1992. During those forty-five years the Christian Democratic Party (DC) governed the country by itself and/or in coalitions with other parties. The Italian Communist Party, the main opposition party, was never allowed to govern.

3. Stuart Hall, "Gramsci's Relevance for the Study of Race and Ethnicity," *European Journal of Communication Enquiry* 10 (January 1986): 20.

4. Claudia Trincheri, "Gli intellettuali che lavorano alla RAI-TV," *Rassegna italiana di sociologia*, date and place of publication not available, 137.

5. Ettore Bernabei and Giorgio Dell'Arti, *L'uomo di fiducia I retroscena del potere raccontati da un testimone rimasto dietro le quinte per cinquant'anni* (Milan: Arnoldo Mondadori, 1999), 148.

6. Francesco Mattioli, president of RAI International Relations directorate, interview with author, tape recording, RAI International Directorate, Borgo S'Angelo, Rome, March 1998.

7. Mattioli, 1998.

8. Bernabei and Dell'Arti, *L'uomo di fiducia*, 146.

9. Sandro Petrone, vice-director of Tg2 foreign department at time of interview, interview with author, tape recording, RAI headquarters, Saxa Rubra, Rome, January 1998.

10. The fact that journalism schools serve to recruit a diverse population of students is supported by research confirming that by 1995 a considerable number of journalism students came from the south and the islands, which were traditionally underrepresented areas. See Gianni Faustini, "I numeri della professione giornalistica," *Problemi dell'informazione* 20, no. 3 (September 1995).

11. In addition to the journalism school, there are thirteen schools of communication sciences in Italian universities. Most of them are located in the north and center-north regions; two are in the center (Rome and Teramo); one is in the southern region of Campania (University of Salerno); one is in Sicily (University of Palermo).

12. Roberto Natale, "Audizione di rappresentanti dell'USIGRAI" (Audition of Usigrai's representatives) to the RAI Parliamentary Committee, December 12, 2000, on the world wide web at www.camera.it/_dati/leg13/lavori/stenbic/21/2000/1206/s020.htm.

13. Faustini, "I numeri della professione giornalistica," 380.

14. This number represents the total number of employees holding a permanent position in RAI. External contractors and *precari* are not included. The total number of full-time employees continued to drop through the 1990s. However, this did not mean that RAI's payroll got slimmer. For instance, to the 10,995 employees accounted for on the *Annuario RAI 1997*, we need to add approximately 1,195 employees on part-time contracts.

15. Data from RAI, Radio Televisione Italiana, *Annuario RAI 1997* (Rome: RAI, 1998), 188-189.

16. Elaborations on data from *Annuario RAI 2001* (Rome: ERI, 2002), 145, and from *Annuario RAI 2000* (Rome: RAI, 2001), 165.

17. However, although the number of female students in journalism schools increased during the 1990s, as did the overall number of female journalists working for a variety of news organizations, the number of women in positions of responsibility remained low. For instance, even though in 1995 females represented 25 percent of professional journalists, only 15 percent of them were editors in chief, and 13 percent were managing editors. See Faustini, "I numeri della professione giornalistica," 379-380.

18. Managing editor is the translation of *"redattore capo."* I followed William Porter's guidelines to translate journalists' titles from the Italian to English. See William E. Porter, *The Italian Journalist* (Ann Arbor: University of Michigan Press, 1983), viii-x.

19. Elaborations on data from Trincheri, "Gli intellettuali che lavorano alla RAI-TV," 144-145.

20. In 1995, the best-paid journalists were those between the age of 59 and 60 (average salary 72,000 euros), the least paid were those under 30 (average salary 26,000 euros). At that time, the average salary of a public school teacher

was approximately 16,000 euros, and the average annual salary of a member of parliament was approximately 96,000 euros. Elaborations on data reported in Valerio Pietrantoni, "Finanziaria, stipendio ridotto ai giornalisti? I partiti si dividono su un emendamento," *L'Unione Sarda* (Cagliari), October 28, 1995.

21. See *Il Mondo*, supplement to *Corriere della Sera* (Milan), August 30, 1997; and Anonymous, "RAI e Mediaset, ecco gli stipendi d'oro di giornalisti e dirigenti," in *Corriere della Sera* (Milan), August 30, 1997.

22. Piero De Chiara, interview with author, tape recording, Olivetti Foundation, Rome, April 3, 1998.

23. De Chiara, 1998.

24. Petrone, 1998.

25. Petrone, 1998.

26. Paolo Giuntella, head of *Tg1 Special* at time of interview, interview with author, RAI headqaurters, Saxa Rubra, Rome, April 1998.

27. De Chiara, 1998.

28. Roberto Natale, secretary-general of Usigrai, interview with author, tape recording, Usigrai headquarters, Saxa Rubra, Rome, March 1998.

29. Natale, 1998.

30. Natale, 1998.

31. Natale, 1998.

32. Stefano Tomassini, head of Tg1 Foreign Department, interview with author, tape recording, RAI headquarters, Saxa Rubra, Rome, January 1998.

33. Giorgio Balzoni, head of Tg1 Domestic Political Affairs department and former secretary-general of Usigrai, interview with author, tape recording, RAI headquarters, Saxa Rubra, Rome, February 1998.

34. Petrone, 1998.

35. Petrone, 1998.

36. Usigrai, "Accesso in RAI tramite selezione, 1978-1993," Rome, July 1993, Usigrai internal publication.

37. Usigrai, "Accesso in RAI."

38. Usigrai, "Accesso in RAI."

39. Francesca Nocerino, Tg2 reporter, interview with author, tape recording, Tg2 newsroom, RAI headquarters, Saxa Rubra, Rome, April 1998.

40. Daniela Vergara, Tg2 anchor, telephone interview with author, RAI headquarters, Saxa Rubra, Rome, January 1998.

41. Valerio Fiorespino, head of the Journalists' Division at the RAI Personnel Office, interview with author, tape recording, RAI headquarters, Viale Mazzini, Rome, April 1998.

42. Fiorespino, 1998.

43. Fiorespino, 1998.

44. Fiorespino, 1998.

45. Fiorespino, 1998.

46. Fiorespino, 1998.

47. Fiorespino, 1998.

48. Nocerino, 1998.

49. For a detailed account of how news programs reported the unfolding events during the Clean Hands scandal, see Maria Grazia Bruzzone, *L'Avventurosa storia del TG in Italia dall'avvento della televisione a oggi* (Milan: RCS Libri S.p.A., 2002), 355-361.

50. Nocerino, 1998.

51. Nocerino, 1998.

52. By saying that he is an *aziendalista*, this respondent wants to underline that he follows the corporation's orders. Indeed, there are rules that forbid RAI employees to release interviews that might harm the corporation. But there are also rules that protect freedom of speech, so there are ways to talk about sensitive issues while protecting oneself from potential problems with the corporation. Anyhow, he was the only one of my respondents who opted not to release an interview on the basis of the rules forbidding to release potentially damaging information.

53. RAI official, telephone interview with author, March 1998.

54. Bettino Craxi, fax letter from Hammamet, Tunisia, April 1998.

55. Craxi recommended that I read his book, *Guerra d'Africa* (Milan: Giornalisti Editori, 1997).

56. Daniele Ronzoni, head of Tg2 Domestic Political Affairs department, telephone interview with author, January 15, 1998.

57. Ronzoni, 1998.

58. Ronzoni, 1998.

59. Fiorespino, 1998.

60. Ronzoni, 1998.

61. Tomassini, 1998.

62. Tomassini, 1998.

63. Nocerino, 1998.

64. The professors' television era refers to the time when RAI board of directors consisted of five intellectuals and academicians (1993-1994).

65. Nocerino, 1998.

66. Ronzoni, 1998.

67. Ronzoni, 1998.

68. Gianni Minà, telephone interview with author, December 28, 2002.

69. Ettore Bernabei, interview with author, Rome, December 6, 1996.

70. Roberto Morrione, interview with author, tape recording, RAI headquarters, Saxa Rubra, Rome, July 24, 2002.

71. Vergara, 1998.

72. Carlo Gallucci, "Eiar Eiar alalà," in *L'Espresso* (Rome), vol. 42, March 1, 1996, 49.

73. Vergara, 1998.

74. Vergara, 1998.

75. Vergara, 1998.

76. Petrone, 1998.

77. Petrone, 1998.
78. Celestino Spada, head of RAI Research Department (*Verifica Qualità Programmi Trasmessi*), interview with author, tape recording, RAI headquarters, Via Teulada, Rome, January 8, 1998.
79. Spada, 1998.
80. Mattioli, 1998.
81. Spada, 1998.
82. Balzoni, 1998.
83. Francesco Siliato, interview with author, tape recording, Milan, January 30, 1998.
84. Siliato, 1998.
85. Siliato, 1998.
86. Balzoni, 1998.
87. Balzoni, 1998.
88. Mattioli, 1998.
89. Mattioli, 1998.
90. Roberto Mastroianni, interview with author, tape recording, RAI headquarters, Via Mazzini, Rome, January 1998.
91. As Giovanni Cesareo writes, those terms do not "put into discussion the ... functioning [of the apparatus]. ... How indeed, could such independence of journalists be claimed? Only on the false notion that journalists are creative intellectuals working in a vacuum," in Giovanni Cesareo, *La televisione sprecata* (Milan: Feltrinelli, 1974), 56.
92. Tomassini, 1998.
93. Tomassini, 1998.
94. Petrone, 1998.
95. Petrone, 1998.
96. Morrione, 2002.
97. Morrione, 2002.
98. Morrione, 2002.
99. Tomassini, 1998.
100. De Chiara, 1998.
101. Enzo Forcella, quoted in Alberto Asor Rosa, "Il giornalista: appunti sulla fisiologia di un mestiere difficile," in *Storia d'Italia*, Annals 4, *Intellettuali e potere*, eds. Ruggero Romano and Corrado Vivanti (Turin: Giulio Einaudi, 1981), 1232.
102. De Chiara, 1998.
103. Romano Tamberlich, director of *TV7* at time of interview, interview with author, tape recording, RAI headquarters, Saxa Rubra, Rome, March 17, 1998.
104. Tamberlich, 1998.
105. Forcella, quoted in Rosa, "Il giornalista."
106. Tamberlich, 1998.
107. Tamberlich, 1998.

108. Forcella, telephone interview with author, December 6, 1996.

109. Massimo Ghirelli, interview with author, Italian Foreign Ministry, Rome, January 1998.

110. Ghirelli, 1998.

111. Ghirelli, 1998.

112. Ghirelli, 1998.

113. Curzio Maltese, "La censura della RAI si abbatte anche su Blob," in *La Repubblica* (Rome), October 10, 2002.

114. Mattioli, 1998.

115. Eva Etzioni-Halevy, *National Broadcasting under Siege*, (New York: St. Martin's Press, 1987).

116. Marco Taradash, interview with author, tape recording, Senate of the Republic, Rome, April 1998.

117. De Chiara, 1998.

118. Natale, 1998.

119. Alberto Severi, interview with author, tape recording, RAI headquarters, Saxa Rubra, Rome, March 10, 1998.

120. Severi, 1998.

121. Paolo Murialdi, interview with author, tape recording, Milan, January 31, 1998.

122. Murialdi, 1998.

123. Rodolfo Brancoli, director of Tg1 in 1996, interview with author, tape recording, *Liberal* headquarters, Rome, March 1998.

124. Spada, 1998.

125. Petrone, 1998.

126. Severi, 1998.

127. Mastroianni, 1998

128. Ghirelli, 1998.

129. Gianni Minà, "L'invasione dei mediacorpi," in *Il Manifesto* (Rome), March 20, 2002.

130. Brancoli, 1998.

131. Murialdi, 1998.

132. Stefano Picchi, foreign correspondent for Tg2 at time of interview, interview with author, tape recording, RAI headquartes, Saxa Rubra, Rome, January 1998.

133. Petrone, 1998.

134. Giorgio Balzoni, "Relazione congresso Usigrai" (Address to Usigrai Annual Convention), internal publication, Boario, Italy, November 19-22, 1996.

135. Balzoni, 1998.

136. Usigrai, "Carta dei diritti e dei doveri del giornalista radiotelevisivo del servizio pubblico" (Charter of rights and responsibilities of the broadcast journalist), Rome, 1990, web document, no page number available.

137. Usigrai, "Accesso in RAI."

138. Ordine Nazionale dei Giornalisti (Journalists' National Body), and Federazione Nazionale della Stampa Italiana (National Federation Italian Press), "I doveri del giornalista" (Charter of Journalists' Responsabilities), Rome, July 8, 1993, no page number available.

139. RAI too was involved in the Clean Hands scandal. Its administration was under judicial investigation for approving illegitimate expenses to its foreign correspondents, for inappropriately commissioning the construction of the Saxa Rubra news production center (according to the initial plans, the cost of the new headquarters was estimated at about 75 billion lira; its final cost was 290 billion), and for allowing party interference in the career advancement of its journalists. *Lottizzazione* itself became sort of a "crime." In the winter of 1992, the Cassation Court declared that to remove a journalist from his or her position in order to offer the position to somebody else according to *lottizzazione* procedures was damaging to the career of the journalist who lost the job. The case was that of a former vice-director of Gr3 (the news program on the third radio channel), who had been removed from his position in 1983. He had kept his title and salary *ad personam*, but had been moved to another department with different duties. In 1995, another radio journalist won his lawsuit for literally losing his voice when he learned on the phone that he had been replaced by somebody else as a result of a *lottizzazione* procedure.

140. RAI, Radio Televisione Italiana, "Carta dell'informazione e della programmazione a garanzia degli utenti e degli operatori del servizio pubblico" (Information and Programming for Viewers and Personnel of the Public Service Broadcaster), March 1995, place of publication and page number no available.

141. Usigrai, "Relazione al Congresso di Sorrento," November 9-12, 1999, on the web at www.usigrai.it/doc/relaz_99.htm.

142. Mastroianni, 1998.

143. Mastroianni, 1998.

144. Forcella, 1996.

145. Wolfgang Achtner, interview with author, tape recording, Rome, July 11, 2001.

146. Forcella, 1996.

Conclusion

Political Power and the Media

Celestino Spada argued that a historical work on *lottizzazione* would be of no interest because the phenomenon itself is becoming obsolete, not as relevant now as it was in earlier times.[1] He further articulated his position by constructing *lottizzazione* as a secondary, derivative phenomenon rather than as a structural one. Other people I interviewed voiced a similar position: *lottizzazione* is an anachronistic practice to the point that, as one of the respondents said, not even newspapers use such a term anymore. Certainly, the financial weaknesses of the broadcaster and other challenges, like securing a public service role in the digital future, are crucial considerations, perhaps more pressing than the (withering) influence of political parties. But, contrary to what Spada and others might have expected, if it is true that political party influence is fading away, the result is not to advantage a citizens' television nor to create a new broadcaster in the interest of the public. When the majority of broadcasting television channels (not to mention other media outlets, including magazines and newspapers) are concentrated in the hands of one political and economic bloc, and one person, one wonders whether *lottizzazione* wasn't just a childish game, almost innocent compared to a situation in which a prime minister is also the owner of a media empire.

Granted, the history of the broadcaster's proximity with the political powers and the tradition of interrelationships among the state, the government administrations, and industry show that, far from the "Berlusconi phenomenon" being an exceptional event, the media magnate is "the purest example of the monopolist's mentality, in its obsession with the trappings of power that remains at the heart of Italian business."[2] But with Berlusconi, the closeness between the media and the political sphere has reached unprecedented levels. In fact, the end of the state monopoly and the liberalization of the airwaves have failed to open up more spaces for civil society and for other broadcasters to compete in the television sector. To the contrary, the "private monopolist has linked the destiny of his business to the political world of which, he and his party have become the protagonists."[3]

The broadcasting market has evolved in a condition of duopoly that has prevented other operators from entering the competition (another noticeable terrestrial television broadcaster is La7, owned by Telecom Italia, with an audience share of approximately 2 percent). Indeed, the Italian market is characterized by the highest level of concentration in Europe. By the end of 2001, the two major television networks shared 90 percent of the audience versus 74 percent in France, 66 percent in Germany, 65 percent in the U.K., and 54 percent in Spain. RAI and Mediaset also shared 96 percent of advertising resources available for television (65 percent to Mediaset, 31 percent to RAI).

Lottizzazione as Organic Ideology

In the introduction I defined my purpose: to objectify the phenomenon of *lottizzazione* and to "retrieve it from the shadow of common sense." The history of *lottizzazione* in RAI, and journalists' perceptions of it, demonstrate that *lottizzazione* has been anything but an impalpable phenomenon ("*problema impalpabile*").[4] Various philosophical elaborations have given *lottizzazione* its legitimating and operating principles, underwriting its power and relevance. Even if its rules were neither codified nor written anywhere, each member of the board of directors, each party representative, knew exactly what to do and which rules to apply when appointing or promoting somebody. *Lottizzazione* developed as an organic ideology, "and indeed [had] the same energy and strength as a material force."[5] Through the years, the political powers became a familiar, close, almost unconscious presence within journalists' professional ideology.

This is even more the case among those junior journalists who refused to acknowledge the existence of *lottizzazione* and who almost religiously underlined how autonomous and independent they are, and how objective their work was. But what can be learned from RAI's history and its involvement with the political system? And what does its history tell us about the broadcaster's role in the democratic life of the country? In order to answer these questions, it is relevant to sum up the history of *lottizzazione*, with an emphasis on the degree of autonomy that the public broadcaster enjoyed and on the consequences of the relationship between *lottizzazione* and the commercial broadcaster.

Lottizzazione and the History of RAI

The degree of autonomy enjoyed by the public broadcaster varied over the decades according to the hegemonic strategies adopted by the ruling elites and their governing paradigms. During RAI's early days the public broadcaster was administered as a direct emanation of the Christian Democratic Party (DC). Already by that time, however, internal resistance against the director-general (traditionally a DC appointee) was strong, centered on the group of the *aziendalisti*, a powerful group linked to the Piedmont management of the old EIAR (Ente Italiano Audizioni Radiofoniche, the radio broadcaster during the Fascist regime).

Things changed during Ettore Bernabei's tenure as director-general (1961-1974). Bernabei was a strategist. He opened RAI to other political forces and created a more autonomous pole of power in continuous negotiation with the *aziendalisti*, on one side, and with the political establishment, on the other. Bernabei established for the broadcaster "relative independence" from the party system and created his own hegemonic model, always careful not to alienate anybody.[6] His model could be defined as an "enlightened monarchy." Indeed, the director-general had all the power centralized in his hands, but he was also able to surround himself with excellent journalists and the best management. Bernabei ruled by consensus.

Therefore, RAI evolved as a center of power in itself, certainly not completely independent from the political sphere, but able to bargain. The Bernabei era was a time when "information on television was the mirror of political evolution, but it was also a bit ahead compared to what was happening in the government coalitions."[7] Rather than being a direct emanation of political power, the public broadcaster set the trends by anticipating evolutions in the political sphere. Although Bernabei's leadership was condemned by the Left, more recently, those times are remembered by most center and leftist journalists as times of pride, times when "talents . . . were valued, promoted, [and] encouraged."[8] Those were also the times of RAI's monopoly on Italian television.

By the end of the 1960s, the hegemony of the DC was in crisis, and the party was corroded by internal power struggles. The overwhelming prodivorce results of the 1974 referendum were the most tangible sign that the influence of the Catholic bloc over social and cultural relationships was ending. Meanwhile, progressive forces asking for a reform of the broadcaster were working to undermine the DC's supremacy inside RAI. At the same time, promarket interests supporting private broadcasting were gaining momentum. The lack of internal cohesion within the Christian Democratic Party made it impossible to coalesce around an apparently common goal: to defeat those forces that wanted to break the centrality of the public broadcaster and its monopoly.

Bernabei's directorship was an enlightened monarchy, but a monarchy nevertheless. The parties wanted to create a more democratic broadcaster instead. Their democratizing intent, however, was not to eliminate party control (the DC's control), but rather to extend a share in such control to other political parties. The Reform Law of 1975 marked a change in the relationship between the broadcaster and the political sphere. It reduced the public broadcaster's autonomy and designed new positions, a new structure to be filled up according to party quotas.

This notwithstanding, RAI never became a fief, a terrain to be purely conquered. Internal groups always had to be taken into consideration during negotiations when appointments were made. Furthermore, journalists and their unions played an active role in the relationship between the public broadcaster and the political sphere.

The first years after the Reform Law of 1975 are remembered by many of the old guard as a time of innovation and excitement. But that pride was doomed to diminish, soon to be replaced by the fear of competition. The monopoly was crumbling. Political parties began to play double roles, espousing conservatism inside the public broadcaster but liberalism (deregulation) outside it, in the commercial broadcasting sector.

Lottizzazione and Commercial Broadcasting

The breaking of RAI's monopoly and the evolution of the commercial broadcasting sector played an important role in the ways in which *lottizzazione* developed. Indeed, its growth was directly proportional to the growth of Fininvest. While *lottizzazione* was becoming relatively "normalized" inside the public broadcaster (a first relative "normalization" occurred two years after the Reform Law of 1975; a more definitive normalization occurred in the late 1980s), the commercial broadcaster was developing. The stronger Fininvest became, the more invasive *lottizzazione* became. By the time Fininvest had established its monopoly, in the mid-1980s, *lottizzazione* had become more pervasive, involving all the major parties. As the parties were struggling to maintain (or gain, in the case of the Communist Party) partial control of the broadcaster, the defense of RAI became the defense of the parties' own space in it. That is one reason why "the defense of public broadcasting in Italy is [often] in bad faith."[9] Parties lacked a unified political culture. For example, the DC, especially its left wing, traditionally more socially conscious and supportive of public services, opposed breaking RAI's monopoly. But other exponents of that party, in particular members of its right wing interested in the business opportunity represented by the private sector, although unofficially, favored the evolving commercial stations. Hoping to create new outlets for more progressive perspectives, the Left also supported the idea of opening up to independent broadcasters. In 1980, the Communist Party (PCI) established its own network of television stations. At first, only a few members of the Socialist Party encouraged local initiatives of television and radio broadcasting; however, by the end of the 1970s, the PSI had become a strong supporter of the pro-liberalization movement.

The "freedom of antenna" movement further legitimated commercial broadcasters as the heralds of freedom from political interference. RAI appeared sclerotic, "carved up among parties," while the new stations allegedly embodied the notion of liberty from political corruption. Surprisingly, in Italy the independent/commercial broadcasters gained the support of leftist groups and became perceived as spaces in which freedom, independence, and democracy could flourish. Instead, the independent/commercial sector flourished as a site where television could "give to the people what the people wanted," that is, mindless entertainment. That was the apotheosis of a populist democracy. The Left and the social movements of the 1970s wanted a new media system. They got a duopoly. The parties wanted more democracy inside the public broadcaster. They fortified *lottizzazione*.

By the early 1980s, the Socialist Party had become Berlusconi's main ally. The PSI supported the so-called Berlusconi decree of 1984, which allowed Fininvest channels to broadcast nationally, thereby reversing previous decisions of the Constitutional Court (which forbade commercial operators from broadcasting beyond regional borders). The decree was especially significant for two main reasons: (1) it layed down the premises for the growth of Fininvest as the sole operator in the commercial sector; and (2) it sanctioned an even stronger grip of the political parties over the public broadcaster by reinforcing the role of the parliament and the Parliamentary Committee. The strategy of the party system was only apparently contradictory: its interest was to support the formation of a monopoly in the private sector, easier to control, while, at the same time, reinforce its own positions within the public broadcaster.

In 1987, the Communist Party was given the third national public channel. Perhaps unconsciously, by increasing its presence within RAI and accepting RAI3, the Left played in favor of Berlusconi. Indeed, the price that the PCI had to pay for obtaining RAI3 was not to obstruct the Socialists's efforts to support Berlusconi's channels. Indeed, one of the main results of *consociativismo*, a term indicating the participation, official and unofficial, of all parties, including the PCI, in government decisions, was the Mammì Law of August 1990, which legitimated Fininvest as the only national commercial broadcaster.

A New Rhetoric

On the occasion of the 1995 referendum, citizens were asked (among other things) whether or not they wanted to eliminate provisions limiting advertising breaks during televised movies on commercial television. The issue was presented by Fininvest (Mediaset since 1996) as a life-or-death question for the commercial broadcaster. To limit advertising revenues, it was argued, would mean the end of Fininvest, the end of freedom and playfulness, and a return to the seriousness of RAI. Italians voted against the restrictions. As it happened during the 1970s, the private broadcaster was once again portrayed as the guarantor of freedom, that which would provide liberation from the state and ensure more choices for consumers. But this time the distinctions were net: the Right was with Berlusconi's channels and the Left with the RAI channels. The commercial broadcaster, conservative ideologues contended, offered "real" pluralism as opposed to party pluralism, the only kind of pluralism that RAI had ever been able to provide. Indeed, according to philosopher Paolo Del Debbio, "real" pluralism is the prerogative of commercial television, representing the modern electronic agora whose primary function is to address consumers' desires. On the opposite side, there is party pluralism, whose central concern, according to the philosopher, is not the citizens, but the well-being of political parties.[10]

In reality, however, the Fininvest channels developed in the shadow of the party system under the protection of the Socialists and the right-wing Christian Democrats. Not only did Berlusconi's televisions enjoy the support of the political establishment, but their expansion was also directly correlated to the normalization of *lottizzazione* inside the public broadcaster.

A Dialectic Opposition

What was, then, the relationship between *lottizzazione* and commercial broadcasting? Certainly, one of the most important lesson that can be learned from the history of RAI is that the support of the party system was important to maintain a certain independence from market imperatives. As my respondents said, the reason for the increasing strength of *lottizzazione* in RAI was so that the public broadcaster could become stronger, supported by all the political parties that mattered. Indeed, the protection that surrounded RAI during the 1980s served the purpose of defending it from outside competition. This was *lottizzazione*'s second important contribution to the evolution of public service broadcasting: the first one occurred in the 1970s, when the parties' *lottizzazione* put an end to the DC latifundium.

Indeed, if we abandon the false belief that journalism should be objective and that public broadcasting should occupy a space separated from both the market and the political sphere, we might agree with media analyst Francesco Siliato when he says that, given the particular condition of public broadcasting in Italy, *lottizzazione* was the lesser evil. Not only was it a guarantee against industrial control, but it was also preferable to that kind of control.[11]

Over all, the public and the private TV channels have proved to be linked in a dialectic relationship. Although the opposition between RAI and Fininvest/Mediaset was powerful in the 1980s, it began to fade away during the 1990s: the result has been a leveled, homogeneous broadcasting market. The 1990s pervasive ideology claiming journalists' autonomy also called into question the distinction between the public and the private broadcaster, as journalists swear they can do whatever they want (public service journalism) wherever they go, regardless of ownership. The movement of television celebrities, producers, program makers, and managers back and forth between RAI and Mediaset (a phenomenon that journalist Gianni Minà has defined as the *Mediasettizzazione* of RAI) is a symptom of the process through which the opposition between thesis (RAI) and antithesis (Mediaset) has apparently been resolved in a synthesis where the initial differences are lost.

The Berlusconi Effect

The 1990s were characterized by Berlusconi's entrance in the political scene thereby introducing an additional level of complexity in the relationship among the public broadcaster, the government, and the commercial competitor. Much has been said regarding the impact of his television channels on the electorate, and, from the time he became prime minister in 1994 and then in 2001, his potential for control of the public service channels. Many have wondered whether such concentration of power does not also mean that news and public affairs programs, in Mediaset as well as in RAI, are being domesticated, biased toward Berlusconi's government and his party, and somehow oblivious of his legal troubles (Berlusconi has been indicted for financial fraud and corruption of judges, among other things). Others, including media scholars Paolo Mancini and Daniel C. Hallin, argue that, at least during the 2001 election campaign, Mediaset channels did not show a preference toward their owner's party, while RAI actually had "something of an anti-Berlusconi slant."[12]

Whereas the alarm that democracy in Italy might be in peril and that we are on the verge of a new dictatorship is perhaps unjustified, there is certainly a "Berlusconi effect" that can be detected—subtly at times, less subtly at other times. For instance, during the 1996 electoral campaign, a study on television news (on public and private channels) found that Silvio Berlusconi was the most cited politician and the one who received the most favorable reports during public affairs programs. Data showed that coverage of Berlusconi from March 9 through 22, 1996, was for the most part on balance (109 positive "citations" out of 194 total) whereas coverage of D'Alema (secretary-general of the Democratic Party of the Left at the time) was for the most part negative (only 33 positive citations out of 85).[13]

Information from another study conducted during the same preelectoral period showed that not only Fininvest news but also RAI news seemed to "slant in favor of the *Polo delle Libertà*."[14] Researchers found that the prime-time edition of Tg1 appeared to be the most impartial program of all—although the night edition of Tg1 showed special consideration for Gianfranco Fini (the leader of *Alleanza Nazionale*). Tg2, instead, showed a preference for the *Polo delle Libertà* coalition, whereas the center-left coalition was usually portrayed as being in continuous internal struggle, "any new piece of information that might have destabilized the credibility of the center-right coalition was followed by optimistic comments."[15] Tg3 highlighted political commentaries and maintained an objective tone. Tg5, the news on Canale5, allocated equal airtime to both coalitions, although the content of what was reported changed considerably. The internal conflicts of the center-left coalition occupied most of the time allocated to the progressive front, while leaders of the center right were given the space to present their political plans. According to the same research, Tg4 (the news on Rete4) was blatantly pro-Berlusconi.[16]

Even though the bias toward Berlusconi and his party has become less overt through the years, the owner of Mediaset continues to be the star of television news and public affairs programs, especially on the commercial channels. In contrast to Mancini and Hallin's account, a study by political analyst Giovanni Pasquino reveals that during the 2001 election campaign the leader of *Forza Italia* was on Mediaset channels for substantially more time than the leader of the center-left, Francesco Rutelli.[17]

Data from the Communications Authority further confirm the inclination of the commercial channels toward *Forza Italia* and Prime Minister Berlusconi. For instance, during the month of October 2002, Mediaset channels dedicated 37 percent of their political news time to representatives of *Forza Italia* and only 24 percent to the main opposition party, the *Democratici di Sinistra*. (In contrast, RAI channels dedicated 30 percent of their political news time to *Forza Italia* and 17 percent to the *Democratici di Sinistra*). In August 2003, the commercial channels granted almost half of their allocated time to the prime minister and his party. (RAI channels, instead, gave 21 percent of their political news time to Silvio Berlusconi and *Forza Italia*).

These data seem to confirm that the liberalization of the airwaves has not served to increase diversity of viewpoints or choice on Italians' TV screens. The end, or at least the demise of *lottizzazione*, has not given birth to more balanced information, either. While discussing the Berlusconi effect on the news, Valeria Ferro, director of *Centro d'Ascolto dell'Informazione Radiotelevisiva* (a Rome-based Observatory of television news programs), explained why the information sector has become "saturated" with reports on the prime minister and his coalition: "it was," she said, "a cumulative effect, which happens when public television's 'natural' attention to the government and state institutions is added to Mediaset's 'obvious' special consideration toward its owner."[18]

The Missing Legislation

Both the center-left government of the late 1990s and the subsequent center-right government failed to pass a conflict-of-interest law that would effectively put some distance between those who hold government positions and their private interests. Toward the end of 2002, Berlusconi's coalition government submitted a bill to parliament that, according to critics, "promised to increase the control of Italy's media held by [the prime minister's] company."[19] The bill, which was introduced by Communications Minister Maurizio Gasparri, plans to lift restrictions on ownership by a single person of more than two national terrestrial television broadcasters, to extend the revenue market for TV stations by allowing any one owner up to 20 percent of the entire media market (thus effectively raising the allowed threshold for every single medium), to allow for the partial privatization of RAI from 2005, and to authorize cross-ownership of broadcast and print media by 2009. In December 2003, Carlo Azeglio Ciampi, president of the republic, refused to sign the bill, and sent it back to parliament for revisions.

Certainly, the consequences of a further concentration of power in the hands of Silvio Berlusconi might be very serious for the Italian democracy. As Sergio Romano, commentator for the daily *Corriere della Sera*, said, the fundamental question is not whether Berlusconi is manipulating the information that Italians receive. The concern is that "he could do it later. It's not a healthy situation, and principles do matter."[20] It is also disturbing that Italy still lacks legislation clearly separating the government of the day from the public broadcaster, and that policies to overcome the stagnant duopoly in the broadcasting market have failed to encourage the formation of a third national broadcaster strong enough to compete. But then, the absence of adequate legislation has been an endemic problem in Italy, and one can hardly blame Berlusconi for continuing to exploit it.

The Global Crisis and the Commercialization of the Media

No discussion of the troubles of Italian public service broadcasting can elude consideration of public broadcasting's global crisis. Around the world public service broadcasters have been criticized for failing to perform their specific function, namely, to offer what the market cannot provide, and for dumbing down their programming output in order to be more competitive. In the United Kingdom, for example, critics have been protesting against the privileged status enjoyed by the British Broadcasting Corporation and Channel 4, a status that is—according to its opponents—unjustified since neither the BBC nor Channel 4 offers unique programs that cannot be found on commercial stations. This is a sore spot, one that is difficult to ignore. In Italy, too, the main ground for opposing public service broadcasting is that, especially since the early 1990s, RAI's programs have become increasingly similar to those offered by the commercial competitor. Therefore, many wonder why RAI should be granted a special public service status. The homogenization of the broadcasting market is a major problem, one that is certainly exasperated by the counter-scheduling strategy adopted by the Italian broadcaster in an attempt to attract more audience. It is a global trend (made worse in Italy by the peculiar conditions of the RAI/Mediaset duopoly): public broadcasters are squeezed between Scylla and Charybdis as they face the challenge of redefining their role in digital and multimedia platforms. They have to reinforce their "core business" (terrestrial television), while, at the same time, they are expected to promote the uptake of integrated TV sets—and, of course, be competitive.

To make things worse, some high-quality pay-per-view and subscription-based channels, in the United Kingdom as well as in the United States, seem to disprove a fundamental tenet of the pro-public service position, namely, that the market cannot provide quality television and cannot "sustain a culture of risk, . . . creativity, [and] innovation."[21] Indeed, such channels as Artsworld, in the United Kingdom, or the Home Box Office, in the United States, provide a wealth of high-quality programs for a variety of audiences and tastes (some of the best programs ever made for television, like *The Sopranos*, *Six Feet Under*, and *Sex and the City*, are produced by the U.S.-based HBO). And quality pays back: while high-end subscription channels have enjoyed rising subscriptions, the rest of the television industry has struggled with the advertising recession of the early 2000s. After all, subscription-based channels can produce excellent programming as their operations are not dependent on advertising revenues, while whether the institutions of public service can take the chance of alienating audiences with high-quality, but perhaps less popular programs, has become an increasingly rhetorical question. But then, of course, subscription-based channels are by definition not universally available, and most people (especially in a country like Italy) still rely on broadcast television for their news and entertainment.

Indeed, given the relatively low circulation of newspapers and the virtual nonexistence of cable television, and despite the advancement of satellite penetration (twenty-three percent by the fall of 2003), broadcast television continues to be quite popular among Italians, especially among the elderly and low-income families. In 2000, for instance, 40.7 percent of adults still relied only on broadcast television for their news and entertainment, whereas 43.5 percent had access to other media.[22] (These numbers have been growing for both groups, suggesting a widening divide along generational, income-based, and geographical lines.)

Moreover, the audience for broadcasting television continues to grow: in 2002-2003 the average number of viewers during prime time was 27.3 million, 800 thousand more than the previous season, with a record average number of more than 9 million viewers daily. And if it is true that viewers tend to prefer the commercial channels for entertainment, they still choose RAI over Mediaset for their news and information (although the gap between the two is closing). In the year 2000, for instance, the total audience share for RAI newscasts was 63.4 percent versus 36.1 percent for Mediaset.[23]

In summary, even though we need to acknowledge that quality programming is not a prerogative of public service broadcasting, institutions such as RAI still have a very important social and political mission given the vast audiences they reach. Compared to this, even high-quality subscription-based channels are only "drops in the ocean."[24]

The Public Sphere Debate

According to the dominant model within the literature on public service broadcasting, the Habermasian representation of a space-in-between the state and the market provides an ideal ground where public service broadcasting could claim a home. For some, it is the only space where public broadcasters could find their raison d'être: "It is only by recourse to the idea of the public sphere that public service broadcasting can be defended."[25] I must disagree: public service media should be defended on the basis of their historical conditions rather than their supposed normative ideal.

This normative ideal has been amply criticized: as is well-known, the Habermasian notion of the public sphere has been questioned by those who advocate multiple, overlapping, pluralist, neo-Marxist, and post-bourgeois public spheres.[26] Nicholas Garnham's articulation of the association between public sphere and public service broadcasting has also been under attack. Political philosopher John Keane, for instance, rejects the linkage between the eighteenth/nineteenth-century concept of the public sphere and the twentieth-century institution of public service broadcasting, which, according to him, represents one of the most conservative embodiments of the public sphere, one that is anachronistic and doomed to disappear.[27] Keane asserts that the bleak destiny of public broadcasting systems can only hamper the many potentialities that a revised notion of the public sphere still harbors. Indeed, he states that the

> elective affinity between public service broadcasting and the "public sphere" is hardening into dogma, precisely because the leading spatial metaphor upon which it rests is now out of touch with long-term media trends in the old parliamentary democracies . . . [and also because] the ideal of a unified public sphere and its corresponding vision of a territorially bounded republic of citizens . . . are obsolete.[28]

Elisabeth Jacka echoes Keane's concerns.[29] She thinks not only that the association between public media and the public sphere is problematic, but that the generally accepted assumption that public service broadcasting makes a "unique and indispensable contribution to contemporary pluralist democracies" needs to be challenged.[30] Indeed, she believes that commercial media are able to serve the functions that are traditionally reserved to public service media, like providing a public sphere of information and debate, fostering national culture, and providing mechanisms of accountability for power holders.[31] John Hartley goes even further in advocating the liberating character of what he defines as cultural citizenship, a kind of citizenship that does not require political participation and is best supported by commercial media.[32] In such a context, it is argued, political participation is no longer needed as individuals create their own identities, choosing from a variety of possibilities offered to them by commercial media. Public service media retain no special role.

Notwithstanding the validity of their critiques, which underline the importance of studying television within a specific media ecology and moving beyond established dichotomies (highbrow versus lowbrow, public television versus commercial), neither Jacka's account nor Hartley's is satisfactory, at least in the Italian context. In particular, Jacka's proposition that commercial broadcasting can provide a sphere for public debate, facilitate accountability of power holders, and foster national culture is simply difficult to prove.[33] As mentioned above, Mediaset news programs, especially those on Rete4 and Italia1, are usually slanted in favor of Berlusconi and his party (*Forza Italia*). Even though it is probably true that "there is little evidence that Berlusconi use[s] his three television networks to broadcast overt propaganda,"[34] there are a variety of studies showing that Mediaset channels spend a considerable amount of their airtime reporting (for the most part in a positive light) about Berlusconi and his political allies.

Moreover, Mediaset channels' daily heavy diet of imported soap operas, imported children's programs, and imported films and television series demonstrates that commercial broadcasters do not just spontaneously "foster national culture" nor encourage domestic production. Their purpose is to maximize profits, not to promote culture, informed debate, or quality entertainment, and is certainly not their responsibility to promote political and cultural pluralism. The brute and perhaps unavoidable reality of market-driven broadcasting, of its structure and essential nature, is that it is characterized by concentration of ownership and a high degree of dependence on advertising, which can adversely affect the content and quality of programming by appealing to the least common denominator. This reality brings with it an increasingly necessary neglect of broadcasting as a vehicle for the enrichment of public, civic, and democratic values, core public service values that, relative to the specific historical and political conditions of Italy, RAI has striven to implement.[35]

Commercial Broadcasting in Italy

An additional problem in Italy is that the owner of Mediaset is also in a position to influence the programming content of the public broadcaster. Indeed, the intrusion of the government of the day on the editorial policies of the public service broadcaster can be gleaned through various episodes. For instance, on the occasion of the antiwar march on February 15, 2003, when an estimated 3 million people demonstrated in downtown Rome against a war on Iraq, RAI's director-general, Agostino Saccà, ordered that RAI channels should not broadcast live. A few days earlier, RAI missed another opportunity to broadcast live, that of the weapons inspectors' reports to the United Nations Security Council on the Iraqi situation. Saccà's official explanation for denying live broadcasting was that it could have "conditioned" the decisions of the members of the Italian parliament, who were scheduled to vote on the issue. But Berlusconi's opponents, inside and outside RAI, as well as political and media analysts, saw the decision as a way to reduce the presence and significance of the public broadcaster in the lives of Italians. In comparison, the Mediaset channels shined. A commentator for the daily *La Repubblica* crystallized the general distrust in RAI's leadership and the suspicion of Berlusconi's own responsibility by suggesting that the board

> secure to Berlusconi the control of public service broadcasting, and purposefully serve it to him as an insignificant, lobotomized, insipid broadcaster. Compared to this flat-encephalogram RAI, Mediaset's rare and domesticated attempts to do information are enough to make [Berlusconi's] "magic box" light up, so that, thanks to this trick, even [Berlusconi] comes out looking like a champion of democracy.[36]

As one of my respondents said, public service broadcasting is the last bastion to be conquered. Certainly, the Italian broadcaster has many challenges to face. But whereas one might conclude that RAI's impure relationship with the political sphere means that it cannot contribute to the advancement of democracy, I propose that, as imperfect as it has been, the Italian public broadcaster has served a very important democratizing function, in spite, and perhaps even because of its close relationship with the political party system.

Democracy and Public Service Broadcasting as Evolving Institutions

Political philosopher Norberto Bobbio argues that Italian democracy, as imperfect as it is, "will always be better than any 'perfect' dictatorship."[37] His conclusion can also apply to the discussion over public service broadcasting. Indeed, even as imperfect as it is (at least in comparison to the ideal public-sphere-public-service broadcasting notion), RAI can still offer a much-needed alternative to commercial media. The argument of the lesser evil can also help us to avoid the tendency to interpret the history and current conditions of both democracy and public media as histories of defeats (as Elisabeth Jacka rightly points out),[38] as institutions doomed to end because not in tune with the prevailing neoliberal and postmodern principles and social philosophies. Quite the contrary, both democracy and public media are works-in-progress rather than once stable institutions now in decline.

Furthermore, one needs to be aware of the motivations of those who take any opportunity to denounce RAI's problems and, in the name of an ideal perfect service, might call for the destruction of what we have. Paraphrasing Norberto Bobbio, one needs to be suspicious of

> those who would like to destroy our democracy, always fragile, always vulnerable, corruptible and often corrupt, [and] want to do so in order to create a new perfect democracy. They are like Pelya's daughters described by Hobbes, who cut into pieces their old father to see him be reborn.[39]

It is well this side of cynicism to suggest that lurking in the shadows is a desire to see the demise of RAI so as to benefit the commercial sector. The suggestion that since RAI is less than perfect, it must therefore be destroyed works to the advantage (as it did in the 1970s with the freedom of antenna movement) of those on the Right who know quite well that perfect public service broadcasting is unattainable.

RAI's Public Service Mission

How has the public service concept evolved in Italy? What kind of influence has the political situation had on defining what constitutes RAI's public service obligation? And how has this changed through the years?

The biannual agreement between the Ministry of Communications and RAI is the place where the definition of the broadcaster's public service mission is regularly negotiated. Overall, there has been a concentrated effort to ensure that more objective criteria are used to identify public service programs, to impose more public service programs, and to establish "separate accounting" procedures for a transparent use of public funds. However, this has created a sense that the public service mission has ceased to be the overall philosophy of the corporation, and has become an addendum to its operations.

In the agreement signed in 2000, the state required RAI to produce more quality programs, at least 60 percent of RAI1 and RAI2's total offerings and up to 80 percent of RAI3's offer. Those provisions were stricter than before. Indeed, according to the previous agreement, RAI was supposed to produce a total of 60 percent quality programs, without specifying on which channel.[40]

Following the necessity to do separate accounting[41] in order to distinguish activities paid for by public money from activities paid for by advertisements and other commercial revenues, the 2000-2002 agreement introduced the concept of "areas" of public service. According to those guidelines, only selected programs could be defined as public service. The programs with a public service mark on them were funded by the license fee and the remaining ones were funded from commercial sources; RAI itself was in charge of defining what constituted a public service program. The result was that the public service mission was mostly relegated to specific time slots and primarily to the third channel.

The 2003-2005 agreement slightly modifies the concept of what constitutes public service beyond a selected area of designated public service programs, and indeed, the contract emphasizes that the public broadcaster is expected to ensure quality programming throughout the day and among all genres.[42] The agreement requires that RAI put in place an internal system to control the quality of its offer, and points out that all programs meet the public service criteria. But the corporation is no longer the only entity in charge of defining those criteria. A committee, consisting of two RAI representatives, two members of the National Consumers Council, and one representative of the Ministry of Communications, is in charge of verifying the broadcaster's compliance with the guidelines established in the contract. Whereas the presence of representatives of the National Consumers Council is an important step in making RAI more accountable to its viewers, the presence of one representative of the government is perceived as an intrusion in the internal affairs of the corporation. The justifiable suspicion is that this might become a legitimate way for the government of the day to have its say about programming. The committee's recommendations are, of course, crucial, as they have a direct impact on determining the amount of the license fee.

The 2003-2005 contract also confirms the principle of separate accounting. But control and sanctions have become stricter. A committee, formed by representatives of the Ministry of Finances and RAI, has been instituted to oversee the implementation of such accounting procedures. This committee too is perceived by critics as a way to ensure additional government control over RAI's internal accounting.

Political Party Influence and Democracy

Another question addressed in the introduction concerned the relationship between political party influence within the public service broadcaster and the country's democratic system. *Lottizzazione* was a child of the blocked democracy in two different but still complementary ways. It first developed as a healthy response to the blocked democracy, as it was born out of the will to oppose the DC's power. The party pluralism that *lottizzazione* promoted was, for the most part, positive. Toward the end of the 1980s, the increasing bureaucratization of the party system, which seriously weakened the role of the parties as mediators between citizens and institutions, became highly problematic, as did the persistence and normalization of *lottizzazione*.

For the most part, those who admit the existence of *lottizzazione* perceive it as a relatively positive phenomenon. Although one could argue that this is merely nostalgia, various respondents claimed abundant benefits in the system. For example, *lottizzazione* introduced more diversity within the public broadcaster's monoculture; *lottizzazione* gave employment to excellent journalists who would not have had a chance otherwise; and without *lottizzazione*, the good quality partisan journalism promoted by RAI3 and Tg3 would never have happened.

Parties were the agents of democratization, "institutions of democracy," as Norberto Bobbio defined them,[43] at a time (which lasted until the 1970s) when political and social life still coincided and parties provided their members with social, cultural, and educational activities. In this context, the sharing among parties of positions and areas of responsibility and influence within the broadcaster can indeed be considered as a positive phenomenon, as a step in the democratizing process. In general, *lottizzazione* can be conceived as a corrupt practice only if we have in mind the ideal association between public service broadcasting and the public sphere. If public broadcasting ought to be a space-in-between the state and the market, *lottizzazione* is obviously a sign of corruption, since it indicates an inextricable relation between the broadcaster and political power.

But the question "What would *lottizzazione* have corrupted?" takes us in another direction. Historically, public service broadcasting in Italy has never approached the normative ideal of the public sphere. In other words, *lottizzazione* is not a corrupt practice because there was nothing, no ideal public sphere and no ideal democracy, to be corrupted in the first place. RAI never embodied the ideal of objectivity and independence as its core values. At times, as in the Reform Law, the concepts of autonomy, independence, and pluralism were brought to the fore. However, such concepts never indicated *absolute* independence and autonomy from the political sphere. Pluralism, a crucial term of the 1975 legislation, meant party pluralism rather than the "social" or "real" pluralism classically associated with the individual citizen. Once the notion of pluralism was introduced into the broadcaster through this legislation, its connotations were shaped by the history and tradition of the role of the parties in the evolution of Italian democracy, where they were the mediators between the collectivity of citizens and state institutions. In the historical context of Italy, *lottizzazione* was better than latifundium; more parties were better than only one party ruling the broadcaster.

Lottizzazione was born out of a rebellious spirit that sought to triumph over Italy's blocked democracy: the spirit of the lay, non-Catholic parties rebelling against the DC and its power inside the corporation. Good things came out of this spirit. The *Catto-Comunista* (Catholic/Communist) alliance inside RAI, for instance, was created to embrace the two main traditions of Italian political culture (the Marxist and the Catholic). This alliance (which was embodied by the close relationship between the director-general, Biagio Agnes [DC], and the head of Channel 3, Angelo Guglielmi [close to the PCI]) was at the foundation of the success of Channel 3 and Tg3 in the late 1980s. It was an instrumental alliance, but at its base there was also the desire, as former codirector of Tg3 Alberto Severi said,

> [t]o create something new, to make concrete the hypothesis of the historic compromise that had been impossible in the political arena. The catto-comunista alliance in RAI—in particular in RAI3—was born out

of the director-general's belief that it was possible to . . . realize something good and new.[44]

While junior journalists emphasize the nonexistence of *lottizzazione* and claim the objectivity of their work, the senior journalists conversely recognize the historical roots of Italian journalism and consider *lottizzazione* a necessary condition (at times a positive and enriching one), a specific aspect of Italian political/advocacy journalism:

> I love political journalism. . . . I consider the political identity of my reporters to be a positive element rather than a negative one. On the contrary, I don't like it when I don't know to which party my reporters belong, or which political ideas they have. Even worse, I can't stand it when journalists claim that they have no political affiliation. I think that is dangerous.[45]

What have been the consequences of this state of affairs for the broadcaster and the journalists? In 1980 Alberto Ronchey envisioned a loss of internal cohesion in RAI because of *lottizzazione*, a state in which each journalist and/or official appointed by a given party would first report his or her activity to the party and would thereby lose connection with the structures and hierarchies of the broadcaster:

> When key positions are distributed on the basis of negotiations among parties . . . those people who occupy those positions tend to feel responsible only toward the parties, their own party, in fact disregarding responsibility to any other body or institution.[46]

But that did not happen. On the contrary, *lottizzazione* at times favored internal cohesion and a kind of affection, a strong sense of identification with the broadcaster. Most of my respondents, especially the senior journalists, claimed pride in working for RAI and declared themselves members of the RAI party. In 1998, one of them said, regarding proposals to privatize RAI or to transform it into a holding company,

> I am convinced that the corporation should never be divided and privatized. The RAI party believes in the mission of public service broadcasting. We are the kind of people who, once called by the competitor offering us triple the salary we make here, did not leave the public broadcaster, because we believe in the system and in the fact that being a journalist for the public broadcaster is something totally different.[47]

By the year 2000, however, RAI had been divided into branches and divisions for partial privatization, and one sensed that the spirit of cohesion that had characterized the broadcaster in previous decades was lost. That feeling of purposeful belonging had served RAI well in times of crisis within the political system, since it allowed the broadcaster to keep working efficiently. At times of external threat, such as the competition with Fininvest during the 1980s, the interior political organization of RAI allowed it to maintain an important level of unity. This is a striking difference with the post-1993 RAI, where one perceives the lack of a shared mission, of a unifying purpose.

RAI and the Evolution of Italian Democracy

To define the continued fact of *lottizzazione* necessarily calls into question the whole designation of RAI as a public service broadcaster in the sense that the phrase is classically used. In light of its history, is it contradictory to define RAI as a public service broadcaster? And, most importantly, what does its proximity with the party system tell us about the larger issue, the debate over the condition of public service broadcasting?

My answer to the first question, in the context of Italian political culture, must be no. As I noted, in Italy there is little familiarity with the classic liberal conceptualization of the public sphere. Public service television was rarely considered to be at the service of citizens. The function of the broadcaster as a forum for public debate and enlightenment was advocated only at the time of the Reform Law of 1975. Public debate has traditionally meant participation by political parties more than by citizens.

Since the 1990s, the notion that public broadcasting serves, or should serve, the public-as-citizens rather than the party system has been widely professed. All shades of political opinion, from left to right, now articulate notions of "citizens' television," rather than "parties' television," and collectivist notions of "the masses" have been nudged aside by a new ideology of the individual-as-citizen. (RAI's counter-scheduling strategy in the race for audience is perhaps the result of this ideology. Unfortunately, it hardly represents an attempt to reinforce public life and political participation.) My suspicion is that such a discourse tends merely to promote a populist democracy. Indeed, both the right and the left, which have been advocating the end of the party system, the beginning of the citizens' state, and the end of corruption, implement the same practices as their predecessors did.

Historically, *lottizzazione* has been associated with pluralism. Those who consider such a pluralism in a negative light (often right-wing politicians and the "new" wave of RAI journalists) define it as "hegemonic pluralism," to indicate a "pluralism that brings along with itself consensus and coercion,"[48] a kind of pluralism that is "cultural, professional, and intellectual obsolescence."[49] What they propose instead is "lay pluralism," which should no longer be based on outdated ideologies tending to hegemonize and control society, but rather on "journalists' personal responsibility and intellectual honesty."[50] Personal responsibility and professional honesty: these notions are offered as the solution to any hegemonic function of political influence. Structural changes are being pushed to the side. The emphasis is on journalists' private conscience, well in tune with the growing personalization of political culture and emergent commitment to notions of autonomy within RAI. The habit of frequently changing members of the board, presidents, and directors-general, as if the problem were one of individual appointees, reinforces the idea that things will improve once the right people come along instead of addressing the question of structural changes.[51]

Future Perspectives

There are a couple of powerful dichotomies that have entrapped the discourse on public service broadcasting in Italy. As a result, RAI has been caught in a rather schizophrenic situation: on one side it has been under intense pressure to perform according to the industry market standards, while, on the other side, there has been a strong expectation for the public broadcaster to cease being competitive in order not to be a threat to Silvio Berlusconi's televisions. What should RAI do then? Should it focus exclusively on its public service mission and forget about its audience share? This is certainly what the right-wing coalition led by *Forza Italia* would prefer. Unless the owner of the Mediaset television channels can convincingly resolve his conflict of interest, a legitimate suspicion that the public broadcaster is being undermined for the benefits of the commercial competitor and of the political coalition that supports it will remain. But, on the contrary, if one wants to oppose this perverse logic (focus on the public service so as to not bother the competition), does that mean that RAI should just focus on audience share and counter-scheduling? It seems obvious that such a strategy would further delegitimate its public service role and fuel the argument of those who advocate the end of publicly funded radio and television channels.

The second, closely related dichotomy is the one that pits audience versus quality (commercial broadcasters chase the audience, whereas public broadcasters focus on quality programming). Behind this dichotomy hides the dangerous proposition according to which public broadcasting should be reduced to a niche service, showcasing only "high" culture and certain "noble" genres (like the Public Broadcasting Service model in the United States). For fifty years, RAI has made a very valuable contribution to the cultural, social, and political life of Italians. It would be a real pity and a complete waste to see RAI's public service reduced to a niche service.

Indeed RAI is still Italy's largest radio and television broadcasting institution. Throughout the years, and notwithstanding the particularly adversarial conditions of the 1990s, it has maintained a high audience share, in fact the highest average yearly audience share as compared to other European public service broadcasters (46.4 percent in 2002, versus 41.8 percent of the German ARD, 36.8 percent of the British BBC, 37.2 percent of France Télévisions, and 32.4 percent of the Spanish RTVE).[52]

What is most important is that the public broadcaster has demonstrated that it can (when it wants) marry quality and audience. Programs like Roberto Benigni's recital of Dante Alighieri's *Paradiso*, aired on RAI1 on prime time on December 23, 2003, and other programs, especially those produced in the 1980s, speak to the point. Reading *The Divine Comedy*'s most elusive canto for two hours, the celebrated actor drew almost 13 million viewers (an absolute record for Italian TV) to a show that many would consider unsuitable for television audiences. Events such as these demonstrate that it is possible to transcend those dichotomies that pit audience against quality programming. But to make sure that the quest for popular programs of high quality becomes the norm, rather than the exception, there must be strong political support and a daring vision. And RAI, of course, should revise its counter-scheduling strategy. This is the challenge to public broadcasting that RAI, given its tradition and its history, can win.

Notes

1. See Celestino Spada, untitled author's manuscript, Rome, August 28, 1997, published as "Della lottizzazione e del 'partito RAI'" (About *lottizzazione* and the RAI Party), *Problemi dell'informazione* 22, no. 4 (December 1997), 485-487.
2. Marco Niada, "Farewell Agnelli—Figure of Another Age," *OpenDemocracy*, February 13, 2003. Available at www.opendemocracy.net.
3. Spada, "Della lottizzazione," 487.
4. Paolo Murialdi, interview with author, tape recording, Milan, January 31, 1998.
5. Antonio Gramsci, *Il materialismo storico e la filosofia di Benedetto Croce*, ed. Istituto Gramsci (Turin: Editori Riuniti, 1975), 59.
6. "Bernabei was a Christian Democrat," said Piero De Chiara, "but he did not take orders from the DC. He was the DC." Piero De Chiara, responsible for the PCI mass communications division, interview with author, tape recording, Olivetti Foundation, Rome, April 3, 1998.
7. Emilio Rossi, former director of Tg1, interview with author, tape recording, *Centro Televisivo Vaticano* (Vatican Television Center), Vatican City, January 4, 1997.
8. Rossi, interview cit.
9. Wolfgang Achtner, interview with author, tape recording, The International Press Association headquarters, Rome, March 3, 1998.
10. See Paolo Del Debbio, *Il mercante e l'inquisitore apologia della televisione commerciale* (Milan: Il Sole 24 ORE Libri, 1991).
11. Francesco Siliato, interview with author, tape recording, Milan, January 30, 1998.
12. Paolo Mancini and Daniel C. Hallin, "Italy's Television, Italy's Democracy," *OpenDemocracy*, July 19, 2001. Available at www.opendemocracy.net.
13. Data from the research conducted by professor Mario Morcellini, reported by Carlo Gallucci, "Letizia missione compiuta," in *L'Espresso* (Rome), April 12, 1996, 54.
14. Data from the research conducted by the professor Roberto Grandi, reported by Carlo Gallucci, "Letizia missione compiuta," in *L'Espresso* (Rome), April 12, 1996, 54.
15. Gallucci, "Letizia missione compiuta," 56.
16. Carlo Gallucci summarized the results of the two studies (the one by professor Mario Morcellini and the other by professor Roberto Grandi) saying that "during the 1994 electoral campaign, TV talked only about the Right. [In the electoral campaign of 1996], . . . TV reported on both, the Right and the Left. Positively about the first, negatively about the second." Carlo Gallucci, "Letizia missione compiuta," 54.
17. See Gianfranco Pasquino, quoted by Raffaele Mastrolonardo, "Media Concentration: The Italian Case-Study," *OpenDemocracy*, March 14, 2002. Available at www.opendemocracy.net.

18. Valeria Ferro, interview with author, Rome, July 22, 2002.

19. "Bravo, President Ciampi," in *The Economist* (London), December 20, 2003.

20. Sergio Romano, quoted in Frank Bruni, "Italy's Leader Balances Ambitions and Trials," in *The New York Times*, February 16, 2003, 3.

21. Roger Graef, "Not Good Enough," *OpenDemocracy*, June 2, 2001. Available at www.opendemocracy.net.

22. Centro Studi Investimenti Sociali (CENSIS), *Il rapporto in breve 2000* (Summary of the 2000 Report). Available at www.censis.it/censis/ra.html.

23. RAI, Radiotelevisione Italiana, *Annuario 2001* (Rome: ERI, no publication date available), 64.

24. Roger Graef, "Not Good Enough."

25. Anonymous source, quoted in Michael Tracey, *The Decline and Fall of Public Service Broadcasting* (Oxford: Oxford University Press, 1998), xiii.

26. See Oskar Negt and Alexander Kluge, *Public Sphere and Experience: Toward an Analysis of the Bourgeois and Proletarian Public Sphere* (Minneapolis: University of Minnesota Press, 1993); Nancy Fraser, "Rethinking the Public Sphere: A Contribution to the Critique of Actual Existing Democracy," in *Habermas and the Public Sphere*, ed. Craig Calhoun (Cambridge, Mass.: MIT Press, 1992), 109-142; and Seyla Benhabib, "Models of Public Space: Hanna Arendt, the Liberal Tradition, and Jürgen Habermas," in *Habermas and the Public Sphere*, ed. Craig Calhoun, 73-98.

27. See John Keane, "Structural Transformations of the Public Sphere," *Communication Review* 1, no. 1 (1995): 1-22; and Keane, "A Reply to Nicholas Garnham," *Communication Review* 1, no. 1 (1995): 27-31.

28. In Keane, "Structural Transformations of the Public Sphere," 8.

29. See Elisabeth Jacka, "Democracy as Defeat: The Impotence of Arguments for Public Service Broadcasting," in "Rethinking Public Media in a Transnational Era," ed. Gerald Sussman, special issue, *Television and New Media* 4, no. 2 (May 2003).

30. Jacka, "Democracy as Defeat," 178.

31. Jacka, "Democracy as Defeat," 180.

32. See John Hartley, *Uses of Television* (New York: Routledge, 1999).

33. See Jacka, "Democracy as Defeat."

34. Mancini and Hallin, "Italy's Television, Italy's Democracy."

35. Hartley's proposition, which celebrates cultural rather than political citizenship, attempts to carve a noble role for commercial television. However, the problem remains that cultural citizenship (which, according to him is replacing political citizenship) is irremediably passive as individuals are not encouraged to share in negotiating the range of their possible identities. Cultural citizenship is an audience-based citizenship, a citizenship of TV viewers whose only freedom is to choose their (always shifting, multiple, overlapping) cultural identities among those offered to them by the media. This analysis is similar to Paolo Del Debbio's apologia, which celebrates the freedoms of the marketplace and compares commercial television to a sort of electronic meeting place where indi-

viduals aggregate and separate continuously (see Paolo Del Debbio, *Il mercante e l'inquisitore*). Both Hartley and Del Debbio, however, seem oblivious to one main identity that all TV audiences share, the one that is neither shifting nor multiple: the viewers' identity as consumers, as packages to be sold to the advertisers.

36. Massimo Giannini, "RAI, il pubblico disservizio," in *La Repubblica* (Rome), February 17, 2003.

37. Norberto Bobbio, *Il futuro della democrazia* (Turin: Einaudi, 1984), 23.

38. See Jacka, "Democracy as Defeat."

39. Bobbio, *Il futuro della democrazia*, xxii.

40. Although stricter than the one before, the new concession was not as strict as the proposal by Silvio Berlusconi, head of the opposition at the time, according to which RAI would have been forced to air 20 percent of educational programming on prime time, thus eliminating Mediaset's competition and allowing the commercial channels to collect billions of additional advertising revenues.

41. In Europe, public broadcasters financed by public and commercial revenues are requested to do "separate accounting" according to European Commission guidelines (European Commission Communication 2001/C 320/4).

42. *Contratto di servizio 2003-2005* (Service Agreement between the Communications Ministry and RAI Corporation), Art. 2. Available at www.sas.rai.it/regolamenti/contratto2003.html.

43. Bobbio, *Il futuro della democrazia*.

44. Alberto Severi, codirector of Tg3, interview with author, tape recording, RAI headquarters, Saxa Rubra, Rome, March 11, 1998.

45. Giorgio Balzoni, head of Tg1 Domestic Political Affairs and former secretary-general of Usigrai, interview with author, tape recording, RAI headquarters, Saxa Rubra, Rome, February 1998.

46. Alberto Ronchey, "La 'Lottizzazione'," in *Corriere della Sera* (Milan), October 12, 1980.

47. Balzoni, interview cit.

48. Emiddio Novi, senator elected on the *Forza Italia* ticket and member of the RAI Parliamentary Committee, speech to the RAI Parliamentary Committee, *Discussione sul pluralismo nel servizio pubblico radiotelevisivo: Audizione contestuale dei direttori del TG1, del TG2, del TGR e del Giornale radio* (Discussion of pluralism in the public service broadcaster: audition of news directors of Tg1, Tg2, TGR and Giornale radio), January 14, 1997. (A summary of the speech is available at notes3.senato.it/ODG_PUBL.NSF/0/18b40092add282bc412564ad00572cf9?OpenDocument).

49. Novi, *Discussione sul pluralismo*.

50. Novi, *Discussione sul pluralismo*.

51. As Renato Parascandolo, former vice-director of RAI Educational, said, in order to liberate RAI from political influence, "We should come up with something very creative, . . . a sort of bureaucratic imagination, in other words, a paradox. It's a paradox because we should invent new forms of structural or-

ganization. We should create a hermaphrodite. But this is very difficult and nobody wants to do it." Renato Parascandolo, interview with author, tape recording, RAI headquarters, Rome, February 1998.

52. Data from RAI, Radiotelevisione Italiana, *Annuario 2002*. Available at www.rai.it.

Glossary

Agenzia Stefani. The Stefani news agency was founded in 1853 in Turin. Under the leadership of Manlio Morgagni (1924-1943), it became a docile instrument in the hands of the Fascist regime. It disappeared after the fall of Mussolini.

Alleanza Nazionale **(AN).** Right wing party founded in 1993 by Gianfranco Fini, former leader of the neofascist Italian Social Movement party. The purpose of this new political formation was to legitimate the Italian right and to promote a new postfascist party. One of the most significant events in this regard was when, in the fall of 2003, during his first official visit to Israel, the leader of AN declared that fascism was part of the "absolute evil" and condemned Mussolini's 1938 racial laws. However, because of this, Fini was bitterly criticized by rank-and-file members as well as by elected lawmakers of his party.

Angelo Rizzoli Editore. Already by the early 1970s, the Rizzoli publishing house was very active in the daily press and television broadcasting businesses. In 1974, it bought the prestigious *Corriere della Sera*; two years later, with the help of some PSI officials, Rizzoli made agreements with the government of Malta to establish a foreign Italian TV station in the Mediterranean island. The goal (never achieved) of Telemalta was to threaten

RAI's monopoly as the Italian national broadcaster. Rizzoli also controlled Primarete Indipendente, the first commercial television station to broadcast a national news program in 1980.

Arnoldo Mondadori Editore. Mondadori was the founder of Rete4, which it owned together with *Editoriale L'Espresso* and the Perrone family. After an intense competition with Berlusconi's two channels, Rete4 was acquired by Fininvest in August 1984.

Aziendalisti. The name indicates RAI's old guard, which originally included the middle and top managers of the old EIAR. Nowadays the term is used to indicate those most loyal to the corporation.

CAF. This acronym indicates the alliance that dominated the Italian political scene during the last years of the old party system, from 1989 until 1992. "C" stands for Bettino Craxi, PSI secretary-general and former prime minister; "A" stands for Giulio Andreotti, prime minister; and "F" stands for Arnaldo Forlani, DC secretary-general. In 1990, the triumvirate was instrumental in passing the Mammì law (named after the minister of post and telecommunications, Oscar Mammì) legitimating the duopoly of RAI and Fininvest in the broadcasting sector.

Centrismo. This refers to the government coalitions of the first postwar era (1947-1962). This form of government, which excluded both the Socialist Party (PSI) and the Communist Party (PCI), included the Christian Democrats (DC), the center-right Italian Liberal Party (PLI), and the center-left Italian Republican Party (PRI).

Centro Sinistra. The DC-PSI center-left coalitions that governed Italy from 1962 to 1969.

Commissione Parlamentare di Vigilanza RAI. The RAI Parliamentary Committee was established in 1947 and remained mostly inactive until the Reform Law of 1975, which established a close relationship between the public broadcaster and the parliament thereby reinvigorating the role of the committee. The committee, whose forty members were appointed by the presidents of the Senate and the Chamber of Deputies and chosen among the representatives of all parliamentary groups, was given the power to supervise RAI's programming and its financial resources.

Compromesso Storico. The historic compromise, a governing formula that was first introduced by PCI secretary-general Enrico Berlinguer in 1973, envisioned a convergence of Catholic, Marxist, and Socialist forces to lead the country. The proposal was supported by Aldo Moro, a prominent DC leader, and, after the victorious results of the Communists at the 1976 national elections, by the rest of the DC left wing. But other forces, including the DC right wing, other left parties, and fringes of the PCI itself, opposed the compromise. The proposal was definitely abandoned in 1979, when Aldo Moro was kidnapped and killed by a Red Brigade command.

Consociativismo. Even though the *conventio ad excludendum* was still in effect, in the late 1980s the Communist Party became an external supporter of government coalitions. During the last years of the first republic, *consociativismo* indicated the practice of including the PCI in government decisions, although informally.

Conventio ad excludendum. A nonwritten agreement among the center and center-left parties (DC, PSI, PSDI, PLI, PRI) aimed at keeping the PCI outside government coalition. This agreement remained in place from 1947 until 1992.

Correntocrazia. This refers to the formation of factions (*correnti*) within political parties and indicates the power exercised by the various factions within the party itself.

Corriere della Sera. The most important Italian daily was founded in Milan in 1876.

Democrazia Bloccata. The term "blocked democracy" refers to the lack of alternate government that characterized the Italian political system from 1947 to 1992. During that period, the PCI, which was Italy's main opposition party, was formally excluded from any government coalition according to a formula known as *conventio ad excludendum*.

Democrazia Cristiana **(DC).** The Christian Democratic Party was founded in 1942 by former members of the *Partito Popolare* (the party founded in 1919 by Don Luigi Sturzo). Its interclass appeal (its electoral basis included the peasants, vast strata of the middle class, small entrepreneurs, and Catholics) was the main reason for the party's success. The DC governed the country from 1947 until 1993, and it disappeared after the Clean Hands scandal. Various parties, including the Christian Democratic Center (*Centro Cristiano Democratico*) and the Italian Popular Party (*Partito Popolare Italiano*), emerged from its debacle.

Dorotei. One of the DC's most powerful factions, it was founded in 1959 by Mariano Rumor. This current, together with the *fanfaniani*, was one of the most influential factions inside the broadcasting community during the 1950s and 1960s.

***Ente Italiano Audizioni Radiofoniche* (EIAR).** In 1928 the government refinanced the private radio broadcaster URI and founded EIAR, which soon obtained the concession for radio broadcasting from the state.

***Federazione Nazionale della Stampa Italiana* (FNSI).** FNSI was founded in 1908 as the first union of Italian journalists. In 1924, the Fascist government decreed the end of the federation and replaced it with a pro-Fascist union. In the summer of 1943, after almost twenty years, the activities of the FNSI resumed.

Fininvest. Silvio Berlusconi created Fininvest in 1978. Two years later, Fininvest established the commercial television channel Canale5 (an offspring of a local television channel owned by Berlusconi) which began broadcasting beyond regional borders. In 1983, Berlusconi acquired Italia1, and in 1984, Rete4. As of 2003, Fininvest owned Mediaset, a media conglomerate; the Arnoldo Mondadori publishing house; Mediolanum, insurance and financial services; Blockbuster Italy, video rental; Medusa Film, a major film production studio; and AC Milan, a national soccer team.

***Forza Italia* (FI).** This highly "personalized party" (as Norberto Bobbio defined it in his *Dialogo intorno alla repubblica*, Bari: Laterza, 2001) was founded in early 1994 by Silvio Berlusconi as a center-right alternative to what he perceived to be the "Communist menace." *Forza Italia*'s values include individuals' freedoms, family values, a rather minimalist conception of the role of the state, and a free market. *Forza Italia* has also been able to appeal to some Catholic voters by emphasizing the Christian heritage of the Italian liberal/conservative tradition.

***Istituto per la Ricostruzione Industriale* (IRI).** The Institute for Industrial Reconstruction was established in 1933 to administer public and state financing for the private sector. IRI survived the fall of fascism, was reintegrated into the new democratic state, and contributed to the reconstruction of the industrial apparatus. The institute was dismantled in the year 2000.

Lega Nord. Umberto Bossi founded the Northern League in 1991 in an attempt to bring together various preexisting regional autonomy leagues. The political platform of the Northern League interprets the dynamics of social struggle as an opposition between highly centralized nation-states and peoples claiming autonomy and independence, rather than as class struggle. In 1992, eighty lawmakers were elected on the *Lega Nord* ticket. Their number more than doubled in 1994.

Libertà d'antenna. The "freedom of antenna" movement of the 1970s advocated independence from state and government control in broadcasting.

Many who led this movement held strong political and social commitments to the left; paradoxically, they were also those who supported the development of commercial radio and television broadcasting.

Lottizzazione. Literally, the term indicates the partition of land in various portions (*lotti*). Figuratively, *lottizzazione* means the sharing of the most prestigious and powerful positions within any agency or public institution carried out by political parties according to criteria based on political opportunism and economic interests.

Mediaset. Because of a debt of more than two thousand billion lira, in 1996 Fininvest decided to raise money by consolidating its most successful media operations within a new company called Mediaset, which, in the summer of that year, successfully entered the stock market. By 2003, Mediaset, of which more than 70 percent was still controlled by Fininvest, owned the three national television channels Canale5, Italia1, and Rete4; shares of the Spanish TV station Telecinco; Albacom, an Italian telephone company; and Publitalia, the company that collects advertising revenues for the TV channels.

Movimento Sociale Italiano/Destra Nazionale **(MSI/DN).** The Italian Social Movement/National Right, a neo-Fascist party, was founded in 1946 by former members of Benito Mussolini's Repubblica di Salò (1943-1944). In 1995, the MSI was dissolved. Most of its members joined the newly born *Alleanza Nazionale.*

Partito Comunista Italiano **(PCI).** After the Communist Party of Italy (PCd'I) was dissolved by Mussolini in 1926, its members created a clandestine organization. During the *Resistenza* (1943-1945), former members of the PCd'I founded the Italian Communist Party (PCI), which was organized as a mass party, well rooted in the country's social fabric thanks to numerous collateral organizations. Soon, the PCI became Italy's major opposition party. After the failure of the *Compromesso Storico* in the late 1970s, the party began its slow decline, until it was dissolved in 1991, when the central committee, after long and intense internal debates, declared the end of the party and changed its name into *Partito Democratico della Sinistra* (PDS).

Partito Democratico della Sinistra **(PDS).** The Democratic Party of the Left was founded in 1991 as the post-Communist successor of the PCI. In the 1992 national elections, PDS obtained 16.1 percent of the vote.

Partito Liberale Italiano **(PLI).** The Italian Liberal Party was founded in 1922 as the heir to the liberal elites that governed the country after its unification. In the period after World War II, the PLI took part in various DC-led coalitions together with other small parties, which included the Italian Socialist Democratic Party (PSDI) and the Italian Republican Party (PRI). The PLI opposed the center-left governments of the 1960s and, in particular, the political economy of the DC, which favored a larger public service sector. The Liberal Party disappeared after the political elections of 1994, once the majority of its electorate migrated to other political formations.

Partito Popolare Italiano. The Italian Popular Party was one of the few small parties born after the end of the DC in 1993. The PPI claims the inheritance to the pre-Fascist Popular Party, founded by Don Luigi Sturzo in 1919.

Partito Repubblicano Italiano **(PRI).** The Italian Republican Party was founded in 1895 as the heir to the democratic and republican tradition of Giuseppe Mazzini and Giuseppe Garibaldi, Italy's founding fathers. This center-left party was characterized by a decisive antifascism and antimonarchy stance, a commitment to social solidarity, and a moderate promarket position. Since the end of World War II, the PRI has participated in various DC-led government coalitions together with other parties, including the PSDI and the PLI. The PRI was one of the very few parties that did not disappear after the Clean Hands scandal of 1992-1993.

Partito Socialista Italiano **(PSI).** The Italian Socialist Party was founded in 1892. Its history was always characterized by schisms and secessions. (In 1921, a group of former Socialist Party members founded the Communist Party of Italy, PCd'I.) During the 1980s, the PSI became the hinge of the party system, the balance broker between the two most powerful parties, the DC and the PCI: as such, the Socialist Party turned out to be essential to the formation of government coalitions. However, its increasingly important role within the party system resulted in the PSI's final collapse in 1993. Italian Socialists, Socialist Renewal, and the New Italian Socialist Party emerged as the heirs to Italy's oldest political party. These new formations failed to constitute a united front: the Italian Socialists, led by Enrico Boselli, and the Socialist Renewal, led by Giorgio Benvenuto, joined the center-left coalition; the New Italian Socialist Party, led by Bobo Craxi, son of Bettino Craxi, late secretary-general of the PSI, joined the right-wing *Casa delle Libertà* coalition.

Pentapartito **(1983-1992).** Government coalitions formed by five parties, the DC, the PSI, the PSDI, the PLI, and the PRI. *Pentapartito* refers in particular to the coalitions that governed Italy in the early 1980s.

Polo delle Libertà. Freedom Alliance won the 1994 national elections. The *Polo delle Libertà* alliance consisted of *Forza Italia, Alleanza Nazionale,* and

Lega Nord. The coalition was led by Silvio Berlusconi, leader of *Forza Italia*.

Il Popolo. Founded in 1923 by Giuseppe Donati, *Il Popolo* was a Catholic, antifascist daily, organ of the *Popular Party*. After being shut down by the Fascist government, it resumed publication in late 1943. It became the Christian Democratic Party's official newspaper after the end of the war.

Radiotelevisione Italiana **(RAI).** On October 26, 1944, decree no. 457 changed the name of the national radio broadcaster from EIAR to RAI; in 1952, RAI obtained the rights for television broadcasting. IRI (the Institute for Industrial Reconstruction) owned the majority of the corporation's shares until the year 2000. By 2003, RAI's offerings included three national broadcasting television channels (RAI1, RAI2, RAI3); RadioRAI, the national public radio broadcaster; RAI NEWS 24, a TV and satellite news channel; RAI International, international distributor of RAI programs; and RAI Educational, provider of educational services. Since the late 1990s, the corporation has also created a variety of commercial branches, including Sipra, the advertising corporation that collects RAI's advertising revenues; RAI Trade, the commercial structure that oversees the international distribution of RAI's products and audiovisual rights; and RAI Cinema, the branch that manages the production and distribution of films.

La Repubblica. *La Repubblica* was founded in 1976 by journalist Eugenio Scalfari and publishers Carlo Caracciolo and Giorgio Mondadori (of the Mondadori publishing house). The new daily newspaper targeted young, urban, well-educated, left-wing readers. It soon became the second most read national daily after *Corriere della Sera*.

Rifondazione Comunista **(RC)**. Reconstructed Communism was founded in December 1991 by a group of former members of the PCI still loyal to the communist idea. At the 1992 elections, *Rifondazione Comunista* obtained 5.6 percent of the votes. Under the leadership of Fausto Bertinotti, the party was able to maintain an important position in the Italian political panorama. RC was part of the coalition that governed the country from 1996 until 2001.

Rusconi Editore. Rusconi was the owner of the commercial television channel Antennanord, which broadcast across the north and northwest regions in 1980. Rusconi also owned the commercial television channel Italia1, which was acquired by Fininvest in the summer of 1982.

La Stampa. This national daily newspaper began its publications in 1867 in Turin with the name of *La Gazzetta Piemontese*.

Tg1. ("Tg" stands for Telegiornale). The news on RAI's flagship channel, RAI1.

Tg2. The news on RAI's second channel, RAI2.

Tg3. The news on RAI's third channel, RAI3.

L'Ulivo. The name of the heterogeneous center-left alliance dominated by the Democratic Party of the Left (PDS), and comprising the influential Italian Popular Party (PPI, which included former left-wing members of the DC, numerous ex-Socialists, and the Green Party) and Reconstructed Communism. The Olive Tree alliance led by Romano Prodi won the 1996 national elections.

Unione Radiofonica Italiana **(URI).** URI was established on August 27, 1924, after the unification of the three major national broadcasters, Radio Araldo, Radiofono, and S.I.R.A.C. (Società Italiana Radio Audizioni Circolari). The decree law of December 14, 1924, granted to URI the state monopoly of radio broadcasting.

L'Unità. Founded in 1924 by Antonio Gramsci, the newspaper was shut down by the Fascist regime in 1925. It resumed publication at the end of 1943 and became the official paper of the PCI after the end of the war.

La Voce Repubblicana. The official newspaper of the center-left Republican party. It was founded in 1921 and shut down by Mussolini. It resumed publications at the end of World War II.

Bibliography

Achtner, Wolfgang. Tape recorded interview with author. Rome, July 11, 2001.
———. Tape recorded interview with author. International Press Association, Rome, March 3, 1998.
Amato, Giuliano. "RAI: la riforma interrotta." In *Informazione e potere*. Milan: Feltrinelli, 1979.
Asor Rosa, Alberto. "Il giornalismo: Appunti sulla fisiologia di un mestiere difficile." In *Storia d'Italia*, annals 4, *Intellettuali e potere*, edited by Ruggero Romano and Corrado Vivanti. Turin: Giulio Einaudi, 1981: 1227-1257.
Balzoni, Giorgio. Tape recorded interview with author. RAI headquarters, Saxa Rubra, Rome, February 1998.
———. "Relazione congresso Usigrai" (Address to Usigrai Annual Convention). Internal publication, Boario, Italy, November 19-22, 1996.
Barbagallo, Francesco. "La formazione dell'Italia democratica." In *Storia dell'Italia Repubblicana*, vol. 1, *La costruzione della democrazia*, edited by Francesco Barbagallo et al. Turin: Giulio Einaudi, 1994.
Benhabib, Seyla. "Models of Public Space: Hanna Arendt, the Liberal Tradition, and Jürgen Habermas." In *Habermas and the Public Sphere*, edited by Craig Calhoun, 73-98. Cambridge, Mass.: MIT Press, 1992.
Bernabei, Ettore. Tape recorded interview with author. Lux headquarters, Rome, December 6, 1996.

Bernabei, Ettore, and Giorgio Dell'Arti. *L'uomo di fiducia I retroscena del potere raccontati da un testimone rimasto dietro le quinte per cinquant'anni*. Milan: Arnoldo Mondadori, 1999.

Bobbio, Norberto. *Ideological Profile of 21st Century Italy*. Translated by Lydia G. Cochrane. Princeton, N.J.: Princeton University Press, 1995.

———. *Il futuro della democrazia*. Turin: Einaudi, 1984.

Brancoli, Rodolfo. Tape recorded interview with author. *Liberal* headquarters, Rome, March 1998.

Bruzzone, Maria Grazia. *L'avventurosa storia del TG in Italia dall'avvento della televisione a oggi*. Milan: RCS Libri S.p.A., 2002.

Buonanno, Milly. "Degenerazione o mutamento?" In *Check up del giornalismo italiano*, edited by Jader Jacobelli, 28-33. Bari: Laterza, 1995.

Carlo Alberto of Savoj. *Statuto del Regno di Sardegna* (Constitution of the Kingdom of Sardinia), March 1848. Available at www.dickinson.edu/~rhyne/232/Four/Statuto.html.

Centro d'Ascolto dell'Informazione Radiotelevisiva. *Monitoraggio televisivo* (Monitoring of television newscasts). October 2002 and August 2003. Reports available on the *Autorità per le Garanzie nelle Comunicazioni* website at www.agcom.it.

Centro Studi Investimenti Sociali (CENSIS). *Il Rapporto Annuale 2000—34 Rapporto sulla situazione sociale del paese* (Annual report 2000—34th report on the social condition of the country). Available at www.censis.it.

Cesareo, Giovanni. *Anatomia del potere televisivo*. Milan: Franco Angeli, 1970.

———. "Privatization: Some Questions and Paradoxes." Paper presented at the "Media in Transition Colloquium." Piran, Slovenia, October 17-21, 1992.

———. "Televisione." In *La cultura italiana del Novecento*, edited by Corrado Stajano, 753-772. Bari: Laterza, 1997.

———. *La televisione sprecata*. Milan: Feltrinelli, 1974.

———. "Tesi," personal correspondence via e-mail, April 7, 1999.

———. "Tesi," personal correspondence via e-mail, March 28, 1999.

Chiarenza, Franco. *Il cavallo morente*. Milan: Bompiani, 1978.

Constitutional Court. *Radiotelevisione e servizi radioelettrici—Radiodiffusione circolare per mezzo di onde elettromagnetiche—Questione fondata di costituzionalità* (Radio and television services—Radio broadcasting via electromagnetic waves—Question of constitutionality). Sentence no. 225, July 10, 1974. Published in *Gazzetta Ufficiale* (Official Gazette of the Italian Republic), July 17, 1974, no. 187. Available at www.telestreet.it/telestreet/doc_legali/consulta225_74.htm.

———. *Radiotelevisione e servizi radioelettrici—Servizi di televisione via cavo—Questione fondata di costituzionalità* (Radio and television services—Cable television services—Question of constitutionality). Sentence no. 226, July 10, 1974. Published in *Gazzetta Ufficiale* (Official Gazette of the Italian Republic), July 17, 1974, no. 187. Available at www.telestreet.it/telestreet/doc_legali/consulta226_74.htm.

Contratto di servizio 2003-2005 (Service agreement between the Communications Ministry and RAI Corporation). Available at www.sas.rai.it/regolamenti/contratto2003.html.

Corriere della Sera (Milan), October 1980-November 1998.

Costituzione italiana. Turin: Piccola Biblioteca Einaudi, 1975.

Craxi, Bettino. Telephone interview with author. April 1998.

De Bernardi, Alberto, and Luigi Canapini. *Storia d'Italia 1860-1995*. Milan: Bruno Mondadori, 1996.

De Chiara, Piero. Tape recorded interview with author. Olivetti Foundation, Rome, April 3, 1998.

De Felice, Franco. "Nazione e crisi: le linee di frattura." In *Storia dell'Italia Repubblicana*, vol. 3.1, *L'Italia nella crisi mondiale. L'ultimo ventennio*, edited by Francesco Barbagallo et al. Turin: Giulio Einaudi, 1994.

De Luna, Giovanni. "Partiti e società negli anni della ricostruzione." In *Storia dell'Italia Repubblicana*, vol. 1, *La costruzione della democrazia*, edited by Francesco Barbagallo et al. Turin: Giulio Einaudi, 1994.

Del Debbio, Paolo. *Il Mercante e l'inquisitore apologia della televisione commerciale*. Milan: Il Sole 24 ORE Libri, 1991.

De Mauro, Tullio. *Storia linguistica dell'Italia unita*. Bari: Laterza, 1962.

Di Nolfo, Ennio. *La repubblica delle speranze e degli inganni*. Florence: Ponte alle Grazie, 1996.

Eco, Umberto. *Apocalittici e integrati*. Bologna: Bonpiani, 1954.

The Economist (London), December 20, 2003.

L'Espresso (Rome), March-April, 1996.

Etzioni-Halevy, Eva. *National Broadcasting under Siege*. New York: St. Martin's Press, 1987.

Farinelli, Giuseppe, Ermanno Paccagnini, Giovanni Santambrogio, and Angela Ida Villa. *Storia del giornalismo italiano*. Turin: UTET, 1997.

Faustini, Gianni. "I numeri della professione giornalistica." *Problemi dell'informazione* 20, no. 3 (September 1995): 379-380.

Ferro, Valeria. Tape recorded interview with author. Centro d'Ascolto dell'Informazione Radiotelevisiva, Rome, July 22, 2002.

Fiorespino, Valerio. Tape recorded interview with author. RAI headquarters, Rome, April 1998.

Firpo, Massimo, Nicola Tranfaglia, and Pier Giorgio Zunino, eds. *Guida all'Italia contemporanea*. Milan: Garzanti, 1998.

Fontana, Sandro. "I nodi della riforma della RAI-TV." In *Il decentramento radiotelevisivo in Europa. La terza rete TV e la ristrutturazione della radiofonia pubblica in Italia*, edited by Franco Iseppi and Giuseppe Richeri, 583-586. Milan: Franco Angeli Editore, 1980.

Forcella, Enzo. Telephone interview with author. December 8, 1996.

Forgacs, David. "The Italian Communist Party and Culture." In *Culture in Postwar Italy*, edited by Zygmunt G. Baranski and Robert Lumley, 97-114. New York: St. Martin's Press, 1990.

Fraser, Nancy. "Rethinking the Public Sphere: A Contribution to the Critique of Actual Existing Democracy." In *Habermas and the Public Sphere*, edited by Craig Calhoun, 109-142. Cambridge, Mass.: MIT Press, 1992.

Gambaro, Marco, and Francesco Silva. *Economia della televisione*. Bologna: Il Mulino, 1992.

Garnham, Nicholas. "A Reply to Elisabeth Jacka's Democracy as Defeat." In Rethinking Public Media in a Transnational Era, edited by Gerald Sussman. Special issue of *Television and New Media* 4, no. 2 (May 2003): 193-200.

———. *Emancipation, the Media, and Modernity: Arguments about the Media and Social Theory*. Oxford: Oxford University Press, 2000.

———. "The Media and the Public Sphere." In *Communicating Politics: Mass Communication and the Political Process*, edited by Peter Golding, et al., 37-54. Leicester: Leicester University Press, 1986.

———. "The Media and the Public Sphere." In *Habermas and the Public Sphere*, edited by Craig Calhoun, 359-376. Cambridge, Mass.: MIT Press, 1992.

———. "Public Service versus the Market." *Screen* 5, no. 1 (1983): 6-28.

Germino, Dante, and Stefano Passigli. *The Government and Politics of Contemporary Italy*. New York: Harper & Row, 1968.

Ghirelli, Massimo. Interview with author. Italian Foreign Ministry, Rome, January 1998.

Giuntella, Paolo. Tape recorded interview with author. RAI Headquarters, Saxa Rubra, Rome, April 1998.

Government Acts. Law June 25, 1993, no. 206. *Disposizioni sulla società concessionaria del servizio pubblico radiotelevisivo* (Regulations on the public service broadcaster). Available at www.medialaw.it/Rai/1993206.htm.

———. Law August 6, 1990, no. 223. *Disciplina del sistema radiotelevisivo pubblico e privato* (Discipline of the public and private broadcasting sector). Available at www.agcom.it/L_naz/L223_90.htm.

———. Law April 14, 1975, no. 103. *Ordinamento del servizio pubblico radiotelevisivo* (Ordinance on Public Service Broadcasting). Available at www.camera.it/_bicamerali/rai/norme/listitut.htm.

Gozzini, Giovanni. *Storia del giornalismo*. Milan: Bruno Mondadori, 2000.

Graef, Roger. "Not Good Enough." *OpenDemocracy*, June 2, 2001. Available at www.opendemocracy.net.

Gramsci, Antonio. *Il materialismo storico e la filosofia di Benedetto Croce*. Edited by Istituto Gramsci. Turin: Editori Riuniti, 1975.

———. *Quaderni del Carcere*, vol. 1. Edited by Valentino Gerratana. Turin: Einaudi, 1975.

Habermas, Jurgen. *The Structural Transformation of the Public Sphere*. Cambridge, Mass.: MIT Press, 1989.

Hall, Stuart. "Gramsci's Relevance for the Study of Race and Ethnicity." *European Journal of Communication Enquiry* 10 (January 1986): 5-25.

Hartley, John. *Uses of Television*. New York: Routledge, 1999.

Hellman, Stephen. *Italian Communism in Transition: The Rise and Fall of the Historic Compromise in Turin, 1975-1980*. New York: Oxford University Press, 1988.

Jacka, Elisabeth. "Democracy as Defeat: The Impotence of Arguments for Public Service Broadcasting." In Rethinking Public Media in a Transnational Era, edited by Gerald Sussman. Special issue of *Television and New Media* 4, no. 2 (May 2003): 177-191.

Keane, John. "A Reply to Nicholas Garnham." *Communication Review* 1, no. 1 (1995): 27-31.

———. "Structural Transformations of the Public Sphere." *Communication Review* 1, no. 1 (1995): 1-22.

Lanaro, Silvio. *Storia dell'Italia repubblicana*. Venice: Marsilio, 1992.

Levi, Roberto. *Le trasmissioni TV che hanno fatto (o no) l'Italia da "Lascia o Raddoppia" al "Grande Fratello."* Milan: Rizzoli, 2002.

Lumley, Bob, and Philip Schlesinger. "The Press, the State and Its Enemies: The Italian Case." *Sociological Review* 30, no. 4 (November 1982): 603-626.

Mancini, Paolo, and Daniel C. Hallin. "Italy's Television, Italy's Democracy." *OpenDemocracy*, July 19, 2001. Available at www.opendemocracy.net.

Il Manifesto (Rome), March 20, 2002.

Mannucci, Cesare. *Lo spettatore senza libertà*. Bari: Laterza, 1962.

Mastroianni, Roberto. Tape recorded interview with author. RAI headquarters, Rome, January 1998.

Mastrolonardo, Raffaele. "Media Concentration: The Italian Case-Study." *OpenDemocracy*, March 14, 2002. Available at www.opendemocracy.net.

Mattioli, Francesco. Tape recorded interview with author. RAI International Directorate headquarters, Rome, March 1998.

Minà, Gianni. Tape recorded telephone interview with author. December 28, 2002.

Monteleone, Franco. *La radio italiana nel periodo fascista*. Venice: Marsilio, 1976.

———. *Storia della RAI dagli alleati alla DC 1944-1954*. Rome: Laterza, 1980.

———. *Storia della RAI dagli alleati alla DC 1944-1954*. Rome: Laterza, 1979.

Moretti, Italo. Tape recorded interview with author, RAI headquarters, Saxa Rubra, Rome, March 1998.

Morrione, Roberto. Tape recorded interview with author, RAI headquarters, Saxa Rubra, Rome, July 24, 2002.

Murialdi, Paolo. Tape recorded interview with author. Milan, January 31, 1998.

———. "Idee per vivere felici, non lottizzati e senza canone" (A few ideas to be happy, *lottizzazione*-free, and without the annual fee). *Reset*, Milan, no. 43 (December 1997): 14-15.

———. *Maledetti "Professori."* Milan: Rizzoli, 1994.

———. "Per una ricerca sulla lottizzazione" (Notes toward research on lottizzazione). *Problemi dell'informazione* 22 no. 1 (March 1997).

———. *La stampa italiana dalla liberazione alla crisi di fine secolo.* Bari: Laterza, 1995.

———. *Storia del giornalismo italiano.* Bologna: Il Mulino, 1996.

———. *Storia del giornalismo italiano dalle prime gazzette ai telegiornali.* Turin: Gutemberg 2000, 1986.

Natale, Roberto. *Audizione di rappresentanti dell'USIGRAI* (Audition of Usigrai's representatives). Speech to the RAI Parliamentary Committee, December 12, 2000. Available at www.camera.it/_dati/leg13/lavori/stenbic/21/2000/1206/s020.htm.

———. Tape recorded interview with author. Usigrai headquarters, Saxa Rubra, Rome, March 1998.

Negt, Oskar, and Alexander Kluge. *Public Sphere and Experience: Toward an Analysis of the Bourgeois and Proletarian Public Sphere.* Minneapolis: University of Minnesota Press, 1993.

Newell, James L. *Parties and Democracy in Italy.* Aldershot, UK: Ashgate, 2000.

Niada, Marco. "Farewell Agnelli—Figure of Another Age." *OpenDemocracy,* February 13, 2003. Available at www.opendemocracy.net.

The New York Times, February 16, 2003.

Nocerino, Francesca. Tape recorded interview with author. RAI headquarters, Saxa Rubra, Rome, April 1998.

Novelli, Edoardo. *Dalla TV di partito, al partito della TV televisione e politica in Italia 1960-1995.* Florence: La Nuova Italia, 1995.

Novi, Emiddio. *Discussione sul pluralismo nel servizio pubblico radiotelevisivo: Audizione contestuale dei direttori del TG1, del TG2, del TGR e del Giornale radio* (Discussion about pluralism in the public service broadcaster: audition of news directors of Tg1, Tg2, TGR and Giornale radio). Speech to the RAI Parliamentary Committee, January 14, 1997. (A summary of the speech is available at notes3.senato.it/ODG_PUBL.NSF/0/18b40092add282bc412564ad00572cf9?OpenDocument).

Ordine Nazionale dei Giornalisti (Journalists' National Body), and Federazione Nazionale della Stampa Italiana (National Federation of the Italian Press). *I Doveri del Giornalista* (Charter of Journalists' Responsibilities), Rome, July 8, 1993. Available at www.medialaw.it/deontologia/doveri.htm.

Ortoleva, Peppino. "Mezzi di Comunicazione." In *Guida all'Italia contemporanea, 1861-1997,* vol. 4, *Comportamenti sociali e cultura,* edited by Massimo Firpo, Nicola Tranfaglia, and Pier Giorgio Zunino. Milan: Garzanti, 1998.

Padovani, Cinzia, and Andrew Calabrese. "Berlusconi, RAI, and the Modernization of Italian Feudalism." *Javnost/The Public* 3, no. 2 (1996): 109-120.

Papa, Antonio. *Storia politica della radio in Italia.* Naples: Guida, 1978.

Parascandolo, Renato. Tape recorded interview with author. RAI headquarters, Rome, January 19, 1998.

Parente, Luigi. *I partiti politici nell'Italia repubblicana (1943-1992)*. Naples: Edizioni Scientifiche Italiane, 1996.

Pasquino, Gianfranco. "Politica e ideologia." In *La cultura italiana del Novecento*, edited by Corrado Stajano, 481-513. Bari: Laterza, 1996.

Petrone, Sandro. Tape recorded interview with author. RAI headquarters, Saxa Rubra, Rome, January 8, 1998.

Picchi, Stefano. Tape recorded interview with author. RAI headquarters, Saxa Rubra, Rome, January 1998.

Pinto, Francesco. *Il modello televisivo. Professionalità e politica da Bernabei alla Terza Rete*. Milan: Feltrinelli, 1980.

Pius XII. *Miranda Prorsus: Circa la cinematografia, la radio e la televisione*. Rome: Tipografia Poliglotta Vaticana, 1957.

Porter, William E. *The Italian Journalist*. Ann Arbor: University of Michigan Press, 1983.

Presidential Decree. January 26, 1952, no. 180. *Approvazione ed esecutoreità della Convenzione per la concessione alla Radio Audizioni Italia Società per azioni del servizio di telediffusione su filo* (Concession between the state and RAI for television and radio broadcasting services).

Radiocorriere. Turin: Ente Italiano Audizioni Radiofoniche, January 1932.

Radiocorriere. Rome: Radio Audizioni Italia, November 1945.

RAI Official. Telephone interview with author. RAI headquarters, Rome, March 1998.

RAI, Radiotelevisione Italiana. *Annuari RAI* (RAI Annual Reports), 1954-2003.

———. *Il Bilancio 2000. La situazione economica e finanziaria* (The financial and economic situation 2000). Available on the RAI website (under "Azienda") at www.ufficiostampa.rai.it/.

———. *Carta dell'Informazione e della Programmazione a Garanzia degli Utenti e degli Operatori del Servizio Pubblico* (Information and programming for viewers and personnel of the public service broadcaster), March 1995. Available at www.medialaw.it/deontologia/rai.htm.

La Repubblica (Rome), October 1980-February 2003.

Richeri, Giuseppe. "Italy: Public Service and Private Interests." *Journal of Communication* (Summer 1978): 75-78.

Ronzoni, Daniele. Tape recorded telephone interview with author. RAI headquarters, Saxa Rubra, Rome, January 1998.

Rossi, Emilio. Tape recorded interview with author. *Centro Televisivo Vaticano*, Vatican City, January 4, 1997.

Rossi, Ernesto. *I padroni del vapore*. Bari: Laterza, 1957.

Salvati, Mariuccia. "Amministrazione pubblica e partiti." In *Storia dell'Italia Repubblicana*, vol. 1, *La costruzione della democrazia*, edited by Francesco Barbagallo et al. Turin: Einaudi, 1994.

———. *Stato e industria nella ricostruzione*. Milan: Feltrinelli, 1982.

Santarelli, Enzo. *Storia critica della repubblica*. Milan: Feltrinelli, 1996.

Scalfari, Eugenio. *L'autunno della repubblica: La mappa del potere in Italia*. Milan: Etas Kompass, 1969.
Scoppola, Pietro. *La repubblica dei partiti profilo storico della democrazia in Italia (1945-1990)*. Bologna: Il Mulino, 1991.
Scuola ed istruzione. Document available at the Risorgimento Italiano website, www.riccati.it/risorgi/1815-49.htm.
Severi, Alberto. Tape recorded interview with author. RAI headquarters, Saxa Rubra, Rome, March 11, 1998.
Siliato, Francesco. Tape recorded telephone interview with author. October 3, 2001.
———. Tape recorded interview with author. Studio Frasi, Milan, January 31, 1998.
———. *L'Antenna dei padroni*. Milan: Gabriele Mazzotta Editore, 1977.
Il Sole 24 Ore (Milan), January 2002-June 2003.
Spada, Celestino. Tape recorded interview with author. RAI headquarters, Via Teulada, Rome, January 8, 1998.
———. Untitled author's manuscript, Rome, August 28, 1997, published as "Della lottizzazione e del 'partito RAI'" (About *lottizzazione* and the RAI Party). *Problemi dell'informazione* 22, no. 4 (December 1997): 485-493.
La Stampa (Turin), September 1993-June 2003.
Studio Frasi. *Stagioni televisive individui giorno medio share*. Milan: October 2001.
Tamberlich, Romano. Tape recorded interview with author. RAI headquarters, Saxa Rubra, Rome, March 17, 1998.
Taradash, Marco. Tape recorded interview with author. Senate of the Republic, Rome, April 1998.
Tomassini, Stefano. Tape recorded interview with author. RAI headquarters, Saxa Rubra, Rome, January 1998.
Tracey, Michael. *The Decline and Fall of Public Service Broadcasting*. Oxford: Oxford University Press, 1998.
Trincheri, Claudia. "Gli intellettuali che lavorano alla RAI-TV." *Rassegna italiana di sociologia* (date and place of publication not available): 133-154.
L'Unità (Rome), February 18, 1995.
L'Unione Sarda (Cagliari), October 28, 1995.
Usigrai. *Accesso in RAI tramite selezione, 1978-1993*, Rome, July 1993, Usigrai internal publication.
———. *Carta dei diritti e dei doveri del giornalista radiotelevisivo del servizio pubblico* (Charter of rights and responsibilities of the broadcast journalist), Rome, 1990. Available at www.medialaw.it/deontologia/usigrai.htm.
———. *Relazione al congresso di Sorrento*, November 9-12, 1999. Available at www.usigrai.it/doc/relaz_99.htm.
Veltroni, Walter. *Io e Berlusconi (e la RAI)*. Rome: Editori Riuniti, 1990.
Vergara, Daniela. Tape recorded interview with author. RAI headquarters, Saxa Rubra, Rome, January 1998.

Wagner-Pacifici, Erica Robin. *The Moro Morality Play: Terrorism as Social Drama*. Chicago: University of Chicago Press, 1986.
Zaccaria, Roberto, ed. "Radiotelevisione," vol. 15, 2nd ed. In *Trattato di diritto amministrativo*, edited by Giuseppe Santaniello. Padua: Cedam, 1996.

Index

Achtner, Wolfgang, 220
Agence Havas, 61
Agnelli, and FIAT, 40
Agnes, Biagio, 110, 113, 115, 120, 247
Aics (*Associazione italiana cultura e sport*), 22
Albo dei giornalisti (List of Italian Journalists), 62
Alleanza Nazionale, 45, 47, 137, 140, 145, 149, 151-52, 187-89, 194, 237, 257, 261-62
Allende, President Salvador, 37
Almirante, Giorgio, 201
Amato, Giuliano, 46
Andreotti, Giulio, 43, 114, 120-21, 140, 169, 203, 258
Angelini, Claudio, 141
anni del riflusso, 40
anni di piombo, 33
Annunziata, Lucia, 152

ANSA (*Associazione Nazionale Agenzie di Stampa*), 19
Antennanord, 106, 263
Antonelli, Giuseppe, 33
Arata, Rodolfo, 72-74
Arci (*Associazione ricreativa e culturale italiana*), 21
Artsworld, 239
Asor Rosa, Alberto, 57
Associazione italiana cultura e sport (Aics), 22
Associazione Nazionale Agenzie di Stampa (ANSA), 19
Associazione ricreativa e culturale italiana (Arci), 21
Augias, Corrado, 169
autunno caldo, 35
L'Avvenire, 59
aziendalisti, 69-71, 73, 81, 90, 113, 181, 206

Baldassarre, Antonio, 150
Balzoni, Giorgio, 171, 191-93, 214
Barbato, Andrea, 76, 94
BBC. *See* British Broadcasting Corporation
Il Becco Giallo, 60
Benigni, Roberto, 251
Benvenuti, Feliciano, 130
Berlinguer, Enrico, 37, 109, 258
Berlusconi, Silvio, x, 40, 42, 86, 92, 106, 120-22, 127, 141, 181, 184, 190, 208, 214, 234-38, 250, 258; as a political figure, 45-48, 137, 140, 142-144, 149-53, 176, 186-87, 191, 204-5, 208, 217-18, 230, 236-39, 242-43, 260, 263
Berlusconi decree, 40, 42, 110-14, 129, 234
Bernabei, Ettore, 28, 33-34, 74-83, 86-87, 89-91, 94-95, 163, 186, 193, 231-32
Biagi, Enzo, 119, 132, 141, 151-52, 186, 204
Billia, Gianni, 138
Bindi, Rosi, 215-16
Blix, Hans, 151
blocked democracy, 4, 7, 13, 23, 47, 161, 193, 246-47, 259
Bobbio, Norberto, 5, 6, 35, 40, 244, 246, 260
Bocca, Giorgio, 34, 123, 202
Bordiga, Amadeo, 60
Bossi, Umberto, 45, 142, 260
Brancoli, Rodolfo, 118, 145
British Broadcasting Corporation (BBC), 5-6, 65, 210, 239, 251
Bruzzone, Maria Grazia, 33

CAF (the trio Craxi, Andreotti, Fanfani), 42, 121, 136, 140-41, 169, 217, 258
Il Caffè, 55

Camera dei fasci (Fascist House), 13
Camera Generale Italiana del Lavoro (C.G.I.L.), 67
Canale5, 42, 106, 120, 131, 152, 215-16, 237, 260-61
Catholic/Communist alliance, 247
Cattaneo, Flavio, 152
Cavani, Liliana, 144
center-left government: of the 1960s, 22, 27, 32-35, 74-75, 81, 163; of the 1990s, 46, 144-45, 149, 153, 188, 237-38
centrismo, 22-23, 26, 74, 258
Centro d'Ascolto dell'Informazione Radiotelevisiva (Observatory of television news programs), 185, 238
centro-sinistra. *See* center-left government
C.G.I.L. (*Camera Generale Italiana del Lavoro*), 67
Christian Democratic Party (DC), x, 27-28, 176, 258, 261, 264; crisis of, 44, 46; history of, 14, 16, 19-20, 22-24, 29-30, 35-39, 47-48, 137, 263; influence on broadcasting, 2, 4, 6-7, 26, 31-34, 36, 42-43, 68-76, 80-86, 88-95, 98, 108, 110-15, 118, 120-22, 126-28, 130, 133, 137, 143-44, 149, 163, 169, 192-93, 207, 231-33, 235, 246-47, 259, 262
Clean Hands scandal (*tangentopoli*), 4, 44, 123, 127-28, 132, 172, 208, 215, 218
Commissione Parlamentare di Vigilanza RAI. *See* RAI Parliamentary Committee
Comunisti Italiani, 145
Il Conciliatore, 56
Confalonieri, Federico, 56
Confindustria, 40

Consiglio Superiore della Magistratura, 16
consociativismo, 42, 44, 109, 234, 259
Continental Telegraphen Compagnie, 61
Contri, Alberto, 149
conventio ad excludendum, 23, 108-9, 259
correntocrazia, 27-28, 259
Corriere della Sera, 18, 34, 58-60, 66, 85, 127, 139-40, 142-43, 166, 199, 238, 257, 259, 263
Corriere Milanese, 55
Costanzo, Maurizio, 106, 120, 215, 216
Craxi, Bettino, 39-40, 43-44, 46, 110-12, 114, 120-21, 125, 134, 140, 142, 169, 179, 181, 187, 189, 258, 262
Critica sociale, 59
Curzi, Alessandro, 113, 119, 137

DC. *See* Christian Democratic Party
De Chiara, Piero, 108-9, 112, 114-15, 117, 167, 169, 170, 173, 199-200, 219
Decreti Delegati, 35
de-*fascistizzazione*, 16
De Feo, Italo, 33
De Gasperi, Alcide, 19, 23
Delai, Nadio, 133
Del Bufalo, Giuliana, 120
Del Noce, Fabrizio, 150
Demattè, Claudio, 130, 135, 137-38
De Mita, Ciriaco, 43, 115, 121
Democratici di Sinistra, 152, 237
Democratic Party of the Left (*Partito Democratico della Sinistra*), 42, 44, 46, 130, 133, 137, 143-45, 149, 194, 237, 261, 264
Di Bella, Antonio, 215-16

Di Lampedusa, Tommaso, 136
Di Lorenzo, Ottavio, 113
Donati, Giuseppe, 60, 263
dorotei, 71, 80, 90, 259
il duce, 60, 161

Eco, Umberto, 21, 70
Editoriale Espresso, 106
EIAR. *See* Ente Italiano Audizioni Radiofoniche
Emiliani, Vittorio, 149
ENEL (National Energy Company), 46, 183
Ente Italiano Audizioni Radiofoniche (EIAR), 17, 62-66, 68-69, 72, 231, 258, 260, 263
Ernesto Rossi, 29
L'Espresso, 43, 85, 188
Etzioni-Halevy, Eva, 206

Fabiani, Fabiano, 70, 81-82
Fanfani, Amintore, 27, 69, 71, 74, 83, 89-90, 128, 140
fanfaniani, 27, 71, 81, 259
Farolfi, Guido, 113
Fascist House (*Camera dei fasci*), 13
Fava, Nuccio, 113, 115
Fede e Avvenire, 59
Federazione Nazionale della Stampa (national press association), 66, 120, 260
Fellini, Federico, 98
Ferro, Valeria, 238
Fichera, Massimo, 94
Fini, Gianfranco, 45, 140, 188, 237
Fininvest, 41-43, 106-7, 119, 121, 128, 137, 139, 214, 237, 258, 260-61, 263; and Berlusconi, 40, 42, 45, 86, 110, 122, 143; and the Berlusconi Decree, 110-12, 234; and *lottizzazione*, 233, 235; and RAI, 113-14,

118, 120, 122, 124, 130-31, 135, 140, 150, 249
Finocchiaro, Beniamino, 94
Fiorespino, Valerio, 176-78, 180, 183-84
Forcella, Enzo, 5, 94- 96, 114-15, 136, 199, 201-3, 205, 220
Forlani, Arnaldo, 43, 114, 120-21, 127-28, 169, 258
Forza Italia, 45-48, 137, 140, 145, 149, 150, 237, 242, 250, 260, 262
France Télévisions, 251
Freccero, Carlo, 149
freedom of antenna (*Libertà d'antenna*), 36, 85, 233, 244, 260

Gallucci, Carlo, 188
Gamaleri, Giampiero, 149
Garimberti, Paolo, 133
Garnham, Nicholas, 2, 241
Gasparri, Maurizio, 150, 238
La Gazzetta Piemontese, 58, 263
Gazzette Letterarie, 55
Il Gazzettino, 19
Gennarini, Pier Emilio, 70
Ghirelli, Massimo, 203, 204, 207
Giolitti, Giovanni, 23
Giornale de' Litterati d'Italia, 55
Giubilo, Andrea, 133
Giulietti, Beppe, 200
Giuntella, Paolo, 169
Government Acts: Law no. 103 (April 14, 1975), 122, 131; Law no. 206 (June 25, 1993), 45, 129; Law no. 223 (August 6, 1990), 122, 131. *See also* Berlusconi decree; Mammì Law; *par conditio* law
Gramsci, Antonio, 9, 38, 57, 58, 60, 161, 264
Gran Giornale de' Litterati, 55
Granzotto, Gianni, 33, 80

Green Party, 149, 264
Gregory, Tullio, 130
Guala, Filiberto, 20, 69-72, 74, 81
Guglielmi, Alessandro, 70, 108, 119, 133, 149, 247
Guidi, Ugo, 113
Guzzanti, Sabina, 205

Hallin, Daniel C., 236-37
Hartley, John, 241-42
historic compromise, 37, 108, 247, 258

Institute for Industrial Reconstruction, 29-30, 46, 68, 71, 90, 148, 260, 263
Intini, Ugo, 125
Iseppi, Franco, 133, 144
Italian Communist Party (PCI), 47-48, 77, 133, 261-63; crisis of, 44; history of, 2, 6-7, 14, 16, 19, 25, 28, 35, 37-39, 41-42, 258-59; influence on broadcasting, 27, 43, 79, 84, 94, 96, 108-9, 111-16, 118, 121, 126, 164, 167-69, 173, 188, 200, 207, 233-34, 247; and *L'Unità*, 264
Italian Liberal Party (PLI), 23, 35, 84, 113, 122-23, 126, 258-59, 261-62
Italian Popular Party (PPI), 143-44, 262, 264
Italian Postal Service (*Poste Italiane*), 46
Italian Republican Party (PRI), 23, 35, 68, 84, 108, 113, 121-23, 126-27, 133, 258-59, 262
Italian Socialist Party (PSI), 181, 257, 258; history of, 2, 14, 16, 19, 22, 27-28, 32, 35, 37, 39-40, 44, 46-47, 68, 259, 262; influence on broadcasting, 6, 22, 26-27, 42-43, 81-84, 89-90,

94, 108, 110-14, 118, 120-22, 125-26, 164, 167, 179, 189, 233-34
Italia1 (Mediaset channel), 42, 106, 139, 242, 260-61, 263

Jacka, Elisabeth, 241-42, 244

Kuliscioff, Anna, 59

La Malfa, Giorgio, 127
Lambertenghi, Luigi Porro, 56
Il Lavoro, 19
Lega Nord. See Northern League
Levi, Arrigo, 169
Libertà d'antenna. See freedom of antenna
Liga Veneta. See Venetian League
List of Italian Journalists (*Albo dei giornalisti*), 62
Locatelli, Luigi, 113, 120
Longhi, Albino, 128, 132
Lotta di Classe Giornale dei Lavoratori Italiani, 59
lottizzazione, 2-4, 8-9, 30, 47, 123, 127, 192-93, 238; and commercial broadcasting, 121, 233-35; definition of, 261; and democracy, 13, 220, 246-50; history of, 6-7, 26, 53, 112, 114, 116, 122, 129-30, 229-31; and the public broadcaster, 28, 45, 48, 82-83, 92, 95, 107-8, 113, 125-26, 132-33, 135, 137-44, 146, 149, 186, 200-1, 209-11, 219; and journalists, 53, 161-63, 166-85, 187-91, 194-98, 202-3, 205-7, 212, 217, 221; theories of, 109-10, 117-18, 123, 173, 220
Luttazzi, Daniele, 186

Malgieri, Gennaro, 200
Maltese, Curzio, 204

Mammì, Oscar, 43, 122, 126, 144, 234, 258
Mammì Law, 43, 122, 126, 144, 234
Manca, Enrico, 33, 110, 113, 123, 133, 173
Marano, Antonio, 150
Marconi Radio Experimental Center Foundation, 63
Mastroianni, Roberto, 136, 142, 194, 210-11, 219
Il Mattino, 18, 19
Mattioli, Francesco, 97, 140, 163, 191, 194, 205
Mazza, Mauro, 151
Media Observatory (University of Pavia), 145
Mediaset, 124, 131-32, 166, 180, 205, 215-16, 234, 260-61; and Berlusconi, 3, 237-38, 242-43, 250; and RAI, 47, 146-47, 149-51, 183-84, 187, 191, 210, 212, 214, 230, 235-36, 239-40
Mediaset news programs (*telegiornali*): *Studio aperto*, 98; Tg4, 237; Tg5, 128, 131, 215, 237
mediasettizzazione (of RAI), 140, 212
Medio Credito Centrale, 32
Mentana, Enrico, 128, 140, 215
Il Messaggero, 66, 149
Milano, Emmanuele, 70
Milano Sera, 19
Mimun, Clemente, 140-42, 188, 211
Minà, Gianni, 186, 212, 236
Minoli, Giovanni, 120, 132-33, 211
Mondadori Publishers, 43, 86, 106, 120, 258, 260, 263
Il Mondo, 166
Montanelli, Indro, 145
Moratti, Letizia, 138, 140-41, 144, 150, 204, 208, 217-18

Moretti, Italo, 113
Morgagni, Manlio, 60, 257
Morrione, Roberto, 77, 187, 197-98
Movimento Sociale Italiano (MSI), 32, 45, 84, 201, 261
MSI. *See Movimento Sociale Italiano*
Murialdi, Paolo, 7-9, 56, 70-71, 114, 130, 134, 162, 207, 209, 212
Mursia, Fiorenza, 144
Mussolini, Benito, 21, 30, 62-64, 68, 257, 261, 264. *See also il duce*

Natale, Roberto, 135, 170-71, 173, 207-8
National Energy Company (ENEL), 46, 183
Nenni, Pietro, 22, 32
NET (*Nuova Emittenza Televisiva*), 84
New York Times, 58
Nocerino, Francesca, 179-80, 184
Northern League (*Lega Nord*), 39, 45, 47, 137, 141-43, 150, 152, 260, 263
Notizie Letterarie Oltramontane, 55
Novelle Letterarie, 55
Nuova Emittenza Televisiva (NET), 84
Il Nuovo Corriere, 19

Observatory of television news programs (*Centro d'Ascolto dell'Informazione Radiotelevisiva*), 185, 238
Occhetto, Achille, 42, 133
Olivares, Federica, 144
Olive Tree coalition. *See L'Ulivo*
Ordine Nuovo, 60
organic ideology, 9, 161, 230
Ortoleva, Peppino, 68

L'Osservatore Romano, 58-59
ostruzionismo di maggioranza, 16

Paese Sera, 19
Panorama, 43, 85, 150
Parascandolo, Renato, 83
par conditio law, 185
partitocrazia, 25-26, 30, 47-48, 116, 124, 126, 128, 140-41, 187, 201, 208

Partito Democratico della Sinistra. *See* Democratic Party of the Left
Pasquarelli, Gianni, 120, 128
Pasquino, Giovanni, 237
pax televisiva, 120
PCI. *See* Italian Communist Party
Pellico, Silvio, 56
pentapartito, 41, 43
Perrone family, 106, 258
Petrone, Sandro, 167, 172, 189-90, 196-97, 210
Petruccioli, Claudio, 151
Picchi, Stefano, 185, 213
Piccoli, Flaminio, 71
Pinochet, Augusto, 37
La Plebe, 59
PLI. *See* Italian Liberal Party
Polo delle Libertà, 47, 137, 140, 142, 145, 149, 211, 237, 262
Pope Pius XI, 20, 63, 69; and his encyclical *Urbi et orbi*, 63
Pope Pius XII, 20, 69
Il Popolo, 19, 60, 65, 72, 75, 81, 192, 195, 263
Popular Party (1919), 19, 60, 263
Poste Italiane (Italian Postal Service), 46
Pozzilli, Gregorio, 81
PPI. *See* Italian Popular Party
Prampolini, Camillo, 59
Presutti, Ennio, 141
PRI. *See* Italian Republican Party

(PRI)
Primarete Indipendente, 106, 258
Principe, Michele, 94
Prodi, Romano, 46, 148, 264
PSDI. *See* Social-Democratic Party
PSI. *See* Italian Socialist Party
Publitalia, 137, 143, 261
Pugliese, Sergio, 81

Qaddafi, President Mohammed, 119

Radio Alice, 85
Radio Antenna Rossa, 85
Radio Araldo, 61, 264
Radio Città Futura, 85
Radiofono, 61, 264
Radio Londra, 65, 67
radio programs: *Commento ai fatti del giorno*, 64; *Conversazioni*, 67; *Cronache dal regime*, 64; *Giornale radio*, 73; *Lezioni di tedesco*, 67; *Notiziario Cattolico*, 67; *Radio Igea*, 63; *Radio Sociale*, 63; *La voce dei lavoratori*, 67; *Voce dei partiti*, 67
Radiotelevisión Española (RTVE), 251
Radio Vaticana, 67
RAI1 (RAI Channel 1), 93-94, 107, 113, 118-19, 125, 128, 132, 138, 149-52, 216, 245, 251, 263-64; and the Christian Democratic Party, 4, 94, 133; and *lottizzazione*, 188
RAI2 (RAI Channel 2), 93-94, 98, 107, 118-19, 125, 130, 138-39, 149-52, 211, 216, 245, 263-64; and the Italian Socialist Party, 4, 22, 108, 120, 133, 179
RAI3 (RAI Channel 3), 47, 107, 118-19, 133, 138, 147, 149, 151, 245, 263-64; and the center-left, 152; and the Italian Communist Party, 4, 42, 109, 114-15, 234; and *lottizzazione*, 125, 246-47
RAI Channel 1. *See* RAI1
RAI Channel 2. *See* RAI2
RAI Channel 3. *See* RAI3
RAI.it (website), 148
RAI NEWS 24, 187, 197, 263
RAI news programs (*telegiornali*), 33, 69, 72-74, 81, 107, 145; *telegiornale regionale*, 119, 131. *See also* RAI news Tg1; RAI news Tg2; RAI news Tg3
RAI news Tg1, 94, 97, 113-15, 131-32, 134, 145, 183, 200-201, 211, 216, 218, 237, 264; and the Christian Democratic Party, 108, 110, 120, 164; and *Forza Italia*, 140; and *lottizzazione*, 117-18, 123, 127-28, 169, 171, 188-89; and the *Ulivo* coalition, 149
RAI news Tg2, 94, 97-98, 115, 128, 132-34, 149, 163, 167, 194, 196-97, 213, 218, 264; and *Alleanza Nazionale*, 140, 145, 151, 188-89; and the Italian Socialist Party, 94, 108, 113, 118, 120, 164; and *lottizzazione*, 117, 123, 125, 142, 179-80, 182, 184-85, 187, 190; and *Polo delle Libertà*, 237
RAI news Tg3, 119, 133-34, 137, 149, 152-53, 187-88, 208, 210, 237, 264; and *lottizzazione*, 117, 123, 140, 246-47; and the Italian Communist Party, 112-13, 115, 118; and the Democratic Party of the Left, 145
RAI Parliamentary Committee (*Commissione Parlamentare di Vigilanza RAI*), 7, 36, 92, 94,

111, 129, 151, 207, 234, 258
RAI *Regione*, 112, 115
RAI SAT Fiction, 148
RAI Trade, 148, 263
Reconstructed Communism, 133, 144, 148, 263-64
Red Brigades, 38
La Repubblica, 43, 124, 128, 142, 199, 202, 243, 263
Resistenza, 65, 261
Rete4, 42, 106, 139, 237, 242, 258, 260-61
Reuter Telegram Company, 61
Richeri, Giuseppe, ix
Risorgimento, 56
Rocca, Gianni, 43
Rodinò, Marcello, 72
Romanò, Angelo, 82
Ronchey, Alberto, 76, 82, 199, 248
Ronzoni, Daniele, 182-87
Rossella, Carlo, 140-41, 150
Rossi, Emilio, 94, 97
RTVE (Radiotelevisión Española), 251
Rusconi Publishing, 106, 263
Rutelli, Francesco, 237

Saccà, Agostino, 150, 204, 243
Sandulli, Aldo, 81
Santoro, Michele, 119, 132-33, 147, 149, 151-52, 168, 186, 204, 211, 214-16
Savelli, Giulio, 200
Savoj monarchy, 14-15
Scalfari, Eugenio, 27-28, 124, 263
Scarano, Domenico, 94
Scoppola, Pietro, 16-17, 26
Il Secolo, 19, 58, 59
Il Secolo XIX, 19
Sellerio, Elvira, 130
Selva, Gustavo, 200
Severati, Marcello, 73
Severi, Alberto, 96, 208, 210, 247
Siciliano, Enzo, 144, 148

Siliato, Francesco, 132, 136, 191-92, 235
Sindacato Giornalisti RAI (Singrai), 208
Singrai (*Sindacato Giornalisti* RAI), 208
SIP (*Società Idroelettrica Piemontese*), 46, 84
S.I.R.A.C. (Società Italiana Radio Audizioni Circolari), 61, 264
sistema incompiuto, 23
Social-Democratic Party (PSDI), 23, 35, 81-83, 113, 122, 259, 262
Società Italiana Radio Audizioni Circolari (S.I.R.A.C.), 61, 264
Sodano, Giampaolo, 120
Spada, Celestino, 7-9, 162, 190-91, 206, 209, 229
Spadolini, Giovanni, 39, 199
La Stampa, 58, 60, 142, 146, 150, 199, 263
Statuto Albertino, 15, 56
Stefani News Agency, 60-61, 257
Sturzo, Luigi, 19, 259, 262

tangentopoli. *See* Clean Hands scandal
Tamberlich, Romano, 200-203
Tambroni government, 32, 74
Taradash, Marco, 207
Tasca, Angelo, 60
Taviani brothers, 98
Telealessandria, 36, 84
Telebiella, 36, 84
Telecom Italia, 46, 230
Telediffusione Italiana, 36
telegiornali. *See* Mediaset news programs; RAI news programs
Teleivrea, 84
Telepiombino, 36
Teleroma-cavo, 36
Televercelli, 84
Tg4. *See* Mediaset news programs

(*telegiornali*)
Tg5. *See* Mediaset news programs (*telegiornali*)
Times, 58
Togliatti, Palmiro, 60
Tomassini, Stefano, 171, 183, 195-96, 198, 202
Tornabuoni, Lietta, 146, 147
La Tribuna, 59
Turati, Filippo, 59
television programs: *Attenti al fiasco*, 72; *Gli atti degli apostoli*, 77; *Blob*, 204; *Il caso*, 119; *I clowns*, 98; *Cronache dai partiti*, 76; *Cronache dal XX secolo*, 76; *Delitto e castigo*, 77; *Dentro la notizia*, 120; *Elettorando*, 119; *Il fatto*, 152; *Gesù di Nazareth*, 98; *Indietro tutta*, 119; *Mastro don Gesualdo*, 77; *The Maurizio Costanzo Show*, 215, 216; *I miserabili*, 77; *Non solo nero*, 119, 203, 204; *L'Odissea* 77; *Padre Padrone*, 98; *Parlamento in*, 119; *Porta a porta*, 128, 132, 149; *Prima pagina*, 76; *I promessi sposi*, 77; *Il raggio verde*, 149; *Il rosso e il nero*, 132; *Samarcanda*, 119; *Satirycon*, 186; *Sciuscià*, 149; *Sex and the City*, 240; *Six Feet Under*, 240; *The Sopranos*, 240; *Striscia la notizia*, 120, 152; *Tempo reale*, 147; *Tocca a noi*, 132; *Tribuna elettorale*, 74, 75, 76; *Tribuna politica*, 75; *Tribuna sindacale*, 76; *La TV delle ragazze*, 119; *Un, due, tre*, 72; *Un giorno in pretura*, 119; *Zoom*, 76

L'Ulivo (Olive Tree coalition), 144, 149, 264
L'Unità, 19, 59-60, 65, 169
L'Unità Cattolica, 59
Unione Radiofonica Italiana (URI), 61-62, 260, 264
URI (Unione Radiofonica Italiana), 61-62, 260, 264
Usigrai (*Unione Sindacale Giornalisti* RAI), 125-26, 133, 135-36, 165, 168-75, 193, 206-9, 211, 214-15, 217-18

Valentini, Giovanni, 128, 130
Vattimo, Gianni, 70
Vecchietti, Giorgio, 33
Veltroni, Walter, 84, 114
Venetian League (*Liga Veneta*), 39
Vergara, Daniela, 187-89
Vespa, Bruno, 120, 127-28, 149
Vigorelli, Piero, 141
La Voce repubblicana, 60, 65, 264
Volcic, Demetrio, 133-34, 140

Zaccaria, Roberto, 149
Zanetti, Livio, 115
Zavoli, Sergio, 77, 110, 169
Zeffirelli, Franco, 98

About the Author

Dr. Cinzia Padovani is assistant professor of the political economy of mass media in the School of Journalism at Southern Illinois University. She received her Ph.D. in media studies from the School of Journalism and Mass Communication at the University of Colorado at Boulder. Her research interest is in historical approaches to the study of the political economy of media institutions, public service broadcasting and global media, diasporic communication and ethnic media, social movements and alternative media, political philosophy, and social theory. She has taught courses on these topics and also worked as a research associate at the University of Colorado, pursuing a study on the conditions of public service broadcasting organizations worldwide. Cinzia has published extensively on topics related to the conditions of public service media.